Gunsmiths
and
Allied Tradesmen
of Alabama

Thomas E. Kilgo
And
James B. Whisker

Published by:
Bluewater Publications
1812 CR 111
Killen, Alabama 35645
www.BluewaterPublications.com

DEDICATIONS

This book is dedicated with love and devotion to our wives, Milani Trannin and Sheila Whisker. Also, we dedicate this book to Dan Wallace, in respectful memory of one of the first serious researchers on Alabama gunsmiths, and to the future researchers and collectors of early Alabama history who may be encouraged by the information in this book.

THE AUTHORS

Thomas Kilgo is a native of Alabama and President of MTT Ltda. , a business development company for the Americas. He is a student and collector of early Alabama firearms and early American and Confederate Bowie knives. He may be reached at tom@tkilgo.com.

James Whisker is Professor Emeritus, West Virginia University, and author of over 60 books on the American Longrifle.

ACKNOWLEDGEMENTS

Very special thanks are extended and acknowledged by the authors to the following people who unselfishly contributed additional research information to this book.

Primary Research Contributors in Addition to the Authors:
Jerry Noble
Dan Wallace (In Memoriam)
William Lindsey McDonald (In Memoriam)

Additional Research information:

Allen Daniels
Andy Mock
Charley Pate
Chris Hirsch
Chuck Torrey
Damon Mills
Elizabeth Moore
George Hebling
Jack Burner
Jim Blackburn
Jim Mitchell
Meredith McLemore, AL Dept. of
Archives and History
Joey Brackner, Dir. AL Center for
Traditional Culture

Lloyd Jackson
Morris Killen
Roger Ballard
Ronald Pettit
Tom McVay
Wayne Elliott
Lee Freeman
Kathy Melvin
Curt Johnson
Dan Hartzler
Elizabeth Claire Moore
Larry W. Yantz
Jack Melton, contributing historical
photographer

Additional Photo Contributions from Present and Past Collections:
Chris Hirsch
Jim Mitchell
Damon and Donna Mills
Andy Mock
Holly Jensen, Curator of Collections, History Museum of Mobile

Contents

INTRODUCTION 1

GUNSMITHS AND ALLIED TRADESMEN OF ALABAMA 4

    A 4

    B 6

    C.. 14

    D 18

    E 20

    F 21

    G 23

    H 26

    I 34

    J 35

    K 36

    L 41

    M 44

    N 49

    O 51

    P 52

    Q 56

    R 57

    S 60

    T 66

    U 69

    V 70

    W 71

    X 74

    Y 75

    Z 76

CONFEDERATE ARMS IN ALABAMA.. 77

PHOTOS 85

INDEX 143

Introduction
By Thomas Kilgo and James Whisker

In 1704, Nicolas de la Salle conducted a census which revealed additional details regarding the settlement of Mobile and its occupants. The structures identified in the census comprised a guardhouse, a forge, a gunsmith shop, a brick kiln, and eighty one-story wooden houses. The occupants included 180 men, 27 families with ten children, eleven Native American slave boys and girls, and numerous farm animals. [Wikipedia]

The French founded the first European settlement in the state with the establishment of Mobile in 1702. Southern most Alabama was French from 1702 to 1763, part of British West Florida from 1763 to 1780, and part of Spanish West Florida from 1780 to 1813, when captured by the United States. Most of Alabama was part of British Georgia from 1763 to 1783 and part of the American Mississippi territory thereafter from 1798.

The Alabama, a Muskogean tribe whose members lived just below the confluence of the Coosa and Tallapoosa Rivers on the upper reaches of the Alabama River, served as the etymological source of the names of the river and state. Alabama's statehood was delayed by the lack of a coastline; rectified when Andrew Jackson captured Spanish Mobile in 1813. Alabama was the twenty-second state, admitted to the Union in 1819. Alabama is bordered by Tennessee to the north, Georgia to the east, Florida and the Gulf of Mexico to the south, and Mississippi to the west. Alabama ranks 30th in total land area and presently ranks 23rd in population.

There is no doubt that French, Spanish, and probably British gunsmiths worked in what is now Alabama long before the beginning of this listing. The French had gunsmiths at Ft. Louis in Mobile. LaSalle noted that there was a gunsmithy there in 1704. That facility evidently repaired firearms for the soldiers and native aborigine. Whether any guns or names of gunsmiths from the pre-1814 period survive is not know for sure. There is little question that there was a small American gunsmith trade in the Mississippi Territory beginning in the 1790's and an active American gunsmith trade from its beginnings as a state.

There was no published study of Southern gunsmiths generally until Jerry Noble undertook his study of Notes on Southern Long Rifles and pistols made in the southeast United States in his four volumes on Southern gunsmiths. Our sources consisted primarily of the U.S. Census and local, state, and regional directories. We have cited only Census in our entries to include U.S. and state census in this work. The internet has proven to be a wonderful source of information, especially of family genealogies and histories. Military histories and war pension papers yielded a number of armorers. Much information came from state, local, and regional histories of the 19th century.

While researching this book we have seen only a few Alabama made guns. All of us should be extremely happy to have this book illustrate many of those few long rifles and pistols.

As you study the photos of the rifles included, you will notice various distinctive traits traditionally associated with known gunsmiths in NC, SC, TN, and GA. There are also traits unique to first generation European gunsmiths who were more adaptive of their own Alabama style. This is clear when you read about the migration of families and groups of gunsmiths from these other areas where they learned their craft.

Examples are the Kennedys and related families from Moore County, NC to Lauderdale County, AL.; the Higgins family and related families from Lauren County, SC to Butts County, GA and on to several counties in AL; the Bull family from MD to TN and then to Marion County, AL; and the Landrum family from Chatham County, NC to the Mississippi Territory, Washington County, later Clarke County, AL.

Other examples are Christian Kreutner, George Balzer, and Ignatious Bender, all first generation European immigrants in South Central Alabama producing excellent guns of their own style.

Of course, many individual gunsmiths migrated to Alabama from many locations and many later would learn their skills in Alabama. The result is that there are many different styles and schools that have influenced and formed varied Alabama styles. This only makes each gun and its maker that much more interesting.

Essentially this book covers gunsmiths who worked in the 19th century and who made muzzle-loading guns before 1900. Of necessity a few gunsmiths who made muzzle-loading long rifles while working deep into the 20th century were included.

Typical of the many difficulties and disappointments one encounters is this. Joey Brackner, Director of the Alabama Center for Traditional Culture made us aware of a letter the state possesses, dated January 21, 1862. It refers to an unnamed English gunsmith, providing us with a tantalizing bit of historical information:

[I am writing you] to state a fact which may be of some importance in connection with the establishment of a foundry and armory here [Selma]. We have here one of the most skillful gunmakers I doubt not in the Confederate States. He has been in the business here for some five or six years and has established quite a reputation for making superior pistols, rifles, and shotguns, and has by his industry and attention to business, accumulated frequently in independent circumstance. He is a

foreigner, Pelanser [?] I think, and is esteemed and respected as a mechanic, industrious, intelligent, and every way [a] reliable citizen. He agreed last spring to take care of an armory if one should be established here as then proposed; and was as willing to go to his native county and employ and bring over as many skillful workmen as might be wanted. Being acquainted there he could get workmen when a stranger could not. I have no doubt his services could now be commanded on fair and reasonable terms, to go to work with such workmen as could be procured in the Confederacy; or if need be to run the blockade and go to Europe for them. Being a foreigner who would be seeking who would be seeking to return to have native land, he would stand a better chance to get through than a national of this country. I consider him very trustworthy and reliable. I have thought this matter of sufficient seriousness to state it to you.

Much is to be said of the work of the late Dan Wallace. The first study of Alabama long rifles of which we are aware was undertaken by him. On 25 February, 1995 Dan gave a presentation at the symposium sponsored by the Huntsville Museum of Art. His talk did not encompass the identification of many Alabama gunsmiths, but it created the intellectual atmosphere in which the study of long rifles made in this state could be undertaken. Thereafter he devoted himself to the identification of these tradesmen. Dan spent many hours going through microfilmed census records. That remains the primary way to locate and identify artisans and craftsmen to this day. Dan studied several families, notably the Higgins and Bull clans, and his objective findings displeased some of the collectors who possessed more monetary resources than historical sense. Such is often the inevitable price of serious scholarship.

Most often as collectors, researchers, and students of history and culture we are just positing facts and theories to be tested, challenged and either accepted, modified or rejected. But that, in and of itself, is the valuable process this book strives to promote. Our hope is that this book stimulates and provokes the future discovery and open sharing of new information that will influence, correct, add to and clarify the information presented.

Gunsmiths and Allied
Tradesmen of Alabama

A

Adams, Stephen Thomas (1847-1926). cotton farmer and gunsmith. Adams was born in Alabama in 1847, migrated to Texas with his pioneering parents as a boy, came to live in the Lampasas River Valley and in or near Tobey Valley and Tobeyville, in Burnet county, just before the Civil War. He and Nathaniel Tobey helped make and assemble rifles for the Confederate Army. In 1867, Tom Adams married Nat Tobey's daughter, Ruth, in Hood County, Texas. They had 16 children, several in Bell County, and more later in Lamar County. He died in Pleasanton, Atascosa County, in 1926.

Adamson, William Colt (1863-1942). gun and blacksmith. Almond, Anderson County. William was born in Anderson County, a son of Nathaniel and Margaret E. Adamson. 1920, William Anderson, blacksmith, 57, born in AL. He was a retired gunsmith who died on 24 April 1942 at Shawmut, Chambers County, at age 79. He was a widower, his wife the former Sarah Robertson having predeceased him [death certificate at Ancestry].

Adare, William Branch (1834) farmer and gunsmith. Madison County, AL. Adare was born on 1 January 1834 a son of John Blain and his wife Elvira Sublett. On 22 March 1870 in Hays County, TX, he married Mary Victortine O'Banion. 1880, Hays County, TX: William B. Adare, born 1834 in AL; Mary V., wife, 49; Charles Joseph, 17; Thomas C., 15; Ethel, 13; Virginia, 11, all born in TX. William died on 12 May 1923 in Hays County [Ancestry].

Allen, Robert (1793-1837) gunsmith Allen married Sarah Cobb (1800-1838). They had 12 children. Both were born in SC, but moved to GA, where their last son was born in 1834. Both died in AL. Their son Columbus became a physician and was the subject of a biography for Weakley County, Tennessee, from which the above information came.

Allen, William (1870-1917) gunsmith 1899-1900, 454 Conti, Mobile. He died at Crealston, Mobile County, on 24 October 1917 [*Dirs.*].

Alley, William (1819-1872). gunsmith. 1860, Southern division, Macon County. William was born on 19 September 1819. William Alley, 41, gunsmith; Mary I., wife, 35; Laura, 18; Mary, 16; Alice, 14, all born in Germany; William, 7; Ernest, 5; Thomas, 1, all born in AL. He died on 9 September 1872, and was buried at Tuskegee, Macon County [Census; Ancestry].

Anderson, James (1805) gunsmith. 1850, Chambers County. James, age 45, gunsmith, born in NC; Sarah M., 47; William C., 19, farmer; John T., 17, farmer; H.J. [female], 15, all born in GA; James A., 12, born in GA [Census].

Anderson, Samuel (1844-1917) gunsmith. 1880, Columbus, MS. Samuel Anderson, gunsmith, 36; Eliza, wife, 36; Ellen, 18; Jennie, 16; Ida, 11, all born in AL; William, 7; Alice, 3, both born in MS. Anderson died on 21 December 1917 in Walker County, AL [Ancestry; Census].

Angel, Elizabeth (1809) gunsmith 1850-60, Huntsville, Madison County. 1850, Joseph Angel, gunsmith, 43, Elizabeth, wife, 41, gunsmith; Joseph P., 12; Albert H., 10, both born in CT; Mariah, E, 2, born in England. 1860, Joseph, age 52, gunsmith, value $1300; Elizabeth, 51, his wife, also noted as a gunsmith in the census; Maria, 12, all born in England; Joseph P. Angel, 21, silversmith, born in CT [Census].

Angel, Joseph W (1808) gunsmith. 1843-48, New Haven. 1850-63, Huntsville. 1860, Huntsville, Madison County. Joseph, age 52, gunsmith, value $1300; Elizabeth, 51, his wife, also listed as a gunsmith; Maria, 12, all born in England; Joseph P. Angel, 21, silversmith, born in CT. Angell was an Englishman who became a U.S. citizen. His shop in New Haven was at the foot of Crown St. He left New Haven c.1848 and took a short trip to England with his wife who was a member of British aristocracy. He then settled in Huntsville. He opposed secession and was harassed until he undertook gunsmithing services to the South. Southern officials wished him to superintend the arsenal at Holly Springs. He was liberated by Union forces under General Mitchell. Upon the latter's withdrawal from Huntsville, Angel accompanied the army, leaving behind his home, shop, and tools. His letters, declaring the Southern cause to be unjust, brought him before a court of inquiry but was saved by the intervention of a highly placed English nobleman, a friend of his wife's relatives [*New Haven Palladium*, 27 February 1863].

Armstrong, Levi (1863) gunsmith. Shelby County. Levi and his wife Catherine migrated to Shelby County, Alabama from SC before 1840. Levi was killed in The Battle of Bakers Creek, MS, on 12 May 1863 [Ancestry].

Austill, Evan. (1773-1818) Trader with Native Americans and gun and blacksmith. Native of NC although both he and his son Jeremiah served in the Georgia legislature. On November 24, 1801, Nancy, "by appearance an Indian woman," gave testimony at Fort Southwest Point, a garrison in eastern Tennessee established in 1792 to defend white settlements against Indian attack. In a statement recorded under the title "The Narrative of Nancy, A Cherokee Woman," Nancy claimed that she had been wrongfully held as a slave in Virginia since the year 1778. One of her last owners was Evan Austill who purchased her from one John Smith about 1808. Fort Madison, Alabama, was commanded by Captain Samuel Dale and Evan Austill after it was abandoned by Colonel Carson. He primarily traded among the Cherokees. His son Jeremiah was born in Pendleton district, South Carolina, in 1794. Jeremiah in 1832 at Tuscumbia spoke out boldly against the removal of the Native Americans to the Far West [Ancestry].

B

Bailey, James W (1853-1908) gunsmith. Beat 11, Conecuh County. Also seen as J. W. 1900, Evergreen, Conecuh County [*Montgomery Adviser*, 10 August 1901] James died on 9 January 1908 at age 55, buried at Evergreen Cemetery [death certificate at Ancestry].

Bailey, W. J.. (1855) gunsmith. 1885, Greenville, Butler County; 1901 signed a petition against the issuance of railroad passes. 1880, William James Bailey, clerk, 25; Josephine, 25; James E., 2 months [Census; Ancestry; *Dir*].

Balzer (Baltzer), George (1826) gunsmith. Hayneville, Lowndes County. George was a son of George and Anna M. Baltzer. 1860, George Balzer, born in Bavaria, Germany; wife, Sarah, 3 children. 1870, Hayneville: George Balzer, 43, gunsmith; Sarah, born in GA, 36, wife; Joseph L., 15; Alice A., 13; George, 11; William, 9; John D, 3; Bernard, infant, all born in AL. Reportedly, he died in Lowndes County, date unknown [Ancestry; Census]. *One rifle is shown in photo section.*

Barber, W. A. (1829) gunsmith. 1860, Stevenson, Jackson County. W. A. age 31, gunsmith, value $800 property, $471 real estate, born in AL; Carolina 31, born in TN; Erasmus 7, born in AL; James E. 4, born in AL; Margaret 2, born in AL; Robert Davidson,16, laborer, born in AL [Census].

Barbour, Richard. gunsmith. Huntsville. Barbour was seriously, but accidentally, shot by an employee named Parish [*Memphis Daily Avalanche*, 17 September 1868]

Barnerd, Elisha Smith (1812) gunsmith. 1850, Southern district, Henry County. E. S. Barnerd, 38, gunsmith, born in S.C., value $300; Oliver Barnerd, age 20, gunsmith, born in AL; Jesse Barnerd, gunsmith, age 37, born in AL; all in household of William Noflin, 34, a farmer, born in GA [Census]. Elisha Smith Barnard, who was a gunmaker of note in southeastern Alabama, and who afterward successfully engaged in the grocery business at Eufaula, Ala. At the time of his death he was part owner in a steamboat plying on the Chattahoochee River, and also owned land near Abbeville, AL.

Barnerd, Jesse (1813) gunsmith. 1850, southern district, Henry County. E. S. Bernerd, 28; Oliver, 20; Jesse, value $300, 37, gunsmith; born in SC; Lison Kelly, 20. 1860, eastern division, Barbour County: E. S. Bernerd, grocer, Oliver, 28; Frances, 10; Martin, 7; Angus, 5; Mary, 3; Jesse, 45, no occupation [Census].

Barnerd, Oliver (1830) gunsmith. 1850, southern district, Henry County; born in AL. See also Jesse Bernerd [Census].

Barnard, William (1826) gunsmith. 1850, Henry County. William, age 24, gunsmith, born in NC; Sarah, age 20, born in GA; child, 11 months, born in AL [Census].

Barnes, Z. A. (1848-1912) gunsmith. Eufaula, Barbour County. Born near Americus, Barnes fought with General Joe Wheeler in the 34th Georgia, C.S.A. He became a telegrapher in Jacksonville and Tampa, Florida, and last an independent gunsmith in Eufaula. He was a Baptist, Mason, and member of Knights of Pythias [*Montgomery Advertiser*, 14 August 1912]

Barnett, Warren Hocksley (1832-1920). gunsmith and machinist. Warren H. Barnett was born Sept. 11, 1832 and died March 12, 1920. He was a gunsmith and a machinist., born in Selma, Alabama. Barnett served with the 37th Infantry, Company D as a sergeant. On his Texas pension application, it states he served under Jack Waterhouse's Company and in Walter P. Lane's Regiment [*Roster of Confederate Soldiers 1861-1865*].

Barton, James A. (1845) gunsmith. 1900, Walker County. He, his parents, and all his children were born in Alabama [Census].

Bates, Riley (1819) gun and blacksmith. 1860, Paulding County, GA: R. Bates, gunsmith; Sarah, wife, 33; Caroline, 11; Mary M., 9; William F., 3; Amanda, 6; Ranson, 2; Nancy, infant, all born in GA. Riley was born in Paulding and moved after 1860 to Winston [now Cullman] County, AL, with a large group of Union Volunteers. [Census; Ancestry; Family Genealogy]. *One rifle is shown in the Photo section.*

Beasley, Abraham (1814-1875) gunsmith. 1880, Covington County. 1880, gunsmith, born in GA, age 65; wife Happy, 70; Linny McGran, 39; John McGran, 13; M. Beasley, 43. Abraham was born on 25 November 1814 in Jefferson County, a son of Solomon and Nancy Henderson Beasley. He died on 25 November 1875 in Red Level, Covington County [Ancestry; Census].

Becker (Beekan), Nicholas (1815) gunsmith. 1854-65, Montgomery. 1850, Montgomery City. Nicholas Beekan, age 35, born in Prussia, gunsmith; Caroline, 24, his wife, born in NY; Alice, 2, born in AL; Joseph Todd, 22, gunsmith, and George Todd, 11, both born in NY. Noted in *Confederate Homefront* "Nick Becker, a German gunsmith, had a shop on Commerce Street." Also seen as Beekan [*Dirs.*; Census]. *Two pistols are shown in the Photo section.*

Belew, John J. (1809-1891) gunsmith. 1840, Lauderdale County. Reportedly he worked at the Kennedy gun factory. 1840, free white inhabitants: 1 male 20-29, engaged in agriculture; 1 female under 5; 1 female 20-29. 1850, Lawrence County, AL: J. Belew, 26, farmer, born in SC; Caroline G., 24, wife; William M., 3, both born in AL. John J. was a son of James Perry and Mary Ann Belew, born on 28 July 1809 in SC. On 20 December 1832 he married Martha Lankester. 1870, Lawrenceburg, Lawrence County, TN: John J. Belew, farmer, 60, born in SC; Martha, wife, 55, born in AL. He was a private in Leighton Rangers in the Civil War. J. J. died on 16 March 1891 and was buried at Second Creek Cemetery, Lawrence County, TN [Census; Ancestry].

Bell, David (1810-1860) gunsmith. 1850, Baldwin County, gunsmith, 40, born in SC; Sophiome, wife, 38, place of birth illegible; Robert, 15; William, 13; Mary, 12; Margaret, 10; Sarah, 8; Andrew, 6; Mark, 4; Catharine, 3, all born in AL [Census; Ancestry].

Bellamy, John gunsmith. 1839-44, Mobile. 1844, Belamy [*sic*] & Gay [*Dirs*].

Beltz, D. C. gunsmith and minister. Shady Grove, Cullman County. Sometime in the late 1880s, D.C. Beltz, a minister from Cincinnati, Ohio, moved to this part of the country. He seemed to have many talents, being a gunsmith, a carpenter, and a great sportsman. He did his work with precision and the trustees employed him as the architect for the building of the present church. He drew the blueprints which were the first to be used in this newly settled area [Ancestry].

Bender, Antonio J. gunsmith. 1892-1927, 52 Dauphin, Mobile [*Dirs*.].

Bender, Ignatius (1833-1920) gunsmith. 1870-87, Mobile. 1870, shop at 3 Dauphin, residence southwest corner of Conti and Conception Sts. Bender was born about 1833 in Germany. He died on 7 May 1920 in Mobile, age 87, widower [Ancestry; *Dirs*]..

Bender, James gunsmith. Mobile. He worked for Gelbke & Brother in 1866 [*Dirs*.].

Bender, John L. (A.?) John L. Bender born in Germany married Mary Byrnes on 09 Jul 1825 in Mobile County, Alabama and in 1830 was listed in the Mobile City Directory. In the 1840 Mobile census is listed with 14 workers living at his property. This was possibly a gun shop or factory. He is believed to be the father of Ignatius Bender who shows up in the Mobile, Alabama City Directory in the 1870's and several other Bender gunsmiths. [Mobile City Directory, Census. Early AL Marriages] *One rifle shown in the Photo section.*

Bender, John. gunsmith. 1861-1904, Mobile. John was a son of Ignatius. He worked for Gelbke & Brother in 1861. 1869, shop at 3 Dauphin, residence southwest corner of Conti and Conception Sts. 1888, 30 Dauphin, residence upstairs. 1897, 52 Dauphin, Mobile. Residence upstairs. Guns, cutlery, notions, sporting goods [*Dirs*].

Bender, Joseph A. apprentice gunsmith. 1888, 30 Dauphin, residence upstairs, Mobile; apprenticed to John Bender, presumably a son [*Dir*.].

Beyseigal, Charles F. (1822-1877) gunsmith. 1860-61, Demopolis, Marengo County [Noble; *Dir*]. 1870, Jacksonville, Calhoun County: Charles Beysiegel, born in Germany, 48, gunsmith; Katie, 31, wife; William, 12; Lula, 5; Charles, 10; George, 3; Robert, 1, all born in AL [Census; Ancestry]. Also seen as Bayseigal.

Biford, William (1808) gunsmith. Franklin County. 1850, district 6: William Biford, 42, gunsmith; Sarah, 40, wife, both born in NC; Benjamin, 19; Jane, 18; Sarah, 13; Henry, 12; James 10; William, 8, all born in AL. Reportedly Biford worked for the Kennedy gun factory earlier [Noble; Wallace; Census].

Binder (Bender), Charles (1830) gunsmith. 1870, Valhermoso Springs, Morgan County. Charles, 40, gunsmith; Maria, 36, his wife; Louis, 13; Eberhard, 9, all born in Prussia [Census].

Birmingham Arms & Cycle. gun and locksmiths. 1916 2nd Ave., Birmingham. E. H. Gast, keys are made & arms repaired by expert gunsmith; air guns; fireworks; garden tools [*Age Herald*, 27 June 1897; 12 July 1898; 7 May 1899; 5 November 1899; 24 March 1900].

Blackburn, Joel (1794-1873) tradesman. Blount County. For his service in the War of 1812, Joel received bounty land in the new territory of Alabama. In November 1816 he took his bride, Anna Fry, and infant son, William Baxter, and headed for the wilderness of northeastern Alabama settling on a stream he called the Blackburn River, now known as the Blackburn Prong of the Warrior River. Starting out on a 160 acre homestead in a log cabin with straw beds on a dirt floor, the hard working couple eventually owned a 600 acre farm where they built a substantial two story house, a cotton gin, and a tannery. A fine blacksmith and gunsmith, Joel Blackburn was dependent on outsiders for very little. The couple raised flax, made a hackle to harvest the flax, and built a wheel to spin it into cloth. To harvest his wheat Joel built his own thresher. 1860, Summit, eastern division, Blount County: Joel Blackburn. born in NC, 66, farmer; Anna, wife, 64, born in TN; James P., 22; Lavinia C., 15, both born in AL. 1870, Blountsville, Joel, born in TN, 76; Anna, 72, wife [Ancestry].

Blackwood, William gunsmith. 1890, Cardova Alley, Birmingham [*Dir.*].

Bluis, James (1839) gunsmith. 1815, Maury County, TN; 1820-36, Limestone County. Father of Jeremiah who was born in Alabama in 1820 [Noble].

Boatwright, Daniel Thomas (1819-1897) gunsmith, farmer, carpenter. 1850, Franklin County. In 1850 he listed his occupation as deputy sheriff. He served as deputy sheriff and jailer of Russellville. Boatright was born 20 August 1819 in Tennessee, and died 20 June 1863 in Catoosa Springs Hospital, Georgia. He married Rachel Lawler on 12 March 1846. She was born on 1 Jan 1828 near Russellville, Franklin County, Alabama, and died on 20 January 1897 in Texas. They moved to Bell County, Texas, in 1852, and settled near Eakin. He traveled by way of Tennessee to cross the Mississippi River, stopping in Arkansas to raise a crop before coming on to Texas. In Texas he bought a farm and operated a furniture shop. He had studied medicine but did not practice. Before the war he had a gunsmith shop as well as mercantile business. The McAulay family had a tanning yard and a wagon shop. Moffett was a busy community. It is not known why Boatright chose Moffett. D.T. Boatright enlisted 28 Jan 1862 at Ft. Hebert, Texas. A Lt. Barton signed him into Company K, 10th Regiment, also called Nelson's Regiment, organized in October 1861. Daniel was captured and placed in a prisoner of war camp on Lake Erie.

Boatwright, James William (1827-1915) armorer. James worked as a gunsmith at Tallassee Arsenal during the Civil War. He worked in the building where the gunstocks were made. He was a son of Daniel and Cecelia (Sentitet) Boatwright. In the 1860 census of Tallapoosa County, he was enumerated as a mechanic. His wife, Mary, is listed as age 27, illiterate. James W, born in 1827 in Aiken, Aiken County, SC, Montgomery in 1850 James Washington, Son of Daniel and Celia [Sentitet] Boatwright born in Aiken, Aiken County, S.C. He died in Tallassee, Elmore County, where he had moved before the war. He married Ann Hartley of Lexington County, daughter of Ellis and Mary Abigail Howard [Census; Ancestry; Family].

Bohna, Joseph. gunsmith. 1873, southwest corner of Conception and Conti, Mobile [*Dir.*].

Bon, Jean (c.1667) gunsmith. 1699-1709, Mobile. Jean Praux was a carpenter from Saint Jean d'Angély, France, who migrated to the French settlement of Mobile, then part of the Louisiana colony, in 1706 aboard the ship, *Aigle* with his wife and four daughters. In 1706 he was 48 and his wife was 43. He died shortly after his arrival and his widow married Jean Bon, a gunsmith from LaRochelle, France who had arrived in the colony in 1699. Anne Prévost, the durable widow married the forty-two-year-old gunsmith and tool-maker Jean Bon of La Rochelle [Ancestry; Jay Higginbotham, *Old Mobile: Fort Louis de La Louisiane, 1702-1711*].

Boyer, ---. master gunsmith 1710, Fort Louis, near Mobile. His wife Catharine Christopher, was a witness to a baptism on 20 July 1710 [Ancestry].

Boyles, James (1832) gunsmith. 1850, Warrenton, Marshall County: James M. Boyles, 18, farmer. 1870, township 8, Marshall County: James M. Boyles, 37, farmer; Sarah G,. wife, 28; Lilly, 9. 1880, township 8, Marshall County. James Boyles, gunsmith, 48; Sarah, 43, wife; Lilly, 19, all born in AL; Jennie, 2, born in GA [Census].

Bozeman, David Wood (1814-1887) gunsmith & farmer. David was born on 16 February 1814 in Twiggs County, GA. On 12 April 1832 in Lowndes County, AL, he married Ann English Browning (1817-1905). 1850, Coosa, Coosa County, AL: David Bozeman, farmer, 37; Ann, wife, 33; James, 14; William, 10; Browning, 6, all born in GA. 1860, southern division, Coosa County: David W. Bozeman, 47, real estate $15,000; personal value $106,000; Ann, 44, both born in GA; William E., 19; D. B., 18; E. A., 9; N. 7; H. J., 5, all born in AL. 1870, Milam County, TX: David W. Bozeman, 56, farmer; Ann E., 53, living with son William, a farmer. 1880, precinct 2, Milam County: David Bozeman, 66; Ann, 64, living with Charles T. Gregory family. David died on 20 May 1887 in Maysfield, Milam County, TX [Ancestry; Census].

Broadnax, H. P. (1800) gunsmith. 1850, Clarke County. H. P., age 50, gunsmith; Jane, 20; James, 7; Francis, 1; R [male], 55, farmer; Hannah, 40, his wife; Frances, 17; Peggy, 5; Augustus, 3; Eliza, 2 months, all born in AL [Census].

Brog, Adolph (1835) gunsmith. 1860, Montgomery County; born in Germany [Census].

Brooks, Dan C. (1796) farmer and gunsmith. 1860, Tuscaloosa County. Dan, age 64, value $7500/ $18.500; Rhonda, 56, his wife, both born in S.C.; Tempe, 18, seamstress; Paula, 15, both born in AL [Census].

Brooks, John Thomas (1837-1918) armorer. Opelika, Lee County. Brooks was born in SC on July 24, 1837. He was a member of Arsenal's Battalion Company A, but detailed to shop work as a gunsmith during the Second War for Independence. He filed for pension in Lee County. Private, July 1861, Company A, Arsenal Battalion. John died on 14 June 1918, age 80, at Bryce, Tuscaloosa County, retired gunsmith, widowed [Ancestry].

Brouse, William gunsmith 1866, residence corner of Royal and Conti, Mobile. worked for J. F. Dittrich [*Dir.*].

Broyles, James C. (1858-1925) gunsmith. James was born in Monroe County, MS, a son of Erasmus S. and Abigail Virginia Moore Broyles. 1886-1901, Tupelo, Lee County, MS; 1902-1925, Birmingham, Jefferson County, AL. In 1902 he married Celeste Victoria Pankey (1866-

1941). 1920, Birmingham: James C. Broyles, gunsmith, 61, born in MS; Celeste Victoria, 53, wife, born in AL. James died in 1925 in Birmingham, age 67 [Ancestry; Wallace; Census].

Bruce, Wilson Pulaski (1836-1912) gunsmith. Bruce was born April 27, 1836 in Greene County, and enlisted as a private in Company D, 47th Alabama Infantry. He was listed as a gunsmith in a report dated December 4, 1862. The 47th Alabama Infantry Regiment completed its organization at Loa-chapoka, Alabama, in May, 1862, and moved to Virginia in June. Most of its members were drawn from Chambers, Tallapoosa, Cherokee and Coosa counties. During the war it was assigned to General Taliaferro, Law's and W. F. Perry's Brigade, Army of Northern Virginia. The 47th fought in many battles of the army from Cedar Mountain to Cold Harbor, except when it was with Longstreet at Suffolk, Chickamauga and Knoxville. It participated in the Petersburg siege north of the James River and the final campaign at Appomattox. Private Bruce died on August 19, 1912 in Troup County, GA, and is buried at Hillview Cemetery in LaGrange, GA [family].

Buchanan, James (1836) gunsmith. Wife Mary McGee born on 23 November 1817 in Jefferson County, AL died about 1865 in Burleson County, TX. He was the first born child of Ralph and Lydia Cude McGee. She married James Buchanan in Jefferson County Alabama in 1833. Mary, James, and her parents moved to Texas in 1834 as colonists of Stephen F. Austin. James Buchanan died at the Battle of the Alamo March 6, 1836 [Ancestry].

Buckner, Walker, Sr. (1806-1882) gunsmith. Winston County. In 1824 in GA he married Seleta Caroline Freeland. 1870, Houston, Winston County: Walker Buckner, blacksmith, 64; Saleta, 64, wife, both born in GA; Manda, 22; Nancy, 3; Caroline, 1, all born in AL. He died in 1882 in Lawrence County [Census; Ancestry].

"December 5, 1877, Petition To the Commissioners of Claims, Under the Act of Congress of March 3, 1871, Washington, D.C. Amount allowed $140. Claimant opposed secession and the war and was known as a union man. The rebels threatened to hang him, took his property without compensation. He went inside the Union lines and was employed several months in Government service in the gun smith shop at Chattanooga. He had five sons and two sons-in laws in the Union army. We find him loyal. The supplies were mostly taken in Pulaski and near Nashville in 1864 by Union troops in the vicinity. The original petition amounted to $207.50 and there was no permission to amend, therefore the amount as stated in the petition must govern and limit the allowance. We allow $140" [Ancestry].

Bull, John Valentine (1777-1848) gunsmith. John was a gunsmith in Maryland, Tennessee, and Marion County, Alabama. John Valentine Bull and Fetnah Bean Bull had eight children John probably arrived in Tennessee shortly before 1800. John Valentine Bull moved his family from Tennessee to Alabama about 1823, first to Walker County, and later to Marion County. Marion County was created from the western part of Tuscaloosa County on December 13, 1818, and contained the land west of the Sipsey River and then ran south from the mouth of the Sipsey River "to the ridge dividing the waters of Lookseopelala Creek, and the first large creek south of the same; and thence with said ridge to the Tombigbee River." This part of Alabama was Chickasaw land at that time. His shop there was near Gains Trace and Jackson's Military Road, a good location for a gunshop in the 1820's. When the Chickasaw lands in Alabama were ceded to the

US in 1832, John and Fetnah moved a few miles east to Bear Creek. Besides being a gunsmith, John V. Bull also followed farming for many years. John Valentine Bull was buried near Old Allen shirt factory, about a mile. west of Bear Creek. Headstone inscription: "Resting till the Resurrection Morn". Methodist Episcopal. John probably apprenticed to Robert Hodgson of Baltimore. The stock architecture of his early rifles support this legend, as they have a slight inward curve on the underside of the buttstock. They also have a curved comb-line, where most upper east Tennessee rifles are straight, or nearly so. John's later rifles have the straighter lines. He could have brought a curved stock pattern from Baltimore after his apprenticeship. Dr. John R. Smith owns a gun which was made to order for his father in 1829, by John Bull, a gunsmith of Warrior Mountain, Alabama. It is a fine specimen of gun craft of those days, is mounted with silver and has a gold powder pan and bushings. The stock is of curly maple and the barrel of a very soft iron. It is a remarkably accurate shooting piece and it was designed as a "target" gun for the pioneers. The mounting has several inscriptions on the silver plating. The doctor values this heirloom very highly [*Past and Present of Greene County, Missouri*]. *One attributed rifle and one attributed pistol are shown in the Photo section.*

Bull, Russell Samuel Sellers (1812-1887) gunsmith. Russell was born on June 17, 1812 in Grainger County and died on March 22, 1887 in Marion County, Alabama. He was buried at Old Factory Cemetery near Bear Creek, Marion County. On 3 January 1858 he purchased 40 acres in Township 9-S. He married Mary (Polly) Wylie. 1850, gunsmith, Marion County. His work is very similar to that of his father, John V. Bull.
[Census; http://boards.ancestry.netscape.com/surnames.bull/647/mb.ashx].

Burke, Solomon. gunsmith Burke enlisted 6 March 1862 at Lafayette AL; Appears on Muster Roll of Company I dated 13 May 1862 at Auburn AL; Detailed at Montgomery Arsenal CSA 31 Dec 1863 Mechanic by trade; Paid 16 Jan 1864; Issued a medical certificate: "Hypertrophy and valvular disease of heart" dated 3 Apr 1865 at West Point GA includes information "Residence: Lafayette, Chambers County AL; Blue eyes, black hair, dark complexion, 5'11"; Appears on Pay Roll dated 29 Feb 1864 at Dalton GA with note "On detached duty in armory at Montgomery by order of Surgeon Gray"; appears on a Record Roll of Company I prepared after the war by Thomas J. Griffin, former Captain of the Company dated 28 June 1866, described as "Single" "Gunsmith", "Residence: Lafayette, Ala" *and* "Detailed Dec 12, 1862, in armory at Montgomery. Noted in *Weekly Enterprise* article of 15 May1902. Burke witnessed the Confederate pension application of Mary C. Beatty, apparent widow of David Daniel Beatty, Confederate pension application (Alabama Pension No. 25531) of Burke's widow, Mattie Burke, witnessed by J. A. Williams and D.M. Spence and dated 23 Aug 1913 at Chambers County is noted S.G. Burke not found on roll on file dated April 28, 1862 of Co I, 37th, which is only roll of company in depart, nor has record been found of service, capture or parole of man of name & org"; appears on Census, Tax Assessor list of Chambers County AL of 1907-08 and noted as having been born 7 April 1834, and according to personal statement "promoted to armorer" and "Served until paroled at West Point (GA)"; Appears on Muster Roll of "Company 'I' 37th Regiment, Alabama Volunteers at Lafayette, Chambers County, Alabama, March 6, 1862" published in 31 July 1901 issue of *Lafayette Sun*, Chambers County, with Privates as "Burke, S.G., detached at Armory, Montgomery, Dec. 1862"; Circumstances indicate he died between 1907 and 1913.

Burriss, Isham B. (1820) gunsmith. 1860, Tuscaloosa County. I. B., 40, gunsmith, value $300/ 1380; Martha, 32, his wife, both born in S.C. Sarah, 14; Mary J., 12; James B., 10; William, 7, all born in AL [Census]. Also seen as Burroughs.

Burroughs, Berny (1820) gunsmith. 1880, Romulus, Tuscaloosa County. Berny, gunsmith, age 60, born in SC; Martha C., 52, born in GA; Mary Huda, 49, sister, born in AL [Census].

Burson, Walter C. (1864) gunsmith. 1897, residence 916 2nd Ave., Birmingham. He was a gunsmith at Salisbury & Bailey. 1910, Justice Precinct 8, Cherokee County, TX; W. C. Burson, farmer, 46, born in AL [*Dir*.].

Buys, Jeremiah (1820-1875) gunsmith. Limestone County. Also seen as Buis. 1850, Jeremiah G., 30, born in AL, gunsmith, personal property $250; wife Sarah Ann, 28; Francis M., 10; Margaret, 8; John W, 6; James K., 4, Sarah, 2. Jeremiah bought 100 acres of land from John Shinpock on 11 November 1854 and sold this land to Ezekeil (*sic*) Hastings on 8 September 1859. 1860, Jeremiah Buis, south west division, Basham's Gap, Morgan County. Jeremiah was born on 25 January 1820, a son of James and Sarah Griffin Buys. He fought for the Glorious Cause and was a POW. Jeremiah died on 1 February 1875 in TX [Ancestry; Census].

C

Campbell, Colin (1797) gunsmith. 1850, township 21, Tallapoosa County: Collen Campbell, mechanic, 55; Nancy, 45; Sarah Ann, 19; Flora, 18; Jenny, 15; John, 12; Almeda, 10; Collen, 8. According to the 1850 Census all but Calin [8] Jr. were born in NC. 1860, Dadeville, Tallapoosa County; Colin Campbell, gunsmith, 65, born in NC; Nancy, wife, 46, born in Scotland; Alamena, 19; Colin, 17, both born in AL. 1870, Talladega County: Collin, born in NC, 70, retired; Nancy, 69, born in Scotland [Census].

Campbell, Hiram W. (1812) gunsmith. 1860, Calhoun County; born in TN [Census].

Cannon, Berry (1841-1928) gunsmith. 1880, Mt. Vernon, Mobile County: Berry Cannon, gunsmith, 36; Amelia, wife, 25; Maurice, 7; Henry, 6; Bessie, 3; Eve, 1, all born in AL. 1900, Mt. Vernon: Berry A. Cannon, lumber dealer, 58; Amelia, wife, 47; 8 children, ages 0 to 20, all born in AL. 1920, Mt. Vernon: Berry Cannon, 78, retired. Berry, son of John Cannon, died at Mt. Vernon on 13 April 1928 [Ancestry; Census].

Cardener, C. (1820) gunsmith. 1850, Montgomery County. Cardener, age 30, gunsmith, value $2500; H [female], 29, his wife both born in Germany; Margaret, 9; Louisa, 5; Joseph, 3; Charles, 1, all born in AL [Census].

Carleton, Charles H. gunsmith. 1871-93, Mobile. 1871, north side of Government between Royal and Water Sts.; 1885, north west corner of Royal and Conti, 1889-93, residence south side of Dauphin; worked for Eugene Voss [*Dirs.*].

Carmichael, Hugh (1813-1864) gunsmith. Clayton, Barbour County. 1860, Hugh Carmichael, 47, gunsmith; Flora, wife, both born in NC; William H., born in AL.. On 1 September 1858 Hugh purchased 80 acres in Barbour County. He was killed in the service of the Glorious Cause [Census].

Carmouche, Jean Baptiste (c.1692-c.1753) locksmith. Carmouche was born about 1692, ancestor of the Avoyelles Carmouche family, was a native of St. Laurent de Pont-de-Mousson, France. Carmouche migrated as a locksmith from the port of Lorient, on the ship *Gironde* in 1720 to Mobile where he married and his son, Joseph Carmouche was born about 1742. Jean Baptiste died before 1753, at which time his estate included a plantation outside the city and a house and lot on Bourbon Street in New Orleans. 1746, he served as a witness in Mobile. 1746; Jean Carmouche *dit* Lorain, locksmith.
[http://www.avoyelles.com/]

Carpenter, Barto Davis (1861-1909) gunsmith. African-American tradesman. Vienna, Pickens County. Davis, single, black, 18, gunsmith, living alone. Davis was born on 3 September 1861 and died on 24 September 1909 [Census]. Evidently he went by davis and did not regularly use Barto.

Carroll, W. B. (1827) gunsmith. 1860, Lawrence County. W. B. Carroll, gunsmith, 33, born in SC, $400 real estate, $200 personal value; Mary, wife, 33; Sarah, 7; Margaret, 4, all born in GA; Nola, born in AL [Census].

Caruthers, Joseph (1795-1845) gunsmith. 1834, Huntsville, Madison County. He was a son of John C. and Sarah Rodgers Caruthers. Joseph married Mary Humes. He was noted in the 1830 census of Huntsville [Ancestry; Noble].

Cedar Creek Furnace iron manufactory South of Russellville, Franklin County. This facility opened in 1818 enabling the AL gun-making industry to have a supply of iron. Before it opened gunsmiths had to obtain iron from furnaces near Iron City, Tennessee North of Lauderdale and Limestone Counties.

Clark, Isaac (1792-1854) gunsmith. 1830, Maury County, TN. 1850, Jackson County. Isaac, age 65, gun smith; Juniata, 53, his wife; Perry, 35, farmer, all born in TN; Preston, 27, farmer; Margaret, 18; Richard, 14; David, 12; Eleanor, 8; all born in AL. 1860, Straightbreek post office, Jackson County, living alone. Value of personal estate $300.00; born in VA, age 81. He was the father of Juliett and Elizabeth Clark who lived next door [Census]. According to the family genealogy Isaac was born in 1792 in Montgomery, Virginia. He married Jemima Welch on 2 April 1812 in Jefferson County, Tennessee. Land Record: 26 Nov 1818 Isaac Clark deeds to James Porter. Land Record: 18 July 1838 sold to Jerusha Clark. Isaac was a son of Thomas William Clark and his wife Jemima Scutt. Isaac's children included Thomas N.; Simeon Perry; William Clay; Elizabeth; Isaac C.; Preston; Maragret; George W.; Richard; David C.; Eleanor; and Juliett. Isaac died on 4 April 1854 in Alabama.

Cole, William F. (1841) gunsmith. 1870, Limestone County. William F. Cole was born in TN, a gunsmith, living in household of John West, 45, farmer, with George West, 39, born in TN, gunsmith [Census].

Coleman & Duke dealers. Agents for Deringer. Cahaba. Cahaba, also spelled Cahawba, was the first permanent state capital of Alabama from 1820 to 1825.

Cone, L. T. (1822) gunsmith. 1850, district 21, Macon County. Cone, gunsmith, 28, born in GA, living with James Carpenter, farmer. [Census]. Ancestry gives his initials in 1850 as Y. L.

Connor, Hugh (1819) gunsmith. 1855-80, Red Store, Mobile County. Worked c.1855-59 for James Ferrie. 1880, Hugh Connor, born in NY, 61, gunsmith; James B., born in AL, 21, farmer. 866-69, 38 St. Michael, Mobile. Residence Shell Road between Pine and Hallett Sts. 1892, 157 Marine, Mobile. The 1870 census makes little sense: Hugh Connor, 63, born in NY; Matilda, wife, 40; James, 11; Emma, 20 [Census; Ancestry; *Dirs*.].

Conner, John M. (1819) gunsmith. 1860-85, Tuskegee, Macon County [Census; *Dirs*].

Conning, James (c.1809) gunsmith. 1841-75, Mobile [*Dirs*]. Conning imported small pistols, dueling pistols, and swords and acted as an agent for Henry Deringer. James Conning, Dauphin and Water Street, Mobile, produced, or at least sold, several edged weapons, including officers' swords as well as cavalry and artillery sabres, He provided these under contract for the State of Alabama. The latter are stamped on the reverse ricasso with firm name and address. This method of marking evidently appeared too commercial to be used on his officer's swords. The maker identified many of these by engraving his name and address on the reverse scabbard throat. A serial number was stamped on the underside of the guard just in front of the blade. A comparison between the products of firm and those marked by Boyle & Gamble indicates a certain commonality. James was born about 1809 in Campbell Hall, Orange County, NY, a son of William and Sarah Booth Conning. Reportedly he died in Mobile, date unknown. This does not fit with the census. 1860, James Conning, jeweler, 45. born in NY, $14,000 real estate; personal value $85,000; Virginia, 28; Sally, 10; John G., 6; Willie, 2, all born in AL. 1870, James Conning, jeweler, 50, born in NY; Virginia, wife, 37; Sally, 18; John, 16; William, 12; Mary, 7; Claude, 5; Sewell B., 2, all born in AL [Census; Ancestry]. *One double barrel Shotgun and one set of cased pistols are shown in the Photo section.*

Corun, Hugh (1820) gunsmith. 1850, Mobile. Corun was born in NY, single, 30, living in a large rooming house [Census].

Coruse, Hugh (1820) gunsmith. 1850, Mobile. Hugh was born in NY and lived in a boarding house or hotel [Census].

Cowen, H. (1819) gunsmith. 1850, Mobile County. L. Pisson, 60, gunsmith; L. Pisson, 21, gunsmith, both born in LA; H. Cowen, 31, born in NY. All living with J. B. Fellows, merchant [U.S. Census].

Craddock, David (1792) gunsmith. 1850, Marshall County. 1860, Youngville, western division, Tallapoosa County: David Craddock, mechanic, 68, born in SC; Judy A. F., 15, born in AL [Census].

Cradner, C. (1820) gunsmith. 1850, Montgomery County; born in Germany [Census].

Craig, John A. (1846) gunsmith. 1870, Bellemont, Sumter County. Craig, born in AL, lived with 2 apparently unrelated harness makers [Census].

Crain, John (1762) gunsmith. Granville County, N.C. Son of Ambrose and Elizabeth (Head) Crain. Although he may have been married once before, on 10 August, 1825, in Limestone County, AL, Joel married Margaret Mitchell (c.1780-1860). Joel's application for a Revolutionary War Pension alleged that he enlisted in the Wilkes County, NC Militia in 1780 and served in the NC Line for three months patrolling at Cross Creek. Joel re-enlisted and served a second term of four to five months. He moved from Wilkes County, NC, to Georgia, where Joel was on the 1792 Tax Roll of Wilkes County. In 1806 Joel sold the land he had acquired in 1789 in Franklin County, GA. Joel and Rachel resided in Franklin County, GA, when they transferred property in Elbert County, GA, on 29 September, 1798. Joel was on the tax rolls of Bedford County, TN, from 1806-1825 where he sold land in 1816 and 1822; and was in Warren County, TN, in 1820. Joel's last move was to Crainville, Hatchie River, Hardeman County in 1825 [family].

Culpepper, David (1825) 1850, Union Springs, Bullock County. David, 25, apprentice to gunsmith [Census]. His age is a bit old to be an apprentice and I have not located with whom he was serving his apprenticeship. David Culpepper, 25, Apprentice to gunsmith, value $30; Sarah Culpepper, 25, Keeping home, both white; Monty Jonnis, 6, [M] black, all born in GA.

D

Dalton, John Washington (1842) gunsmith. Limestone County. Dalton was born in AL. He married Nancy Elmira Nash (1845). They had eight children. John's occupation was a gunsmith and his wife was a milliner. He served in the Glorious Cause. 1880, Shelbyville, Bedford County, TN: John W. Dalton, gunsmith, 38, born in AL; Nancy, wife, 35; Martha, 14; Nancy, 12; Frances, 10; Margaret, 8; Sallie, 6; John, 3; William, 1, all born in TN. His mother's name was Nancy E. Dalton [Census; Ancestry; Family].

Danley, James, Jr. (1799) gunsmith. 1842, Lauderdale County. 1850, James Danley, 51, born in SC; wife Eliza, 41; Martha, 17; Susan, 14; Perry, 12; James, 10; Adaline, 9; Amanda, 1?; Elizabeth,1, all born in AL [Census; *Dir*].

Danne & Zepernick gunsmiths. 1868, Mobile. Danne & Zepernick, have removed their Gunsmith Shop from No. 13 S. Water to No. 21 Dauphin St., 2nd store below J. Conning & Co. [*Mobile Register*, 12 November 1868].

Danne, Arthur O. gunsmith 1875-85, 24 Dauphin, upstairs, Mobile. On 20 October 1872 Danne enlisted in the National Guard. 1890-92, Isabella, widow of Arthur Danne [Ancestry; *Dirs*.].

Danne, John W. gunsmith 1859-89, Mobile. 1859, Danne & Zeppernick. 1871, shop at 24 Dauphin; residence 3 N. Hamilton St. On 20 May 1880 he married a lady named Wilhelmina in Mobile. In 1875 Danne rented pistols to various people the day before elections [*Dirs*; Congressional Record]. There were apparently two gunsmiths named John W. Danne, neither located in the censuses. The first man was born about 1819 and emigrated to Mobile, AL, in 1857.The second John died in March 1937.

"Removal. Danne & Zaepernick has removed their gunsmith shop from No. 13 S. Water to No. 21 Dauphin street, second store below J. Conning & Co." [*Mobile Register*, 15 November 1868] *One double barrel shotgun is shown in the Photo section.*

Davidson, A. S. (1816) teacher, gunsmith. 1860, Florence, Lauderdale County. A. S. Davidson, teacher, 44; Margaret A., wife, 37, both born in NC; Nancy, 16; Sarah, 14; John, 12; Martha, 10; William M, 7; James T, 6; Carmelia, 1, all born in AL. Reportedly, Davidson worked at the Kennedy gun factory [Wallace; Census].

Davidson, William Riley (1813) gunsmith. 1850, Lauderdale County. William, age 37, born in N.C., value $200, gunsmith; Matilda, his wife, 30, born in TN; Leroy, 6; Mary, 5; Hiram, 3; Wiley, 2, all born in AL [Census].

Davis and Bozeman's Gunshop 1864, Coosa County. This gunshop served as a Confederate recruiting station during the Second War for Independence. Baseman was probably Bozeman. Henry J. Davis and David W. Bozeman made approximately 900 rifles and 89 carbines for the state of Alabama. In addition, they repaired arms for the state. In November 1864 their contract had expired. The well made barrel are identical to the ones on the Dickson, Nelson & Co. and the Hodgkins arms. It appears the barrels were made in Columbus, Ga. for all three gun makers."

Deene, William (1819) gunsmith 1860, Mobile County; born in France [Census].

Dittrich, John F. (1827-1875) importer and manufacturer 1850-59, St. Louis; 1861-68, Mobile; 1868-75, New Orleans. 1861, 18 S. Water St.; 1866, 156 St. Francis St. [*Dirs.*; Census; Noble].

Dobson, W. (1820) locksmith Perry St., Montgomery. Also bell hanger. 1850, ward 2: William Dobson, born in England, 20, living in a boarding house with a variety of other tradesmen, including a bee keeper, a carriage trimmer, and a basket maker [*Alabama Journal*, 26 January 1851; Census]

Dod, Jonathan (1784-1859) gunsmith. 1850, Choctaw County. Dod, 66, gun smith; Lusinda, 48, his wife, both born in S.C.; William, 32, planter; Henry, 27; Caroline, 11; Isaac, 9; all born in AL [Census]. He died before the 1860 Census was taken. The primary lead we have to his parents is that there was a John Dodd who was a gunsmith in Charleston, South Carolina, during the First War for Independence. The second possibility is that he may have been a son of William and Henrietta Dodd. Jonathan may have married Lucenda Martin McDowell. Jonathan Dodd lived in Johnston County, North Carolina, for a period of time and may have married there a woman of the Ashley family. Jonathan lived around Bladon Springs. Unknown burials. There were four U.S. Censuses showing him in Clark County, Washington County, and Choctaw Counties, all in Alabama. The apparent change of location is due to the succession of counties, not to his having moved [family].

Dolphus, Adam (1815) gunsmith. 1850-60, southern division, Talladega County. 1860, Mardisville, Talladega County: Adam Dolphus, gunsmith, 45, born in France, property value $300, personal worth $50, living alone [Census]. Also seen as Dolphus.

Doty, James J. (1822) gunsmith. 1850, Marengo County. James, gunsmith, age 28; Henrietta, 25, his wife; Julia, 5, all born in AL [Census].

Dudley, Oliver (1791) gunsmith. 1850, division 23, Barbour County. 1850, Oliver Dudley, gunsmith, 59, born in CT; Jane, wife, 50; Sarah, 22; Sidney, 11; Mary C., all born in GA. Oliver was born in Guilford, New Haven County, CT, in 1790, a son of Luther and Mary Chidsey Dudley. 1860-65, Topeka, Shawnee County, KS. He died in Kansas City, MO [Ancestry; Census].

Duncan, Jonathan (1765-1845) gunsmith. Lauderdale County. Duncan was born in Laurens County, SC, a son of Alfred Duncan, a prominent gunsmith later of Sullivan County, TN. Jonathan married Jane Jones. He died in Lauderdale County in 1845 [Ancestry]. According to Dan Wallace, Duncan worked at the Kennedy gun factory in Green Hill.

E

Eckard, George (1820) gunsmith. 1850, Mobile County. All in same household: F. Gibb, born in France, gunsmith, age 30; Charles Gibb, age 28, gunsmith, born in France; John Farrin, age 30, born in France, gunsmith; George Eckard, 30, gunsmith, born in Germany; and William Eckard, age 15, gunsmith [probably an apprentice], born in Germany; all living in a boarding house or hotel with many others [U.S. Census].

Eckard, William (1835) gunsmith. 1850, Mobile County. All in same household: F. Gibb, born in France, gunsmith, age 30; Charles Gibb, age 28, gunsmith, born in France; John Farrin, age 30, born in France, gunsmith; George Eckard, 30, gunsmith, born in Germany; and William Eckard, age 15, gunsmith [probably an apprentice], born in Germany; all living in a boarding house or hotel with many others [Census].

Edgar, James (1825) black and gunsmith. 1850, district 5, Franklin County: James Edgar, farmer, 28, born in TN; Margaret, wife, 28; Jesse, 6; Barton, 1, all born in AL. 1870, Thorn Hill, eastern division, Marion County: James Edgar, born in TN, 45, blacksmith; Margaret, wife, 48; Martha, 18; Dorcas, 18; Joseph, 14; Benjamin, 12; Mary, 10; William C, 8, all born in AL. On 2 April 1857 he purchased 200 acres in Marion County [Census; Ancestry]. According to Dan Wallace, Edgar worked 1852-72, in R. S. S. Bull's shop in Marion County.

Edwards, Henry B. (1810) gunsmith. 1850. Madison County; born in NC [Census].

Edwards, Thomas (1828) gunsmith. 1880, beat 12, Madison County. Edwards, gunsmith, 52, living alone, born in TN [Census].

Eiland, Judge Stephen (1788-1853) jurist and gunsmith. On 1 August 1788 Stephen was born in Washington, Hancock County, GA. On 15 November 1810 he married Mary Allen in Salem, Lee County, AL. He died on 9 April 1853 in Russell County, age 64 [Ancestry].

Eldridge, Charles (1798) gunsmith. 1842, Irwinton, historic district in Eufaula, Barbour County, AL. Charles advertised seeking a journeyman gunsmith to employ. 1870, Silver Lake, AR: Charles Eldridge, farmer, 72; Rebecca, wife, 80, both born in AL [Census; Ancestry; Macon (GA) *Weekly Telegraph*, 15 January 1838].

Elston, Allen (1792) gunsmith. 1820, Lincoln County, Tennessee; born in New Jersey. He charged $15 for his rifles [Census of Manufactures]. 1850-60, Talladega County, Alabama. 1850, Allen Elston, gunsmith, age 68, born in N.J., value $15,000; Ellen, 58, his wife, born in S.C.; Jonathan, 27 no occupation, born in TN; Mary, 15, born in AL [U.S. Census].

Estes, Henderson (1807-1864) gunsmith. Jackson County. Estes died in Columbia, TN. 1860, Henderson Estes, farmer, 53, born in VA; Nancy, wife, 40; William, 24; John, 19; Martha, 17; Mary, 15; Solomon, 12, all born in TN [Noble]. Henderson Estes may be the son of Elisha Estes and Lucy Blankenship who were married in Nov 1806.

F

Farrin, John (1820) gunsmith. 1850, Mobile County. All in same household: F. Gibb, born in France, gunsmith, age 30; Charles Gibb, age 28, gunsmith, born in France; John Farrin, age 30, born in France, gunsmith; George Eckard, 30, gunsmith, born in Germany; and William Eckard, age 15, gunsmith [probably an apprentice], born in Germany; all living in a boarding house or hotel with many others [U.S. Census].

Faulkner, William L. (1835-1898) gunsmith. Shoalford, Limestone County. William was born in Virginia on 6 January 1835, a son of Henry Isaac Faulkner and his wife Mary Ann Virginia Holbert. In 1851 in Giles County, TN, he married Allie Frances Riddle. 1860, Shoalford, Limestone County: William L. Faulkner, gunsmith, 28, born in VA; Arisey [?], 24, wife, born in AL; Jacob, 4, born in TN; Thomas, 1, born in AL. William died on 15 July 1898 in Limestone County[Census].

Ferguson, Bartholomew (1803) gunsmith. 1850, Huntsville, Madison County; born in Virginia. Bart was single and lived in a rooming house or hotel with a number of other professional men [Census].

Ferrie, James. gunsmith. 1855-59, Mobile [*Dirs*]. Not located in censuses.

Fisher, W. B. (c.1813) armorer. sergeant in 44th Alabama Regiment, CSA. Fisher enlisted at Westmorelandville, Lauderdale County [Ancestry].

Fisher, William (1820) armorer. Wetumpka, Coosa County. In civilian life he was a gunsmith. In 1860-64 he lived in Coosa County; but was born in SC. 1860, Fisher, 40, living in a huge boarding house, apparently single [Census].

Flautt, Jerome (1883) cooper and gunsmith. He married Sarah Freeman. Jerome lived two years at Mobile where he was experimenting in gardening early vegetables for the Northern markets. He was born in Hagerstown, MD [Ancestry; Family].

Fleming, William gunsmith. 1873, Montgomery [*Dir*].

Flynn, James (1793) gunsmith. 1850, Dale County; born in GA [Census].

Foley, Watson (1837) armorer. 1850, Washington County, GA: Foley, 17. Enlisted March 11, 1862 in Chambers County by Capt. Powell, Company E, 46th Alabama Infantry. Mustered in at Loachapoka April 21, 1862. Appears on Muster Roll of Detailed Soldiers employed at Atlanta, Georgia Arsenal, commanded by M. H. Wright from September through December 1863. Employed as a gunstocker. Captured near Nashville December 15, 1864 and sent to Camp Douglas, Illinois. Applied to take Oath of Allegiance in January 1865. Remarks: "Claims to have been loyal was conscripted Deserted to avail himself of the Amnesty Proclamation." 5'-5 1/2" tall, hazel eyes, dark hair and complexion. 1870, ward 1 Holly Springs, MS, Watson Foley, single, living alone, carriage maker, born in GA. 1880, Forest City, St. Francis County, AR: Foley, carriage maker, 38, born in GA [Ancestry].

Forem, G. (1816) gunsmith. 1850, Mobile. G. Forem, 34, born in France, gunsmith, single, living in a rooming house with many other men from France [Census].

Foster, James Daniel (1830-1914) gunsmith. James was born on March 28, 1830 in Wilkes County, GA. He enlisted in the Glorious Cause at Greenville, AL, in the spring of 1862 and served at Pensacola and at the Battle of Corinth. Because of disability he was assigned to the Arsenal at Montgomery. He became a lock and gunsmith in Chattanooga. Foster who went to the Huntsville area after the Civil War. On 11 May 1851 he married Caroline Baker in Coosa County. He was listed as a gunsmith and in a later census record, his sister, Fanny, was living with him. He was the son of Joseph Shephard Foster and Charlotte Daniel of Wilkes County Georgia and later Montgomery County Alabama. He died on 30 April 1914 [Genealogy; Family].

Foster, Walter V. (1814-1900) gunsmith. Halpins, Randolph County. Walter was born on 6 March 1841 in Carroll County, GA, a son of William Thomas Foster and his wife Lucy Stribling. He married Betsy Ann Traylor in 1839. 1850, Randolph County. Walter, gunsmith, age 34 born in S.C.; Elizabeth, born in GA, 26, wife; William, 10; John, 8; Green [male], 6; Thomas, 4; Sophia, 1, all born in AL The following households of gunsmiths were enumerated one after another: Foster, Ivy, Southerland, Nunis, Thompson, and Walls. 1850, Foster, born in S.C., age 34, gunsmith; Elizabeth, 26, his wife, born in GA; William, 10; John, 8; Greene, 6; Thomas, 4; Sophia,1, all born in AL. Walter died in Halpins, AL, on 15 December 1900 [Ancestry; Census].

Franks, Benjamin R. inventor. Scottsborough [Scottsboro], Jackson County. On 22 March 1881 Franks received U.S. patent number 239,238, for an extractor.

Freeman, Fineas (1823) gunsmith. 1860, Jackson County: Fineas Freeman, gunsmith, 37, born in TN; Mary Ann, wife, 33; John W, 10; Adam P, 4; Thomas W., 2, all born in AL. He lived beside Young Sellers, gunsmith [Census].

G

Gamble, Harry (1863) gunsmith. 1880, Montgomery. Mary Gamble, mother, 37; Harry, 17, apprentice gunsmith; Charles, 14; Katie, 5; Albert, 3; Thomas, 1, all born in AL [Census].

Ganmiel, George (1837-1922) gunsmith. 1880, Montgomery. George Ganmiel, gunsmith, 43, born in GA; Sallie B., 25, born in Ireland; William, 13; Perly, 10; Calie, 4, all born in AL. Residence Clayton west of Dickerson. 1903, 827 Goode St. George died on 15 October 1922 in Tallapoosa County [*Dirs.*; Census]. Also seen as Gammell and Gammiel.

Gammell, Harry M. gunsmith 1891-1907, 404 Madison Ave., Birmingham [*Dirs.*].

Garner, Lewis (1800-1860) gunsmith. 1818-42, Lauderdale County; employed at the Kennedy gun factory. He married Mary Ritter. 1850, Moore County, NC: Lewis Garner, gunsmith, 55, born in NC; Mary, wife, 44; Henry, 21; Lucy, 17; Gideon, 15; William, 13; John, 10; Samuel, 8; Marcus, 7; Elizabeth, 4, all born in NC. On 1 August 1853 Garner purchased 40 acres in Lauderdale County. About 1857 he moved to Lee County, MS. Dan Wallace said he moved from Moore County, NC to Lauderdale County, about 1818, then back to Moore County about 1847-52. He moved to Tupelo, MS, in late 1853. 1860, Mooresville, Itawamba County, MS; Lewis Garner, gunsmith, 60; Mary, wife, 55, both born in NC; Lemuel, 17; John, 20; Mary H., 11, all born in NC. Lewis Garner, born on 3 March 1788 at Howards Mill, Moore County, NC, a son of Bradley and Barbara Andrews Garner, died in Tishomingo, Tishomingo County, MS, in May 1860 [Wallace; Census; Ancestry].

Gast, E. H. gun and locksmith. at the Birmingham Arms & Cycle. Birmingham. E. H. Gast, expert gunsmith [*Age Herald*, 7 May 1899]

Gay, Alexis (1787-1847) gunsmith. Mobile. Gay died at age 60 in Mobile, born in France [*Mobile Death Records*].

Gelbke Brewery, Mobile. This brew house was operational from roughly the end of the Civil War until the 1880s in a Springhill Avenue location just west of Broad Street for about 12 to 15 years. The facility had a brewery, a saloon and a gunsmith shop all in one.

Gelbke, Charles (c.1820-c.1895) gunsmith. Charles arrived in Mobile in 1868. 1870, ward 8: Charles W., brewery, 50; Madaline, 40, wife, both born in France; Charles, 16; Madaline, 14; Lewis, 7; Louisa, 4, all born in AL. 1880, Mobile; in household of Frederick Gelbke; born in France. Charles died before 1900. His wife Madeline predeceased him. Charles Jr. in the 1900 census claimed both his parents were born in Germany [Ancestry; Census].

"Military Companies having old Styles of Muskets, can have them converted into RIFLE MUSKETS at moderate expense and with little delay, at GELBKE & BRO., GUN MAKERS, No. 14 DAUPHIN STREET -- those gentlemen having the most experienced workmen that can be procured. Also, Cannon Rifled on the most improved principle, and Patterns made for Balls." [1861, reprinted in *Mobile Press Register*, 8 July 1911]

Gelbke, Frederick L. (1819) gunsmith. 1869-84, Mobile. 1870, ward 3: F. L., gunsmith, 51, born in Italy, real estate $1600; Mary, 25, single, born in Italy. He was listed as married and Mary as single, but in 1890 his widow was Marie. 1869, 14 Dauphin St.; 1875, north side Dauphin Way, between Pine and Hallett; 1885, north side Dauphin. His last directory entry was in 1885 and in 1890 Marie, widow of Frederick. Later descendants claimed that Fred was born in Germany [Census; *Dirs.*].

"F. L. Gelbke, gunsmith and dealer in Guns, Rifles, Pistols, Gun Materials, and Ammunition. Fishing Tackle for sale cheap. Also Engraving – fine silver plated door plates, steel and stencil cutting, Government, Lodge, and Notary Public Seals, Facsimiles &c. executed promptly" [*Mobile Register*, 10 March 1868]

Gesslin, Robert. gunsmith. 1921, Dauphin St., Mobile. Gesslin shot and killed a Negro who claimed that Gesslin had his gun for repair and refused to return it. Gesslin told him that he was in the wrong shop. They argued and reportedly the Negro attempted to hit Gesslin with an iron rod. Gesslin got a revolver and shot him dead [*Times Picayune*, 19 October 1921].

Giesel, Jacob. gun and locksmith. 1872, Tuscumbia, Colbert County. "gun & locksmith and general repairs" [Noble]. Not located.

Gorgas, Josiah (1818-1883). armorer. The Confederacy utilized Josiah Gorgas as its chief ordnance officer throughout the war. A graduate of West Point, Class of 1841, Gorgas resigned from the U.S. Army on April 3, 1861. He was initially commissioned major and chief of Ordnance on April 8, 1861. He made lieutenant colonel on March 16, 1861; colonel in 1863; and brigadier general on November 10, 1864. After the war, he was engaged in an iron works business in Alabama and still later in education. Frank E. Van Diver's *Ploughshares into Swords*, a biography of Gorgas, is mandatory reading for those interested in arms in the Confederacy.

Goubil, Benjamin (1830). gunsmith. 1855-78, Mobile. 1870, Benjamin, gunsmith, 32; Artemise, 28, wife. 1870, Benjamin, 40, gunsmith, value $5000 real estate, $3000 personal; Artemus, 42, wife. 1880, Benjamin Goubil, gunsmith, 50; Artemise [Rogers], 48, wife; Mary Ann Boyle, 15, niece; Benjamin Henry, 11, nephew, all born in AL, all listed as mulatto. The 1873 city directory calls him Creole. 1861, 3 Dauphin; residence at 58 S. Cedar. 1866, 77 S. Broad St. 1870, southeast corner of Dauphin and Commerce Sts. 1873, east side Broad between Government and Commerce Sts. 1876, 12 Dauphin Way; residence 17 S. Broad St. [*Dirs.;* Census].

Graves, Charles Henry (1821-1863). farmer and gunsmith. Blount County. Graves was born about 1821 in TN, died 5 November. 1863 of yellow fever in Ross Hospital, Mobile, AL, and was buried in an unmarked grave in Magnolia Cemetery. His family continued to live in Blount County, AL. He was a farmer, and served as a gunsmith during the war [Ancestry; Family].

Graves, James C. (1829). gunsmith. Graves was born in GA. He first married Melinda L. Willis (1830-) on 7 February 1850 in GA. Their first child was born in Troup County, GA; the last one in Washington County, Texas, and all the others in Macon County, AL. He secondly married Clara P. (1859-) on 26 January 1883 in Limestone County, TX, where all their children were born [family].

Graves, James Lewis (1898-1962). clock repair, and was a gunsmith, tinkerer, trapper, and farmer. Hayden. Jim Graves was born 8 August. 1898 in Blount County and died on 22 August 1962, and was buried in Graves Gap Cemetery, Blount County. He married Alice Zadie Barber (1910-) [family]. He reportedly knew of an Amerindian cave called the Devil's Tater Patch or The Devil's Graveyard, in which gold was plentiful. The cave is about one-half mile east of the Bangor-Blountsville road in the Gum Springs Community.

Gray, Adolphus. gunsmith. 1842, Mobile [*Dir*].

Greenberry, Franklin (1827-1881). gunsmith and farmer. Franklin was born on November 20, 1827 in Kentucky and died December 13, 1881 in Jefferson County, Alabama. He served in the Civil War as a private in the Truss Company, Barberres Battalion of Alabama, CSA. He married Arletha McDaniel in Gandrud; daughter of Mary and Jeremiah McDaniel. He and his wife raised 10 children, 7 sons and 3 daughters. He was buried at Nichols Cemetery, Lake Purdy, Jefferson, Alabama. After he had been dead for 26 years his wife applied for a pension in Jefferson County, on June 7, 1907 [family].

Griffin, Green (1821). gunsmith. Lauderdale County, age 42 in 1863 Enlisted in the Union Cavalry, 3rd Arkansas, on 22 March 1864 at Lewisburg, AR. Height 5' 10", eyes blue, hair light, complexion fair, gunsmith. 1860, Murfreesboro, Thompson Twp., Pike County: Green Griffin, blacksmith, 38; Mahala, wife, 37; S.T., 19; H., 13; M.M., 9; Jane, 7, all born in AL [Census; Ancestry; Family Bible].

H

Haag, G. gunsmith. 1873, Mobile. Haag worked for Christian Kreutner. Haag arrived on 8 May 1852 from Ireland [*Dir.*; Noble; Ancestry].

Hanley, Michael (1809). armorer. 1850, Mobile County. Hanley, 41, armorer; Catharine, his wife, 33; Eliza, 13, all born in Ireland. Hanley arrived on 5 December 1836 at New Orleans [Ancestry; Census].

Hanna, John (c.1780-after 1850). gunsmith, patriot, farmer. According to one family genealogy and the 1850 census, Hanna was born in VA. Another genealogy suggested that he was born in Ireland between 1766 and 1780.. Both genealogies agree that he married Mary Adarene in 1835 in Benton County. He was a soldier of the American Revolution, listed as a private in the 2nd Company of Colonel Nathaniel Gist, Virginia Regiment [T. Saffel, *The Revolutionary War*]. Hanna's occupation was gunsmith. He came from TN to Benton, now Calhoun County, AL, in 1832, and settled at the foot of Chosea Mountain. 1850, subdivision 30, Benton County: John Hanna, blacksmith, 70, born in VA, living with his son Woodford R. Hanna. John Hannna died after 1850 in Chosea Springs, Benton County [Census; Family; Ancestry].

Hardin, Morris (1788). gunsmith. 1850, Tuscaloosa County; born in Germany [Census].

Harris, Andrew Green (1830-1867). gunsmith. Mobile County; he died at the age of 37 according to the Mobile County death records.

Harris, John H. (1836-1863). gunsmith. Harris enlisted on 9 April 1862 at Auburn. He appears on muster roll dated 13 May 1862 at Auburn. He was hospitalized in General Hospital at Lauderdale Springs MS on 22 April 1863; Signed for clothing at Lynchburg, VA, Hospital No. 1 on 3 June 1863; Appears on Pay Roll dated 31 October 1863 at Montgomery with notation "Detailed in Ordnance Department in Montgomery." Another notation in one record reads "Detached for duty in Gun Shop by Governor of Alabama"; Detailed to C.S. Arsenal at Montgomery on 31 December 1863. On 26 March 1864 he was noted as a gunsmith age 27; 5'10" tall with blue eyes, dark hair and fair complexion. He appears as a private on muster roll of Company I published by Carlisle in 1902 *Weekly Enterprise*. He appears on a muster roll of Company I 37th Regiment, Alabama Volunteers at Lafayette, Chambers County, Alabama, March 6, 1862 published on 31 July 1901 issue of the *Lafayette Sun* with privates as "Harris, John, died at Lauderdale Spring 1863, MS [Ancestry; Family].

Harris, Virginius C. (1846-1889). gunsmith. Huntsville, Madison County. 1880, V. C. Harris, 34, carpenter; Julia, 29, wife, both born in VA; Lena, 11; Eva, 7; Willie, 4; Oscar, 1, all born in AL [Census]

"The city was thrown into a state of shocked excitement last Thursday on learning that Mr. V. C. Harris was shot and killed about 5:30 o'clock while out hunting. From the statement of Mr. John Organ, his brother-in-law, who was with him at the time, Mr. Harris had stopped to rest at the bridge on the road leading to Maysville about half a mile from the city limits, and seeing a few peaches on a tree growing up out of the ditch, rested the butt of his gun on a rock wall and reached for the fruit. The breach of the gun slipped over the wall and allowed he hammer to strike against the rocks, discharging both barrels into his thigh. The charge entered his thigh a few inches above the knee, ranging up, severed the femoral artery and mangled the flesh terribly. He lived only a few minutes – bleeding to death. Mr. Harris was a gunsmith by trade and was proficient in the use of firearms, and it is a strange fatality that one so accustomed to the use of a gun should be fatally injured from careless handling. He was vice-president of the Madison county gun club. . . .he leaves a wife and family of small children" [*Huntsville Gazette*, 10 August 1889]

Hasting, John P. (1800). gunsmith. Friendship, Butler County. 1860, John P. Hasting, gunsmith, 60, born in SC. On 15 July 1854 John acquired 40 acres in section 9-N, Butler County. On 30 November 1856 in Butler County John Hasting married Nancy Benson. Although technically too old for military service John served the Glorious Cause in the 17th AL Infantry [Ancestry; Census].

Hatcher, Jordan (1809-1882). Slave artisan. Cahaba, Dallas County. Jordan Hatcher, was considered in slave days a very well-to-do colored man. He hired his own time and that of his boys from his master at so much per day and taught them the trades, blacksmithing, wheel righting and carpentry which these boys as fathers have handed down to their posterity and some of their children are now teaching these trades in the schools and making a fair living for their own families. Jordan Hatcher was also a teacher in the public schools of Dallas County, and was ten years postmaster at Cahaba, the first permanent capital of AL, now a ghost town. He was also one of the three colored members of the first Constitutional Convention after the Civil War. 1870, Jordan Hatcher, 60, postmaster, widower, black, born in GA. 1880, Jordan Hatcher, mulatto, 70, postmaster, widower. He was a devout Christian and lived to be 73 years of age, dying in Dallas County on 15 September 1882 [Ancestry; Family].

Hatcher, S. G. (1860). blacksmith and silversmith. African-American tradesman. Mitchells, Dallas County. After some years, owing to ill health, abandoned that occupation, taking up gunsmithing and silversmithing, having successfully run in two different towns a wholesale and retail grocery business and bar-room. After some years' reflection, his decision was that the sale of whiskey was not for Christian men, and he, without hesitation, gave up the same. He was married four times, first, to Laura English, second, Miss Eliza English, third, Virginia Tarte, fourth, Fannie Mumford. To these unions were born sixteen children. At the time of his death he was class leader and trustee, having held all other positions connected with the church. His example in church work was worthy of emulation, and among his last admonitions while on his deathbed was, "Conference meets here in a few weeks, and be sure to pay my dollar money." He was over sixty-three years of age at the time of his death. 1880, S. G. Hatcher, 20, merchant, single, born in AL [Census; Sara Duncan, *Progressive Mission in the South and Addresses*].

Haughton, W. A. gunsmith. 1861, Mobile. Gunsmith at Gelbke Brothers [*Dir.*].

Haughton, William W. gunsmith. 1884-87, shop 26 Dauphin; home south west corner of Palmetto and Jefferson, Mobile [*Dir.*].

Hennington gunsmith (1833-). 1870, Livingston, Sumter County. The census is totally blank as to name but gives age as 37, born in VA, gunsmith, in household of George Hennington, 40, born in N.H., household 959 [Census].

Henry, Edward (1810). gunsmith. 1850, Madison County. Edward, age 40, gun smith, value $150; Delilah, 25, both born in N.C.; Mary, 1, born in AL [Census].

Hidle, John B. (1821-1875). gunsmith. John was a son of John Hidle and his wife Mary Blakely. He was born about 1821 in Edgefield District, SC, and died about 1875 in Sellersville, Geneva County, AL. He married (1) Martha Ann Minerva Whitehurst on October 25, 1843 in Tallahassee, Leon County, FL; (2) Mary Elizabeth Marshall about 1864. Masonic record: J. B. Heidle Lodge #108 Oak Bowery of Chambers County, Alabama on September 25, 1850 E A Degree. He joined the 15th Alabama Partisan rangers but was detailed as a gunsmith October 31, 1862, by order of Major Boyles to work in an unspecified armory [Ancestry; Family].

Higgins, Alexander (1790-c.1862). gunsmith, blacksmith, whitesmith, and farmer. Alexander was born in the Old 96 district, SC, and moved to Lauderdale County, AL in 1818. Alexander Higgins was the father of Josiah Higgins and Michael Higgins. Alexander Higgins was a pioneer gunsmith at Waterloo, Lauderdale County. Alexander Higgins later moved his small gun factory and blacksmith shop from Florence to Waterloo. He established his blacksmith and gun shop on Bumpass Creek Road east of the town. Alexander died in Waterloo and was buried in the Culver Cemetery [Ancestry].

"Adron (L. Lindsey) furnished his own weapons which included a long hunting knife (Confederate Bowie) and a Kentucky rifle (Alabama long rifle), both made by Alexander Higgins at the blacksmith shop on Josiah Higgins' farm on Second Creek. Old Alexander Higgins was Martha Jane Lindsey's grandfather. Adron also brought along his own bullet mold, shot pouch, and powder horn. Adron and Martha had been married a little over eight months when he went to war. He was sworn in on Christmas Eve, 1861, by General Samuel Weakley of Florence. Adron L. Lindsey was assigned to the 27th Alabama Infantry. One of the privileges at that time was that volunteers could select their Company. Adron picked Company "C" commanded by Captain Thompson who operated a large plantation near Oakland. All but three members of his Company were killed in the Battle of Franklin." [Sharp Family History]

Higgins, Benjamin F. (1845). gunsmith. 1880, Travelers Repose, Coosa County. The large family included Ben, age 35 and his wife Josephine, age 30 [Census].

Higgins, [William] Fleming (1838). gunsmith. 1850, district 19, Chambers County. Fleming was born in June 1838, a son of Joseph and Julia Higgins. On 29 May 1859 he married Virginia Dennis in Harris County, GA. 1860, Dadeville, Tallapoosa County: Fleming Higgins, 21, in household of Joseph and Julia Higgins. gunsmith, value $300 real estate, $300 personal, born in GA. 1870, Oxford, Calhoun County: W. F. Higgins, gunsmith, 31, born in GA; Virginia, wife, 26; Uriah Higgins, both born in AL, 26, apprentice. 1880, Oxford: William, farmer, 41; Virginia, 34. 1900, Oxford: William, 61, born in June 1838; Virginia, 56 [Census].

Higgins, James (1806-). blacksmith. 1850, Chambers County. James Higgins, blacksmith, 44; Lavinia, wife, 27, both born in SC; Polimond, 9, born in GA; Julia, 6; Josephus, infant, both born in AL [Census].

Higgins, John (1807). black- and gunsmith. 1850, district 19 ½, Chambers County: John Higgins, blacksmith, 43, born in SC, value $1500; Sophera, wife, 43; James Higgins, 21, blacksmith; Wylie Higgins, 20, student; Williamson Higgins, 18, farmer; Martha, 16; Walker Higgins, 13; Oliver Higgins, 12, all born in GA [Census].

Higgins, Joseph (1818-1880). gun- and silversmith. Joseph was born on 23 May 1814 in Laurens County, SC. On 16 October 1834 in Butts County, GA, he married Judith Watts. Joseph was noted in 1840 in Butts County, GA, census. 1850, Chambers County. Joseph, 32, $700 real estate, gunsmith; Judith, 30; Grier, 11; Fleming, 10; Cordelia, 9; Frank, 7; Nancy, 6, all born in Georgia; Josephine, 4; David U., 2, born in Alabama [Census]. 1860, Tallapoosa County. 1st Regiment, Georgia Regulars. Private Joseph M. Higgins, Company "B",1st Regiment, GA Regulars. Enlisted July 17, 1861 at Savannah by Colonel Williams for 3 years. On Nov/Dec 1863 roll he is listed as absent on detached service Provost Guard at Fort Gaines Ga. by order of Gen. Cobb. A pension inquiry dated April 1,1915 states; the record shows that Joseph M. Higgins (also known as J. Marion Higgins) 1st Regiment, Georgia Regulars, enlisted April 17, 1861 at Blairsville, Georgia, and that he was discharged November 24,1861. His enlistment date differs from his pension inquiry note. He was born in North Carolina, was age 18 years, 5 foot 7 inches tall, fair complexion, blue eyes, Light hair. Occupation noted as a student. He was enlisted on April 17, 1861 byCapt Fair (sp?) at Blairsville Georgia. He was discharged by order of the Secretary of War. Noted in Calhound County censuses of 1870 and 1880. He died in July, 1880 in Oxford, Calhoun County, AL. *One rifle is shown in the Photo section.*

Higgins, Josiah (1812-1890). gunsmith. Lauderdale County. Alexander Higgins was the father of Josiah Higgins and Michael Higgins. Josiah moved from Green Hill to Waterloo, Lauderdale County, AL, in 1818 along with his father, Alexander and other family members. Josiah was born about 1812 in Old Ninety-six District, Laurens County, SC. He died on 12 November 1890 in Lauderdale County, and was buried near Waterloo. He was twice married: (1) Charlotte Chealty Smith on January 4, 1831 (2) Kate Hill on July 12, 1883. He was usually listed as a blacksmith. In the later part of July 1862, Higgins led a group of elderly militiamen and fired on the U.S.S. Cottage at Waterloo, Alabama. In retaliation Federal Gunboats shelled Waterloo. Higgins and nine others were arrested and sent to Civil War Prison at Alton, IL [Ancestry].

"Will of Josiah Higgins. Know all men by these presents that I Josiah Higgins a Citizen of Lauderdale County Alabama, being in feeble health but of sound mind and disposing memory and knowing the uncertainty of human life, and wishing to make some disposition of my property both Real and personal do make and constitute this my last Will and Testament, hereby revoking all former Wills by me at any time heretofore made. 1st I hereby Appoint my Two Sons D. B. Higgins and Richard Higgins my Executors and having full confidence in Their integrity, desire that they be not required to give bond as Executors 2nd I desire at my death that all my Real Estate of whatever it may consist be Sold to the highest bidder for cash after giving Legal Notice of time and place of Sale also that all my personal property at my Death be sold in the same Terms and after paying all Court and other expenses out of proceeds of Sales the balance be disbursed as follows viz, That my wife Kate B Higgins Receive from Executors the sum of

$5.00. The balance whatever it may be I will to be divided equally between my Several children Calvin Higgins, Katharine Parker, Martha J. Lindsey, Izillar Simons, Margaret Hairell, d. B. Higgins, Richard Higgins and Elender E. Tune. Signed in the presence of the following Witnesses, who after hearing this Will read signed it as Witnesses in my presence and in the presence of each other, Waterloo Alabama October the thirteenth A. D. 1890" [Estate Packet # 1012]

Higgins, Michael (1808). gun- and blacksmith. Before 1818, Old 96 district, South Carolina. Married Jane Donaldson in 1825 in Lauderdale County, Alabama. 1860, moved to Mississippi.

Higgins, Michael II (1854). 1880, Gadsden, Etowah County: Michael Higgins, born in KY, 26, gunsmith; Victoria, wife, 27; James, 6; Leon, 4, all born in AL [Census].

Higgins, Palmer (1803-1889). gunsmith. 1850, Trigg County, KY. Palmer, 47, gunsmith; Hannah, 46, William 23, silversmith; all 3 born in S.C.; Charlotte, 19, born in Alabama; Mary, 9, born in Kentucky; William Jr, 2, born in Louisiana [Census]. Palmer was born in 1803 in Laurens County. Palmer died on 14 February 1889 in Gadsden, Etowah County, Alabama. His father was William Higgins and his mother: Nancy Ashley; his wife was Hannah Farrow (1804-1883) whom he married c.1819 in Laurens County, South Carolina. Palmer had a son William (1827-1870) who was a silversmith [family genealogy].

Higgins, Robert (1830). gunsmith. 1850, district 19, Chambers County. Robert was born in SC, a son of Sterling Higgins. 1860, Troy, Pike County: Robert J. Higgins, silversmith, 30, born in SC; Martha, wife, 20; Loulia [?], infant. In 1880 he was noted as a cotton broker, age 50, born in SC, in Troy [Noble; Census].

Higgins, Sterling T. (1802). gunsmith. Born in Laurens County, SC. 1825-42, Iron Springs district, Butts County, Georgia. 1846-50 or later, Chambers County, AL. 1850, district 19, Chambers County: Sterling, 48, gunsmith, $3000 real estate; Harriet B., 44; Robert, 20, gunsmith, all born in SC; Simon, 17; Sterling Jr., 14; Parmelia, 9; Joseph, 7; Benjamin, 5; all born in GA; Mary, 3, born in Alabama. Also Amanda Beavers, 21, born in GA [Census; Jerry Noble].

Higgins, Uriah D. (1847-1909). gunsmith. Uriah was born on 25 April 1847, a son of Joseph and Judith Watts Key Higgins. 1870, Oxford, Calhoun County, apprentice in household of W. Fleming Higgins. In 1873 Uriah married Carrie Walton. 1880, Travelers Repose, Coosa County. U. D. was living with Benjamin F. Higgins as a boarder. U. D., gunsmith, 25; Susan C., 26, wife; Mary, 2. Uriah died on 7 October 1909 [Ancestry; Census].

Higgins, William H. (1817-1868). blacksmith. 1850, Chambers County. William H. Higgins, born in SC, $800 real estate, 32, blacksmith; Adeline, 33, wife; Lavina, 7, both born in GA; William, 4; John, 1, both born in AL; John Lavin, 26, born in GA [Census].

"William H. Higgins was born August 4, 1817. The family resided in Butts County, Georgia, a few years and then moved and settled in Chambers County, Alabama, twelve miles north of LaFayette. Mr. Higgins was an excellent mechanic and conducted a smithy, providing well for the support and comfort of his family. In religious faith the family were Baptist. He was esteemed by his neighbors as a just and upright man. He was an affectionate husband and a kind and indulgent father and his wife, Adaline, was a most estimable woman, a congenial companion and devoted mother. They were the esteemed friends and neighbors. . . . [William] died September 5, 1868 of cancer. He suffered a great deal. . . . [He was buried] at the cemetery at old Bethel Church. . . ." [from the Clark family genealogy, 1905 on Ancestry].

Hill, Joseph (1789). gun maker. 1850, Lawrence County. Joseph, 61, gunsmith; Margaret, 24; Robert, 1 [Census].

Hill, Wiley Williamson (1825-1892). gunsmith. Hill was born January 4, 1825 in Alabama, near the Mississippi state line. His father was probably Wiley W. Hill who had land dealings in Neshoba County, Mississippi. In the Census of 1850 Wiley Sr owned land valued at $6000 and he and his wife had both been born in South Carolina. On June 19, 1851 our gunsmith married Mary West (1831-1921) in Noxubee County. Mary, 19 years old, was the oldest child of Benjamin and Jane (Blasengame) West. Her brother William B. West, was also a gunsmith. Wiley and Mary had nine children. In the Census of 1860 Wiley Jr is noted as a wagon master in Pickensville, Pickens County, Alabama. Wiley W. Hill served the Glorious Cause from 1861 until the close of the war. His wife and four children were left in Alabama when he enlisted in the Pickensville Blues. The enlistees were organized into the 5th Alabama Regiment of the Volunteer Infantry and sent to northern Virginia. The Census of 1870 shows Wiley Jr as a blacksmith in Oktibbeha County, a rural county located in the east-central portion of Mississippi. In 1876 he paid off a debt with produce raised on a farm known as the Harmon Place, in Colfax, Caly County. The 1880 Census listed Wiley as a carpenter in Clay County. In 1884 Wiley W. Hill moved his family from West Point, Mississippi to Hamilton. Their oldest daughter, Ella, and her husband, Bill Perry, had settled on Bear Creek on the outskirts of Hamilton. Mary's brother, William B. West, had also moved to Hamilton County. Wiley established a family home on Bear Creek. Wiley was a carpenter and blacksmith. During much of his Confederate military service he was assigned to the Armory near Richmond, Virginia because of his skill as a gunsmith. In 1890, he was in business in Hamilton as W.W. Hill and Son, with his son John. Wiley died December 27, 1892 a few days before his 68th birthday and was buried in Hamilton, Texas.

Hobbs, Charles II. (1807). gunsmith and farmer. Charles was a son of George J. Hobbs and Mary Burkhalter, born in Sampson County, NC. Charles married Rebecca Tamlinson before 1830 in Monroe County, GA. By 1830, he was in Butts County, GA, and by 1840 in Talledega County, AL. In 1850, while in Talladega County, AL, he lived two houses from his father, George Hobbs, age 78, a farmer. Also living in home of George Hobbs were "R," a 48 year old female, born in NC; "P", a 44 year old female born in SC; and "C", an eleven year old female born in GA. "R" is a daughter, "P" a daughter-in-law, and "C" a granddaughter. Living in the same neighborhood was "Y" Hobbs, age 37, born in GA, and W.W. Hobbs, age 56, a gunsmith, born in NC. This is William Horton Hobbs, Charles' brother, who was living in Talladega County, AL, in 1850. The "W.W." is an error on the part of the census taker. Charles and family appear in the 1870 census in Ashland, Clay County, AL, farmer, and owned real estate valued at $300 and personal property valued at $990. [Census].

Hobbs, Erasmus Marion "Rad" "Rasby". gunsmith. Clay, Talladega County. Hobbs made guns during the Civil War for the Glorious Cause. In 1863 he was serving in the 31st AL Infantry Letter written by "Rad" Hobbs while encamped near Vicksburg, MS, April 5th 1862. "The other

Day and bought one quarte of goober and I had to pay Fiftay sence for them and I bought too dozon eggs and a half and Four pound of butter and I paide $15 dollars and a half for them I pade 5 dolar and half for too dozan and nine I want you all. To be shore to wright to me and wright All the newse." [Ancestry; Historical Society].

Hobbs, James W. (1825). gun maker. 1860, Huntsville, Madison County. James, age 35, gun maker, born in NC, value $2500 property, $2500 personal; Mary, his wife, age 30; Henry, 3; Joseph, 1, all born in AL [Census].

Hobbs, William Horton (1805-1895). gunsmith. Hobbs was born in Samson County, NC, on 11 December 1805 a son of George J. Hobbs and Mary Burkhalter. 1820, Sampson County, NC, living with his father. On 10 May 1827 he married Martha Davis on 13 May 1827 but she soon died. 1830, Monroe County, GA, near Wiley Higgins, with whom he may have apprenticed or worked. He married second Elizabeth Reid McCullough (1821-1906) whose husband had been killed by a mule's kick. 1840, Troup County, GA. 1844, moved to Talladega County, GA. 1850, northern district, Talladega County: William, age 44, gunsmith, value $700, born in NC; Martha, 37; William, 17, laborer; Solomon, 14; Malinda, 13; Matilda, 11; Sarah, 7; Aira [female], 5; Emily, 3; Parisade [female], 7 months, all born in AL. 1860, northern district, Talladega County: William, 56, born in NC, gunsmith, value $500 real estate; $800 personal value; E., his wife, 37; L., 19, R., 15; E, 13; P., 11; V., 7; M., 9; McClellan, 18; 6; McClellan, 14, all born in AL. 1862-64, working with his son George Thomas manufacturing arms for the Confederacy. 1870, Clay County, farmer, real estate $1000, personal value $500. There is no evidence of a formal arms contract with the Confederate government , so it is likely that, during the Civil War, he worked for either Wallis & Rice or Lewis G. Sturdivant & Company, both of whom had C.S. contracts and were located in Talladega. Production ended when on 15 July 1864 General Rousseau reported to General Sherman that two gun factories had been destroyed. Hobbs died in Clay County on 26 May 1895. [Murphy & Madaus; Census; Family]. *One rifle shown in the Photos section.*

Hobbs, William George Thomas (1833-1906). gun- and blacksmith, distiller. Talladega County. G. T. worked with his father during the Civil War manufacturing arms for the Confederacy [Family; Wallace].

Hodges, James (1812). gunsmith. 1860-86, Limestone County. 1860, James Hodges, gunsmith, 48, born in TN; Elizabeth, wife, 46' Virginia, 22; Arthur, 19; Alabama, 18; Napoleon, 17; James D., 16; Columbus, 12; Buena V., 9; T.W., 3, all born in AL. 1880, James Hodges, blacksmith, 67, born in TN; Elizabeth, wife, 61; Newton, 18; Bedford, 15, all born in AL [Census; *Dirs*].

Holder, John L. (1796-1873). gun- and blacksmith. John was born in 1796, a son of John Holder. On 7 February 1832 he married Martha Suttles.. John was a gunsmith and blacksmith by trade, remained in his native state until about twenty-four years of age, when he removed to Winston County, MS, where he owned a large farm, and remained until his death, which occurred on 31 March 1873. In this family were nine children [Ancestry; *History of Franklin County, Arkansas*].

Honiker, W. H. (1832). gunsmith. 1860, Barbour County; born in GA. In 1863 he served in the 1st battalion, State Guards in Georgia [Census].

Horton, Henry (1825). gunsmith. Mobile. 1860, ward 4: Henry Horton, gunsmith, 35, born in England; Laura, wife, 26; Elizabeth, 2; William H., infant [Census].

Horton, James R. (1812). gunsmith. 1850-60, Barbour County. 1850, district 23: James Horton, farmer, 38; Eliza, wife, 26; Mary, 8; John, 3, all born in GA; James, 1, born in AL [Census].

Houston, Alex G. (1859). gunsmith. 1880, village of Madison, Madison County. Alex G. Houston, gunsmith, 21; Lucinda, 25, wife, both born in TN, both mulatto [Census].

Houston, Hartwell (1836). gunsmith. African-American artisan. 1880, Huntsville. Hartwell Houston, gunsmith, 46, born in TN; Hattie, wife, 18, born in AL; Louisa, daughter, 11, born in TN, all black [Census].

Howard, John H. (1800-1853). gunsmith. 1820-53, New Market, Madison County. John was born on 18 January 1800 in TN, a son of Baldwin and Eliza Howard. John married Catharine Weaver. He died on 20 August 1863, in New Market, Madison County [Census; Ancestry]. *One rifle is shown in the Photo section.*

Howard, Jno. (1828). gunsmith. 1850, Huntsville; born in AL. John was the oldest child of Michael and Lucinda Howard [Census].

Howard, William (1827). gunsmith. 1860, Madison County. William, age 33, gunsmith, value $1400 real estate, $1500 personal; Elizabeth, 32; John, 6; Newton, 4; Ann, 2; David, 1; William, 8 months, all born in AL [Census].

Hudgins, Ambrose (1842). gunsmith. 1880, Seals, Mobile County. Ambrose, gunsmith, 38; Joseph, 35; William, 62, all born in AL [Census].

Humphries, Benjamin (1800-1860). gunsmith. 1850, district 27, Cherokee County: Benjamin Humphreys, gunsmith, 52, born in GA; Jerusha, wife, 47, born in SC; William, 24, farmer; Matilda, 26; Sarah Ann, 22; Martha, 20, all born in GA; George, 17; John, 14; Benjamin, 12; Joseph, 10, all born in AL. 1860, St. Clair County. He died in a part of St. Clair County, that is now Etowah County. Humphries was age 60, a gunsmith, born in GA, died in August 1860 of apoplexy [Census; Federal Mortality Schedule; Ancestry]

Hunt, William H. (1816). gunsmith. 1860, Clay County. His children between 5 and 11 years of age were born in AL [Census].

Huroy, George (1827-1904). gunsmith. Heorge was born in Belgium on 27 April 1827. 1850, Mobile County; born in Belgium, age 23, gunsmith; apparently lived in a hotel. By 1880 George had moved to Columbus, MS, where he was listed as a confectioner. He died there on 31 July 1904 [Ancestry; Census].

Hurt & Schevenel smiths Marion. The firm ran an advertisement in the *Cincinnati Enquirer* on 4 December 1871 seeking to employ several skilled tradesman, including a gunsmith.

I

Irons, H. R. (1870). gunsmith. 1901, Decatur, DeKalb County. Noted in 1901 State Constitutional Convention. On 4 September 1906 Irons married Mary Willie in Montgomery, AR [Ancestry].

Ivy, John (1818). gunsmith. 1850, Randolph County. The following households of gunsmiths were enumerated one after another: Foster, Ivy, Southerland, Nunis, Thompson, and Walls. 1850, Ivy, age 32, born in GA, $150 value; Polly, his wife, 28; Herbert, 10; Cynthia, 8; Lucinda, 7; William, 6, all born in GA; Washington, 3, born in AL. 1870, Wahoga, Cleburne County: John Ivy, farmer, 54, born in GA [Census].

J

Jacobs, B. gunsmith. 1866-85, Selma, Dallas County [*Dirs*].

Jessel, Peter (1826). gunsmith. Selma, Dallas County. 1860, C. Suter, gunsmith; L. Suter, wife, 64, both born in Switzerland; Peter Jessel, 34, born in France, gunsmith [Census]. For reasons best to known to him, Sellers listed Jessel as Lessier

Johnson, Arcy (1878-1918). gunsmith. Selma, Dallas County. 1910, Arcy H. Johnson, jeweler, 30, owns his shop; Nellie M., 20; Beulah, 6; Ghent, 6; Stella, 3. He was a son J. A. Johnson, and was married when he died at Selma, age 40 [death certificate at Ancestry; Census].

Jones, A. S. gunsmith. 1840-50, Montgomery. He was a gunsmith in Columbus, MS,, where he had gone from AL. There he was killed and buried in Friendship Cemetery [Ancestry; Family]. *One rifle is shown in the Photo section.*

Jones, J. W. (1835). gunsmith. 1860, Columbia, Henry County; value $400, single, age 25, living with several other professional men, born in AL [Census].

Joplin, A. (1800). gunsmith. 1850, Mobile County. Joplin, age 50, born in Ireland, gunsmith; Marcella, 36, his wife; Vanie, 15; Emily, 11; Mary, 9; Gaspar, 7; Leon, 4, all born in Louisiana [Census].

Joulin, Jacques (1768-1844). gunsmith. Joulin died in Mobile County in 1844 at age 76 [*Mobile Death Records*].

Juallain, François C. gunsmith. 1842, Mobile [*Dir*].

K

Keable, W. B. (1833). gunsmith. 1860, Jackson County; born in NC [Noble].

Keeling, William (1859). gunsmith. 1880, Holmans, Baldwin County. William Keeling, 21, gunsmith; Mary, sister, 17; Emma, sister, 14; Lilly, 10, all born in AL [Census].

Keesee, William gunsmith. before 1828, Huntsville; sold his shop that year to Hyrum W. Ryburn; 1840, Randolph County, Arkansas, with 12 slaves. On 30 March 1837 William purchased 40 acres and on 4 January 1841 Keesee purchased 80 acres, both in Pickens County [Noble; Ancestry].

Keipp, S. P.. (1867-1919). gunsmith. Selma, Dallas County. S. P. was a son of Geo9rge Keipp. He died on 13 March 1919 in Selma [Ancestry; *Dirs*]. Erroneously listed in 1885 as P. C. Keip.

Kelly, Samuel S. (1826-1873). gunsmith. 1860-70, Cherokee County. Samuel was born on 30 August 1826. 1860, Samuel, age 33, gunsmith; Eliza A. Hawkins Kelly, 33; both born in SC. In 1870, Samuel Kelly was appointed administrator of Elizabeth Landrum's will. On 26 April 1850 he married Eliza A. Hawkins at Benton, AL. On 1 January 1859 he obtained 40 acres in Cherokee County. Samuel died on 11 September 1872 at Etowah, Mill Creek Twp., Cherokee County [Census; Family].

Kennedy, Alexander. Ann Eliza was married to her late husband, June 6, 1833. He was a native of Moore county, N. C., born March 29, 1807, a son of Alexander Kennedy. His paternal grandfather was a native of Scotland (of Irish descent), and a pioneer emigrant to North Carolina, who, being shipwrecked on his voyage to America, was rescued, but lost his two brothers, who embarked with him and never knew whether or not they were saved. J. S. Kennedy's maternal grand-father was a Williamson, who was a soldier in the war of the Revolution, and who died at the age of one hundred and thirteen years. Alexander Kennedy reared a large family of children. He was a gunsmith and carried on an extensive manufacturing establishment at Mechanic's Hill, North Carolina, and at his death was succeeded by Josiah S. Kennedy and two brothers, who conducted the business successfully for several years. J. S. Kennedy emigrated from North Carolina to west Tennessee, thence, coming to Bibb county, Ala., in 1837, to visit his brother Lewis, who was a practicing lawyer at Centreville, he decided to remain, and engaged in the grocery business and farming, and was also proprietor of a large blacksmith shop until 1865, when he formed a partnership with J. P. Taylor in the mercantile business. He was a Revolutionary War soldier. Reportedly, some of the guns he made were used in the Continental armies. Alexander's son, David Kennedy, gunsmith, carried on the gun-making business, and had at one time the largest gun factory in this part of the south. At times he employed as many as seventy to ninety men.. The town, now known as Robbins, actually began in 1795 when gunsmith Alexander Kennedy and his family left Philadelphia to settle along Bear Creek. Kennedy set up a factory, which produced long rifles for American soldiers, near the site of the present day Robbins Water Plant. The Kennedy rifle works continued in operation until 1838 and the place became known as Mechanics Hill. Other gunsmiths in the country were John Kennedy, William Williamson, Captain John Ritter, Phil Cameron and James Ray. To obtain water power to operate the emery wheels and drills that were used in the gun making business, a dam was constructed across Bear Creek. Later, the dam was used as a mill site. Alexander Kennedy reared a large family of children, but one of whom is now living-Thomas S., a resident of Springdale, Texas. He was a gunsmith and carried on an extensive manufacturing establishment at Mechanic's Hill, N. C., and at his death was succeeded by Josiah S. Kennedy and two brothers, who conducted the business successfully for several years [family genealogy]. Alexander had an interest in the gun manufactory belonging to William Williamson, which, at the peak production, employed as many as 75 men. Kennedy bought Williamson out after the war.

John Kennedy, son of Alexander Kennedy [# 1], had three sons and four daughters. The names of the daughters are no recorded, but the sons were John, Robert, and Alexander [# 2]. John died near Philadelphia, issue, if any, unknown; Robert drowned at sea. Alexander married an lady, name and issue, if any, unknown, but she died. He remarried to Mary Tandy Thomas, widow of John Thomas. They had issue: Nancy, Alexander [# 3], John, David, and Mary. Mary Tandy Thomas Kennedy then died in Philadelphia and Alexander [# 2] married a third time, to a lady who last name was Levin, also a widow. They had issue: George, Annie, Joseph, Robert, Nathan, and Esther. When the British occupied Philadelphia Alexander who was a sword and gun maker, fled south to North Carolina, settling in Moore County [family genealogy; Noble].

Kennedy, David (1768-1837). gunsmith. 1810-20, Moore County, NC. David was a son of Alexander Kennedy and succeeded him in the gunmaking business. He was born in Philadelphia in January 1768 and died on 2 May 1837. On 24 May 1788 he married Joanna Moore (1766-1857). On 9 August 1799 he received a patent on 100 acres of land [*Deed Book* 104: 242]. He moved to Lauderdale County, AL, around 1835. David was also a mill-owner and fiddler. Mechanic's Hill in Moore County took its name from the large gun factory operated there by Alexander Kennedy and his son David Kennedy. Alexander Kennedy's son, David, gunsmith, mill-owner and fiddler, carried on the gun-making business, and had at one time the largest gun factory in this part of the south The four sons of David Kennedy, all thought to have become gunsmiths, were: John (1790-1857); Hiram (1792-1862); Elias (1803-1835); and Enoch (1805-1835). [family genealogy]. There were no tools of the gunsmith's trade in his estate inventory made on 17 July 1838 [*Lauderdale Inventory Book* A-3: 54-55]. Kennedy Gun Factory existed between 1823 and 1837 in Florence, Alabama**.** About 1823 his son David moved the factory to Green Hill, Alabama, locating 400 yards east of the Tabernacle Cemetery. Green Hill became an early gun manufacturing center with the advent of other gunsmiths. McDonalds, Garners, Stutts, Keys, Higgins, Richardsons, Davidsons, and Myricks. Property willed to the City of Florence by Hiram Kennedy Douglass, a Kennedy descendant, became the Kennedy-Douglass Center for the arts. There were a number of early gun factories in Lauderdale County, mainly around Green Hill. The best known of these was owned by David Kennedy and his son Hiram [Lauderdale County posting].

Kennedy, Enoch Spinks (1805-1826). gunsmith. Moore County, North Carolina. Enoch was born on 19 February 1805. He married Lucy McNeil, sister of his brother's wife. On 25 August 1826 he died in Lauderdale County, AL [Dan Wallace].

Kennedy, Hiram (1792-1862). gunsmith. Born in Moore County, North Carolina. He was a son of David and Joanna [Moore] Kennedy, born 22 October 1792. He married Mary Spinks (1793-1875). When the federal government opened land in Lauderdale County for purchase Hiram was one of the first buyers, in 1818. In 1824 he moved from Moore County to Lauderdale County,

Alabama. 1850, Lauderdale County, Hiram, 58, gunsmith; Mary, 58, both born in N.C.; Hiram, 17, student; Olive, 14 [Census]. He eventually owned 2000 acres on Shoal Creek, near Green Hill, 15 miles from Florence. Hiram died on 20 August 1862 in Lauderdale County, Alabama. [Dan Wallace; *My Southern Families*, 391]. *One rifle is shown in the Photo section.*

Kennedy, John Spinks (1816=1899). black- and gunsmith. John was born on 1 October 1816 in Moore County, NC, a son of Hiram and Mary Spinks Kennedy. About 1853 he married Mary Emaline [?]. He emigrated from NC to west TN, thence, coming to Bibb County, AL. John came to Lauderdale in 1825 with his father who was a gunsmith and planter. He read the law at Lagrange and was admitted to the bar in 1842. He served in the legislature in 1841, 1842 and 1847. He served in the 7th AL Infantry, enlisting as a private and rising to captain and serving as commissary. He left the practice if law, becoming a cotton manufacturer. Dan Wallace listed a John S. Kennedy, son of Hiram Kennedy, a gunsmith in Tuscaloosa before the Civil War. His brother Oliver S. Kennedy learned the trade if gunsmith but left it to read and then practice law at Lauderdale. 1870, John S. Kennedy, 51, cotton manufacturer, $40,000 real estate, $50,000 personal value; Mary E., wife, 44; Edward J., 19; B. Patton, 18; Mary S., 12; Ophelia, 12. John died in May 1899 in Tusaloosa. [Ancestry; Census; *Tuscaloosa County History*, 569].

Kennedy, Josiah S. gun manufacturer. Bibb County. Josiah was born at Mechanic's Hill, NC., a son of Alexander Kennedy. He married Ann Eliza McNeil. Josiah took over his father's business, working first in west TN, then Bibb County, AL. In 1837 he came to visit his brother Lewis, who was a practicing lawyer at Centreville and he decided to remain, and engaged in the grocery business and farming, and was also proprietor of a large blacksmith and gunsmith shop until 1865, when he formed a partnership with J. P. Taylor in the mercantile and textile business. Writing of early days in Hiram's shop, Josiah wrote in the *Florence Gazette* in 1881, "My father got his chief supply of iron from these mills [in Wayne and Lawrence Counties] out of which his Negro men made the rifles' gun barrels." He continued, "Me, myself, and Father, put together some 800 rifle guns using the old flint and steel locks during the year." [Ancestry].

Kelper, John. gunsmith. 1861, boards at 7 Conception, Mobile [*Dir.*].

Key, Calvin Domas (1828-1899). gunsmith. 1850-69, Lauderdale County. Calvin Key was a gunsmith and worked for Jacob Stutts and possibly David Kennedy while in the Green Hill area, c. 1849-69. 1850, Jacob Stutts, 53, gunsmith; Nancy, 49, his wife, both born in N.C.; Wesley, 23, blacksmith; Elizabeth, 21; Asa, 18, laborer; John, 16, laborer; James, 12; Mary, 10; Nancy, 8, all born in AL. Also Calvin Key, 20, gunsmith, born in N.C. [U.S. Census]. before 1877, Turners Point, Kauffman County, Texas. Key died in Allison, Texas. Stutts operated a gun factory, probably formerly David Kennedy's. In 1869 Key left Lauderdale County for TX. Calvin D. Key, born in Moore County, NC He worked for David Kennedy at his gun factory in Lauderdale County, AL. He worked in AL between 1850 and 1869, before he left and moved to TX. Calvin Domas Key was the fourth child born to James Key and Sabeilla Britt in Moore County, NC. He was born February 22, 1828. His main work would center around blacksmith shops in both AL and TX in which gunsmithing was a second occupation. By 1850 at age 22, Calvin left home and migrated westward to AL. This first move in conjunction with his brother Thomas and others from NC, ended in Lauderdale County, AL, near the small community of Green Hill. In the 1850 census of that county, we find one Jacob Stutts and family, formerly of NC. Living with them according to the census is a young North Carolina gunsmith, Calvin Key. He married Mary Evaline Thomas on March 15, 1854, and they had children: James Alexander born January 22, 1855, Eliza Jane born April 22, 1857 and William Andrew born October 20, 1858. During this same time, Calvin's younger brother Crawford migrated to Alabama and took up residence in the area near Calvin and Mary. Both Calvin and Crawford worked as blacksmiths during their stay in Alabama. Calvin Domas Key died on December 12, 1899,. and he was buried in the Baptist Cemetery located near Lipan in Hood County, Texas. His wife, Mary Evaline, lived with her son Samuel and his wife on the farm until her death on August 11, 1914. She is buried next to Calvin in the Baptist Cemetery. His rifles resemble the later work of John Bull, often signed in script on the barrel *C K* [Ancestry; Family].

Key, Thomas (1819- 1857). gunsmith, blacksmith, and farmer. Lauderdale County. He was the first of the Key children to leave Moore County in 1849-50. Tom worked c.1847-56 at the Kennedy gun factory in Green Hill before moving to TX. He died from typhoid fever in 1857 in Cookeville, Titus County, TX. He married Martha Hussey (1815-1892) of Moore County [Ancestry; Family].

King, Joseph. gunsmith. 1874, boards at City Hotel, Mobile [*Dir.*].

King, Samuel D. (1825-1864). gunsmith. King was born in Buncombe County, NC. On 4 December 1863 he enlisted in the 1st Alabama Cavalry, C.S.A. He died of typhoid pneumonia on 19 January 1864 and was buried at Corinth National Cemetery [Ancestry].

King, William Rufus DeVane (April 7, 1786 – April 18, 1853) was an American politician, diplomat, plantation owner and overseer of gun making. He was the 13th Vice President of the US for about six weeks in 1853 before his death. Earlier he had been elected as a US Rep. from NC and a Sen. from AL.. .King was the only Vice President from AL and, as such, held the highest political office of any Alabamian in American history. King was born in Sampson County, NC to William King and Margaret DeVane. King was a delegate to the convention which organized the AL state government. Upon the admission of AL as a State in 1819, he was elected by the legislature as a Democratic-Republican to the US Senate. He was reelected as a Jacksonian in 1822, 1828, 1834, and 1841, serving from December 14, 1819, until April 15, 1844, when he resigned. He served as President pro tempore of the US Senate during the 24th through 27th Congresses. He was appointed as Minister to France from 1844 to 1846. After his return, King was appointed and subsequently elected as a Democrat to the Senate to fill the vacancy caused by the resignation of Arthur P. Bagby; he began serving on July 1, 1848.
King was elected Vice President of the US on the Democratic ticket with Franklin Pierce in 1852 and took the oath of office on March 24, 1853, in Cuba, twenty days after he became Vice President. He had gone to La Ariadne plantation, owned by John Chartrand in Matanzas, due to his ill health. This unusual inauguration on foreign soil took place because it was believed that King, then known to be terminally ill with tuberculosis, would not live much longer. Congress passed a special act to enable this in recognition of his long and distinguished service to the government of the US. Although he did not take the oath until 20 days after the inauguration day, he was legally the Vice President during those three weeks.

Shortly afterward, King returned to AL to his Chestnut Hill plantation near Selma, AL at King's Bend, Dallas County, AL where he died within two days. He was interred in a vault on the plantation and later reburied in Selma's Live Oak Cemetery.

King, a slave owner, oversaw the making of a "Goose Gun" from old English parts at his plantation blacksmith shop. He had the stock made from apple wood harvested on his plantation. [wiki, US hist., family hist.} *One rifle is shown in the Photo section.*

Knight, James Allen. gunsmith. Sylacauga, Talladega County. Son of Enoch and Farthy Parker Knight (1829-1899). James married Martha Ann, daughter of Mark and Balzora Jackson of Troup County, GA. James opposed secession, but after war came he was an armorer for the Glorious Cause. He was a Mason and Methodist [Ancestry; *Notable Men of Alabama*].

Knowles, William J. (1857-1929). gunsmith. Andalusia, Covington County. William was a son of Thomas J. Knowles, born about 1857 in GA. Knowles was married and died on 4 June 1929 at Andalusia at age 72 [death certificate at Ancestry].

Kreutner, Christian (1819-1884). gunsmith. Kreutner was born on October 26, 1819, and died on October 9, 1884. Born in Baden, Germany, he came to New Orleans in 1840 and to Cincinnati, Ohio, then in 1846 to Memphis, TN, and finally to Montgomery, AL, in 1847 at the age of 28, and soon thereafter established himself as a master gunsmith. In the 1850s he partnered with Henry Beathner. One Deringer and several rifles known and are both marked *C. Kreutner and H. Beathner.* Kreutner made exceptional fine percussion hunting rifles both before and after the Second War for Independence. He also made quality percussion pistols, and example was a large specimen, 15 inches in overall length, .58 caliber with a nine-inch octagon barrel, and featuring a silver fore-end cap and barrel escutcheon. His pistols bore the characteristics of his rifles. During the war, Christian Kreutner maintained a small gun factory at 14 North Court Street in Montgomery, where ten or twelve workers were employed to manufacture firearms for the Confederacy. He had a contract with the State of Alabama for the production of Mississippi Rifles at thirty-five dollars each. The total number of rifles produced and delivered by Kreutner is unknown, but between October 1, 1863 and November 1, 1864, when his contract expired, the factory had delivered thirty-six Mississippi Rifles for which Kreutner was paid the sum of $1,260.00. Christian Kreutner also served as Captain at the Montgomery Arsenal and supervised the repair and modification of arms in support of the Confederate Army and stamped " C. Kreutner of Montgomery, AL ". It is not known if the rifles produced during the war displayed the stamping. After the war, Kreutner established a gunsmith business at No. 5 North Perry Street (on the east side of Perry Street and between Dexter Avenue and Monroe Street). He continued his trade at this location until the time of his death at the age of 65. He is buried in Oakwood Cemetery [Ancestry; Family]. *Six rifles and two pistols are shown in the Photo section.*

Kreutner, Christian, Jr. gunsmith. 1880-81, 7 Court St., Montgomery [*Dir.*].

Kreutner, Henry (1887). gunsmith. 1880-87, Montgomery. 1880, boards with C. Kreutner, Sr. His death was sudden and unexpected and he left a wife and 2 children [*Columbus Daily Inquirer*, 21 August 1887].

L

Laborne, J. T. gunsmith. 1881, Good Hope, Cullman County [*Dir*].

Lamberth, A. F. (1848-). gunsmith. 1880, Uniontown, Perry County. A. F. Lamberth, gunsmith, 32, born in NC; Eudora, wife, 30; Percy, 8; Maude, 3, all born in AL [Census].

Landrum Family. About 1803, Benjamin, John, William and Zachariah Landrum moved from Warren/Franklin Counties, GA to the vicinity of St. Stephens, Washington County, Mississippi Territory (M.T.). About 1810, George and Meridith Landrum moved from Edgefield District, SC to the vicinity of St. Stephens, Washington County, M.T. The Landrum's (Landram/Landrem/Landrom/Landrin/Lendrum) of St. Stephens vicinity, Washington County, Mississippi Territory (M.T.).   Washington County, M.T. contained most of current Southern Alabama. St. Stephens was located approximately 58 miles north of Mobile on the Tombigbee River [sources for information on Landrum family: AL Archives, *History of Mobile*, Family Records, Tax; Ancestry].

Landrum, Benjamin (1756-1825). blacksmith, farmer. Benjamin was born in 1756 in Chatham County, NC, a son of John Landrum (1696-1770). He married Mary Gross. He moved to LA after 1816 and was noted in the census and on tax lists, 1811-19, in Washington County. Benjamin died in 1825 in Quachita Parish, LA. He was a veteran of the Revolutionary War and the Creek War [SAR 73956; DAR 284306].

Landrum, George (1768). gun- and blacksmith. George was born in 1768 in Chatham County, NC. He was a veteran of the Revolutionary War, the War of 1812, and the Creek War. 1850, district 21, Macon County: George Landrum, 80, blacksmith, born in NC. 1860, Eufaula, eastern division, Barbour County: George Landrum, 88, born in NC, no occupation. He died in Barbour County, AL [Census; Ancestry].

Landrum, John (1748-1816). blacksmith, farmer. John was born in 1750 in Orange County, VA, a son of Joseph and Mary Buckner Landrum. He was a veteran of the Revolution, and the Creek War. John assisted in building a stockade and blockhouse known as Fort Landrum during the Creek War. John's name was noted on early tax and census records for Washington County, 1808-11. John died on 5 February 1816 in Washington County, M.T. (now Clarke County, AL), age 68 [Ancestry].

"John brought his family from Warren County, GA, to the Tombigbee Territory, in 1803. John, Zachariah, William, and Joseph all brought their families and settled near St. Stephens, in Washington County, MS Territory [which became Clarke County, AL]. Zachariah lived across the Tombigbee River, in Washington County AL. Zachariah must have arrived prior to the rest of the Landrum's, since he signed a memorial to Congress 25 November 1803, about the time his brothers were applying for passes through the Creek Indian nation. John was there by 27 November 1804, when he signed a petition to President Jefferson. William and Joseph returned to Georgia in 1808. The first court held in Clarke County was held in the home of John Landrum. During the Creek War of 1813, John's home became Ft. Landrum, a place of refuge for area settlers. John married Catherine Hill in Ft. Landrum AL After John Landrum died in 1816, Catherine married Samuel Wilson. . . .Their uncle Zachariah took his family to Montgomery County, Texas, in 1829" [Family Genealogy on Ancestry].

Landrum, Meridith (1780). blacksmith. Merideth was born in 1780 on the Edgefield District, SC. He was a veteran of the Creek War and the War of 1812. 1830, Merideth Landrum, Greene County, MS. 1850, Merideth Landrum, blacksmith, 70, born in NC, living alone. On 1 March 1859 some Meredith Landrum purchased 35 acres in Washington County. He died after 1850 in Washington County, AL [Census; Ancestry].

Landrum, William Ellis (1754-1815). gun- and blacksmith, farmer. William was born in 1754 in Chatham County, NC, a son of Joseph and Mary Buckner Landrum. He was a veteran of the Revolutionary War; served in 1793 in the GA Militia, and in the Creek War. William died in Clarke County, Al in 1815. *One attributed rifle is shown in the Photo section.*

Landrum, Zachariah (1762-1833). gun- and blacksmith, farmer. Zachariah was born in 1766 in Chatham County, NC, a son of Joseph and Mary Buckner Landrum. He was a veteran of the Revolutionary War, the Creek War, and the War of 1812. Zachariah married Letitia Tynes in George c.1794. He was noted in tax and state census records in Washington County, 1808-16. He moved his family to TX in 1829 and received Spanish Land Grant in 1831. Two of his sons fought in Texas War of Independence in 1836. Zachariah died on 19 July1833 in Lake Creek, Coahuila, Spanish Texas Territory (Montgomery County, TX).

Leonard & Day. arms suppliers. Mobile. There is an iron mounted rifle with a wide butt and wooden patchbox lid marked *Leonard & Day, Mobile* [Noble].

Leslie, J. D. (1853-1912). gunsmith. Union Springs, Bullock County. Leslie was born on 26 June 1853 at Union Springs, then in Macon County. Noted as a gunsmith in 1885 directory. He died on 31 July 1912 at Union Springs and was buried at Oak Hill Cemetery [Ancestry; *Dir*].

Lewis, Thomas D. (1848-1931). gunsmith. Lewis was born on 11 October 1848 in AL. He died on 16 November 1931 in Morgan County at age 83, a retired gunsmith, buried at Basham Cemetery [death certificate at Ancestry].

Ligon, E. T. (1830). inventor. 1860, Demopolis, Marengo County. Ligon was a dentist, single, born in Maine, living in a boarding house. On 24 September 1861 the Confederate government issued Ligon patent number 24 for a breech-loading pistol[Gardner; Census].

Liles, John Madison (1829-1898). gunsmith and merchant. Andalusia, Covington County. John married Eliza Campbell, born June 27,1831. John Madison Liles was born April 3, 1829 to Sherod and Rebecca (Smith) Liles. John Liles obtained 4 separate land tracts between 1854 and 1855 totaling 160 acres. John Liles did very well for himself as a merchant. In the 1860 census he had a real estate value of $2200 and a personal property value of $9215. Before the Civil War began, John Liles joined up with the Covington County Company of Volunteers on July 16, 1860. By 1870 he had moved his family to Escambia County where he worked as a gunsmith. His personal property value was now just $160. John and Eliza had ten children. After the death of her sister Eliza, Amanda married Eliza's husband John Madison Liles. As mentioned before the War left

John Liles picking up the pieces of his life and starting over again. He moved once more to Conecuh County in the Old Towne area by 1880 where he continued to work as a gunsmith. John and Amanda had three children. He was a democrat, a member of the Masons, and was in the service as a confederate soldier; during the last 2 years of the war, he was captured and sent to Ship Island at Gulfport, MS. He died on April 27, 1898 [Ancestry; Census].

Liles, William (1803-1879). gun maker and farmer. Lauderdale County. William was born in Laurens County, SC, on 25 March 1803. On 8 August 1822 in Laurens County he married Frances America Weaver. Liles migrated to Lauderdale County to work at the Kennedy gun factory at Green William died in Lauderdale County on 31 March 1879. William Liles was one of the 1st land owners in Lauderdale County. William purchased the land through the Federal Government shortly after the Indians were removed on the Trail of Tears. Hill. On 1 August 1839 he purchased 40 acres of land in Lauderdale County and thereafter farmed for a living. On 10 March 1852 Liles added another 40 acres. The property was just west of Highway 43 and North of County Road 8 in Green Hill. William is buried at Kennedy Stutts Cemetery in Green Hill. This cemetery is not maintained and is located in the middle of a cow pasture [Wallace; Ancestry; Census].

Liles, William (1816). blacksmith. Milltown, Chambers County. William was born in Union County, SC, in 1816. 1850, Milltown: William Liles, blacksmith, 34, born in SC; Margaret, wife, 28, born in GA; Elizabeth, 5; Randall, 2; John, infant, all born in AL. On 1 May 1850 Liles purchased 40 acres in Chambers County. 1860, southern district, Randolph County: William Liles, farmer, 45; Sarah, wife, 27, both born in SC; Elizabeth, 15; Randolph, 13; John, 11; Jesse, 9; Amos, 5, all born in AL [Ancestry; Census].

Liles, William (1855-1895). gunsmith. 1880, Monroeville, Monroe County. William Liles, gunsmith, 24; Mary, wife, 18; Bessie, 1, all born in AL. William was born on 27 September 1855, a son of John and Eliza Liles of Andalusia, Covington County. He married Mary Henderson. John died on 19 January 1895 [Census].

Lindfors, John F. gunsmith. 1888-90, boards at 212 16th, Birmingham. Gunsmith for William A. Ricketts. 1890 residence Third Ave., between King and Spring Sts., Avondale. Lindfors was born in Finland [*Dirs.*].

Lindsey, W. H. gunsmith and veterinarian. 1907, Thomasville, Clarke County. Lindsey killed T. J. Kiernan, a railroad employee. Lindsey claimed self defense. Lindsey was to be an important witness in the trial of Kiernan for killing his wife [*Augusta Chronicle*, 13 December 1907].

Ling, O. C. (1857-1937) black- and gunsmith, wagon maker. 1897, Guin, Marion County. Ling was born on 18 November 1857 and died on 2 March 1937. "Wagons made to order and ready tilled wheels always on hand. Horse shoeing a specialty. All work done cheaper than the cheapest for cash" [Ancestry; *Guin Gazette*, April 23, 1897].

Linkham David W. (1804). gunsmith. 1865, Troy. Pike County. David W. Linkham, born in MA, 51, gunsmith [State Census; *Dir.*].

M

McClanahan, William (1807). farmer & gunsmith. Lauderdale County. Reportedly, McClanahan worked at the Kennedy gun factory at Green Hill. 1850, Division 2 East of the Military Road: William McClanahan, farmer, 43, born in KY; Mary, wife, 35; Sarah, 13; Mary, 11; John, 9; Martha, 8; Rebecca, 6; William, 4; James, infant, all born in AL, born in TN; James, 33, laborer, born in TN. 1860, William McClanahan, farmer and miller, 52, born in KY; Mary, 40; John, 20; Martha, 18; Rebecca, 17; William, 14; James U., 10; Robert, 6, all born in AL [Ancestry; Census; Wallace].

McClung, John Richard (1856-1823). farmer, black- and gunsmith. Blount County. John was the third child of Benjamin Franklin McClung and his wife Elizabeth Tapp Barry, born on 6 February 1856. On 23 October 1880 in Logan, AR, he married Julia Beulah Vesta Lowery (1862-1937), daughter of Elijah Mason and Sarah Elizabeth Lowery in Short Mountain Twp., Logan County, AR. 1910, John R. McClung, blacksmith, 54, born in AL; Julia B., wife, 47, born in GA; Johnnie, 11; Earl, 18, both born in AR. John died on 28 August 1923 in Havana, Yell County, AR [Census; Ancestry].

McCravy, Jonathan (1836). gunsmith. 1860, Limestone County. born in AL [Census].

McCravy, William (1838-1911). gunsmith. McCravy was born on 18 Jan 1838, and died on 19 Apr 1911. He enlisted in Confederate Army in 1861 as a gunsmith. His wife, Nancy E. was born on 18 Jun 1840 and died on 13 February 1879. William was a gunsmith during the civil war. He made guns in a shop behind where the cemetery is located. 1880, beat 6, Limestone County. William McCravy, gunsmith, 42, widower; John C. McCravey, 20, son; Mary, 18, daughter; Corlena, 14; George, 5; William S., 4. Although McCravey was a gunsmith, he never intended his guns to be used in war since reportedly he was a staunch pacifist His grave is marked with a Confederate stone. This cemetery is located in the northwest corner of Limestone County on what once was the McCravy farm [Ancestry; Census].

McDaniel, Archie (1826). gunsmith. 1880, Archie McDaniel, gunsmith, 54; Margaret, wife, 56; Archie, 23, farmer; Luther, farmer, 14, all born in TN [Census].

McDennat, Matthew (1817). gunsmith. 1860, Lawrence County; born in TN [Census].

McDonald, Archibald (1801-1875). gunsmith. 1850, Lauderdale County. Arch, 49, gunsmith; N [male], 52; Henry, 24, laborer; James, 17, laborer; Willis, 12; Mary, 9. The census gives a female, age 52, whose name appears to be Ferryby, although the correct name of Arch's wife was Margaret. 1870, Township 1 Range 9, Lauderdale County, Archy, 69, living with his son James. Archibald MacDonald was born in.1801 in North Carolina and died in 1875 in Killen, and wife Margaret Duncan died in 1855 in Killen, Lauderdale County. Archibald was a gunsmith from Moore County NC. He and other NC gunsmiths came to Lauderdale County to work at the Kennedy Gun facility in Green Hill [Census; Wallace, Ancestry].

McDonald, E. B. (1745-1843). gunsmith. Lauderdale County. McDonald migrated from Moore County, NC, to work at the Kennedy gun factory at Green Hill [Wallace; Noble].

McDonald, Elias (1819-1897). carriage maker. 1870, Green Hill, Lauderdale County. Elias McDonald, born in TN, 50, carriage maker; Elmira, born in SC, 49, wife; Fernando, 22; Josephine, 16; Mattie, 13, all born in AL. It is probable that Elias had once worked at the Kennedy gun factory in Green Hill. On 1 April 1852 he purchased 40 acres, and on 1 March 1858 he purchased another 80 acres, in Lauderdale County. [Ancestry; Census].

"Elias McDonald owned three hundred acres of land on both sides of the Old Military Road north of Green Hill, and in 1854, he built a two story log house on this property. He used popular logs in the construction of the house and built the fireplace in the center of the house so that the rooms on both sides could be heated by the one fireplace. This style of structure is referred to as a saddle-bag log house by some historians. The house was almost directly across the road from an older house called the Holland Stand. Elias was a wagon-maker by trade and built and repaired buggies, wagons, coaches, and carriages in a workshop near his home. He was also called upon to do much of the coach repair work for the Holland operation across the road. Entries in his shop ledger show that he also made coffins, sharpened plows and hoes, and even sold bacon and other food items on the side. He also had the reputation of being an outstanding gunsmith and produced Kentucky Rifles at his workshop. This type of rifle had either a hexagon or octagon-shaped barrel with a trigger guard made of polished brass. Elias' obituary in the local newspaper stated that he was one of the oldest members of the Green Hill Masonic Lodge" [Atkins on Ancestry]

McDonald, John (1792-1861). gunsmith & farmer. Before 1815 John married Sarah Margaret Emory in SC. On 10 March 1852 John purchased 40 acres, and on 2 April 1857 240 acres in Lauderdale County. Reportedly, John worked at the Kennedy gun factory at Green Hill. John died in 1861 in Lawrence County, TN [Ancestry].

McGee, David G. (1824). gunsmith. 1860, Greenville, Butler County. D. G. McGee, 36, gunsmith; L., wife, both born in NC; children 2 to 13, only initials for first names, all born in GA [Census].

McGee, Jacob (1765-1839). gunsmith & farmer. Green Hill, Lauderdale County. Jacob was born in 1765 in Moore County, NC, a son of Joseph and Mary Chiles McGehee. About 1815 Jake married Elizabeth Richardson in Moore County. Reportedly, Jacob came to AL to work at the Kennedy gun factory in Green Hill. On 8 June 1833 he purchased 80 acres of land, and on 10 September 1838 he purchased 40 acres, in Lauderdale County. Jacob died on 31 December 1839 in Green Hill. Extant is a bill of sale for a slave Milly and her children issued by McGee [Wallace; Ancestry].

McKinney, John (1806). gunsmith. Madison County. John was born in Roane County, TN, a son of Thomas and Jane Sharpe McKinney. On 16 February 1824 John married Edith Edy [?]. 1850, John, 44, gun smith, born in TN, value $250; Edy, 45, his wife, born in KY; Elizabeth, 21; Thomas, 20, farmer; Mary, 18, all born in KY; Margaret, 16, born in TN; William, 10; Susan, 6; Amy, 3, all born in AL. 1860, Johnson Twp, Carter County, MO: John McKinney, 53; Edy, wife, 54, both born in TN; Mary A., born in KY; Amy, 12, born in AL [Ancestry; Census].

McLauren, Dan (1858-1921). gunsmith. 1921, Mobile. Dan was born on 4 November 1858, at State Line, MS, a son of Frank and Catharine Pitman McLauren. Noted as having been indicted for killing a deputy sheriff. The deputy was arresting McLauren's son for a violation of the liquor laws when he became irate and attacked the deputy. McLauren was physically handicapped in some way [*New Orleans Times*, 18 April 1921]. Dan died on 15 May 1921, living at 1320 Davis Ave., Mobile, at age 62 [Ancestry; AL Death Certificates]. Also seen as McLaurin.

Marin, Edmund C. (1875-1933). gunsmith. Montgomery. Successor to Oscar Marin. The family ran a sporting goods and gun shop. E. C. was arrested and charged with miscegenation for attempting to marry a bright young colored woman named McCue [*Montgomery Advertiser*, 3 September 1907; Ancestry].

Marin, Oscar E. (1869-1904). gunsmith. 312 Herron St., Montgomery, Alabama. Marin was a native of, and had apprenticed in the gunsmith trade in, Savannah, GA. Oscar was a son of Emily and Nicholas Marin, Chatham County, GA, born in December 1869. On 6 February 1894 he married Ann T. Sievers. He moved to, and was a popular gunsmith in, Montgomery. Marin died of injuries sustained when he was run over by a horse which was escaping from a fire at the Roman Cotton Warehouse [*Montgomery Advertiser*, 8 November 1904].

Mattei, Peter (1870-1905) gun- and locksmith. 1896-99, 256 Palmetto, Mobile. 1898, residence at 457 S. Franklin St. 1900 ward 7: Peter L. Mattei, born in LA, 29, locksmith; Sally, wife, 27, born in AL. Peter was born on 12 May 1870 in Muro, Corsica, France, a son of Jean B. and Angele Luciana. On 4 April 1888 he married Susannah E. Barlow. Peter died on 17 February 1905 in Mobile [Ancestry; *Dirs.*].

Pierre Mattei

May, William Green. gunsmith. 1862-65, C.S.A. service as an armorer. He enlisted into service in AL and later migrated to Simpson County, MS [Ancestry].

Mayhall, William (1802-1879). gunsmith. 1850, Somerville, Morgan County: William Mayhall, 48, cabinet maker; Rachel, wife, 46, both born in SC; Delila, 18, Louisa, 16, born in TN; Jessie, 14; John, 12; Marcus, 8; Lucinda, 10, all born in AL. 1870, Decatur, Morgan County: William, born in SC, gunsmith, age 66; Mary, 48, his wife; Martha, 15; Henry, 13; Francis, 9; Susan, 7, all born in AL. William was born c.1802, a son of William and Margaret Landerman Mayhall. William died in Itawamba County, MS, in May 1879 [Ancestry; Census].

Mazagne, Oliver. importer/ dealer/ gunsmith. c.1810-60, Dauphin Street, Mobile. Ovide Mazange's son continued to operate in Mobile until the 1860's at the corner of Commerce and Exchange Sts. [Ancestry; *Dirs.*].

Merrell, Benjamin (c.1791-1853). gunsmith. Ben was born about 1791 in Laurens County, South Carolina, and died 1853 in Marshall County, Alabama. He married (1) Nancy Thompson in 1819, daughter of John and Nana (Merrill) Thompson, of partial native American heritage and by whom he fathered 8 children. He married (2) before 1838 he married a woman named Martha. He was a blacksmith and gunsmith. He acquired 640 acres of Cherokee land through his marriage to Nancy Thompson, which was called the Merrill Reserva**tion [Ancestry; Family]**.

Michant, Peter (1775). gunsmith. 1850, Wilcox County. Peter, age 75, gunsmith; Frances, 44, his wife, both born in France; Andrew, 19; James, 16, farmer; Martha, 15; Rebecca, 13; Peter, 10; Eliza, 6; Richard, 4; Mary, 2, all born in AL [Census].

Millican, Benjamin F. gunsmith. Ben married Rebecca Howell. The father, a native of TN, removed to Alabama when a young man, settling in Jackson County, where he died in 1840, at the age of thirty years. He was a blacksmith and gunsmith by trade, and followed the same all through life [Ancestry; Family].

Millican, Francis Marion (1810-1840). farmer and gunsmith. Jackson County. Millican was born in TN, moved "at an early age" to AL, died at age 30 [Ancestry; Family].

Millican, Francis Marion II (1832-1907). gunsmith. Jackson County, AL and Tarrant County, TX Francis was born on 6 October 1832 in AL. 1850, district 19, Marion Millican, 16, at home. 1860, township 3, Marion Millican, blacksmith, 26, value $100, living with James Lawless. On 9 June 1870 he married Martha D. Ferguson. 1870, precinct 3, Dallas: Francis Millican, gunsmith, 31, born in AL; Martha, wife, 22, born in MS; Mary J., 20; Nancy D., 8, both born in AL.1880, Francis M. Millican, well driller, 49; Martha D., 33; Joseph, 8; Walter, 6; Martha, 2. Millican died in Grapevine, Tarrant County, TX, on 18 December 1907 [Family; Ancestry; Census].

Milican, John (1807). gun and blacksmith. 1860, southwest division, Morgan County. 1870, township 9, Blount County. 1880, beat 5, Morgan County. Jackie (John) Milican was a blacksmith and also a gunsmith. He made a rifle with multiple silver inlays in the stock. An Amerindian who worked for him as an apprentice wanted the gun badly. The savage tried to steal the rifle by killing Jackie with it. The rifle misfired and Jackie shot back, killing the aborigine. The body was hidden in a hollow tree stump and never found. His fellow aborigine went as far as burning the entire wooded area to find the body but it was never recovered [Gary Saunders in Ancestry; Census].

Miller, Henry. gunsmith. 1839, Mobile [*Dir*].

Montgomery Arms. dealers. 1892-93, Montgomery. This is a marking on lowest grade shotguns supplied by Crescent Firearms of Norwich, CT, 1888-1931.

Mooney, John (1806). gunsmith. 1846-50, Coosa County. Mooney, age 44, gunsmith, born in N.C., in the penitentiary, serving 10 years, starting 1845 for "Negro stealing" in Montgomery County [Census; also November 1846 prison census].

Morales, ---. 1796, Mobile.

"1796 July 1. Morales . . . saw Navarro run out of the hospital to the house of the gunsmith, Mr. Antonio and then to the church where Morales saw him at the door a quarter of an hour later when he was sent to call the pastor to hear the confession of the wounded man; that he had head Romero say nothing about the motive; that they had had an argument about 8 o'clock of the same night which Lattre quieted and he heard nothing between them until dawn; that he knew that they had a big knife in the kitchen; that he had not seen Navarro with a knife in the 6 years he had known him . . . Pasos and Bermudes sign as witnesses before Olivier."

Morris, James B. (1821). gunsmith. Morris was born in Alabama. He married Nancy Jane Harrison in 1844 in Coosa County, Alabama. They evidently left Coosa County before the 1850 census. By 1860 they are in White County, AR [Ancestry; Census].

Morrison, John C. (1815). gun maker. 1860, Marengo County. Morrison was born in SC. 1862, private, 43rd AL Infantry, enlisted in Marengo County [Census; Ancestry].

Mullins, Albert Clay (1853) gunsmith Maysville and Huntsville. Mullins married Ola Turner. Later he worked for Alabama Bike Shop in Huntsville, as a gunsmith. That store was owned by H. N. Mullins, the son of Wesley Mullins and his first wife. H. N. also at one time, leased and ran Saltpeter Ave, a cafe and bait shop near Scottsboro.

Mycick, James C. (1791). gunsmith. 1850, Lauderdale County. He was apparently a widower, age 59, born in N.C., value $350, gun smith; his children, ages 9 to 20 were all born in AL [Census]. Also seen as Myricles.

N

Nalors, B. N. (1818). gunsmith. 1850, district 28, Benton County: B. N. Nalors, farmer, 33, born in NC; M. C., wife, 27, born in VA; C.A., 7, born in NC; M. E., 3, born in GA; H.E., 1, born in AL. 1880, Allens, Calhoun County. B. N. Nalors, 68, gunsmith, living with his son D. D. Nalors [Census].

Norwood, Thomas Edward (1868-1953). tradesman. Courtland, Lawrence County. Norwood was born on 13 February 1868 in Mt. Moriah, AL, and died on 28 May 1953 in Tuscumbia, Colbert County. Thomas and his wife Minnie lived all their married life at Courtland. When he was a young man, Thomas worked with his father making furniture and carriages. Later, he had a repair shop, specializing as a gunsmith. He had a collection of antique guns and old books. After Minnie died, he stayed with his daughter, Alice Norwood Sherer, in Tuscumbia, Colbert County, and commuted to work at Courtland. He was a deputy sheriff for many years. For several years, he kept a pair of bloodhounds named Duke and Duchess used for trailing criminals. He was proud of the fact that as a deputy sheriff he had helped destroy over six hundred "moonshine" stills. He still had his shop when he died in 1953 at the age of eighty-five. He had worked in the shop the day before he died. A relative left the following at Ancestry:

"I remember him so well as a man with a mustache stained by the years of clamping a pipe in his teeth. He was a dead shot with guns and could fire a rifle from hip and never miss. Dad told me this when I was 5-7 years old. Papa repaired guns and taught his sons to shoot, and they were experts. They would get all awards at shooting contests. Papa only shot one man, a prisoner trying to escape. He shot him in the leg to stop him. When I was a pastor in Memphis one day I met an old man from Courtland, Ala., and I asked him if he ever knew my grandfather, Thomas E Norwood. He asked, "O you mean the sheriff?" Yes, I said. He instantly said, "That man could shoot a rifle from the hip and never miss." So this confirmed what Dad had told me about his father when I was s kid. Isn't that amazing? Papa used to take me hunting for Amerindian arrowheads in a plowed field in Court-land. He was a man of few words as I recall, would say, "Yeah," often. Must have been quite a man when young. I took several photos of him when I was very young with a little camera. He and grandmother are buried not far from my Mother in Oakwood Cemetery, Tuscumbia, Alabama. I have many memories of him and my grandmother, having stayed with them several times in their house in Courtland when I was only a small child."

Thomas Edward Norwood

"Prominent Citizen of Courtland Dies. Thomas E. Norwood, prominent Courtland citizen, died at the home of his daughter, Mrs. O.W. Sherer, Tuscumbia, Thursday, May 28, 1953. Mr. Norwood was 85 years of age and had lived more than 65 of those years in Courtland. He belonged to one of the pioneer families of Alabama. His grandparents came with their slaves and belongings to Morgan County shortly after 1800. His father, Richard W. Norwood, moved to Lawrence Co. in a few years, living near Moulton. He moved to Courtland about 1880. Mr. Norwood was a deputy sheriff of Lawrence County for several years. He was a gunsmith and ran a shop in Courtland for 61 years" [*Moulton Advertiser*, June 6, 1953].

Nunis, Samuel Unis (1802). gunsmith. Randolph County. Samuel was a son of David Nunez Cardozo. On 5 July 1824 Nunis married Sarah Jordon in Elbert, GA.1850, Randolph CountyL Samuel, age 48, born in SC., gunsmith and farmer; Sarah, 45, born in GA; Martha, 20; Matilda, 15; Alfred, 13; Benjamin, 11, all born in GA; Sarah, 9; Clementine, 7, both born in AL; and Dehlia Jordan, 90, born in SC, mother of Sarah [Census]. The following households of gunsmiths were enumerated one after another: Foster, Ivy, Southerland, Nunis, Thompson, and Walls. 1860, northern division: Samuel Nunis, farmer, 56, born in France; Sally, 54, wife; Ben, 21; Matilda, 18; Clementine, 15, all born in GA [Census; Ancestry].

Nunn, Elijah (1828) gunsmith. 1860, Morgan County. 1850, division 10, Morgan County: Elijah Nunn, 23, farmer, living with Winsford Nunn, 61. 1860, Cedar Plains, southwest division, Morgan County: Elijah T. Nunn, gunsmith, 32; Margaret J., wife, 28; Henry J., 4; William G. 2, all born in AL. [Census]. He may be the E. F. Nunn, born in AL, 53, dry goods merchant, in Beat 4, Noxubee, MS, in 1880.

O

Ogleby, Jesse L. (1819). gunsmith. 1850, district 19, Chambers County. Jesse, age 31, gunsmith; Matilda, 27, his wife; Ruth J., 1, all born in GA [Census].

Opelika, John Thomas Brooks (1837). armorer. John was born on July 24, 1837 at Anderson, SC. He was enlisted as a private July 1861 at Opelika, AL, in Company A, Arsenal Battalion. He was immediately detailed to shop work as a gun smith and continued to close of war [Ancestry].

Orr, William C. (1815-1860). gunsmith. Talladega district, Talladega County. 1850, William C. Orr, born in SC, 37, gun maker; Cynthia A., 31, wife; Laura C., 8; Wilson M., 6; Mary C., 4, all born in GA; William C., 1, born in AL. Orr, 45, gunsmith, born in SC, died from the effects of a fall in his house in July 1860 [Census; Federal Mortality Schedule].

P

Palmer, Amansa Marlin "Mace" (1832-1895). gunsmith. Cleburne County. Amansa was born on 5 October 1832 in Loganville, Walton County, GA, a son of Elijah and Mary Moore Palmer. He married Sarah Jane Baker on 22 July 1860 in Walton County. He was killed on 15 May 1895 in Oak Level, Cleburne County. Ben Crawford was jointly indicted with Henry Evans for murder in the second degree, for killing one Amansa M. Palmer, a man. They were convicted of manslaughter in the first degree, and sentenced to nine years' imprisonment in the penitentiary. The general character of Wright Williamson was excellent and Palmer's character for truth and veracity was bad. The defendants went there to get the deceased, who was a blacksmith and gunsmith, to fix his pistol, as the deceased had told him to bring it to him [Ancestry; *Southern Reporter*, 21].

A.M. "Mace" Palmer

Palmer, Joseph Washington (1845-1933). farmer & gunsmith. 1880, Marion County. Joseph, 34; Rebecca, 30; Elizabeth, 10; Washington, 8; Rebecca, 5; Hester, 3; Robert, 1, all born in AL. He married Rebecca Ann Brown. Noted also in censuses of 1900, 1910, and 1920. Burial was in the Pleasant Ridge Cemetery. Soon after the Civil War, Plummer Williams and a man named Miller were arrested and placed in jail in Fulton, Itawamba County, MS. Joseph Palmer and several other men from Marion County rode to Fulton and broke the men out of jail. During the process of getting them out and getting away the Miller man was shot and killed. The rest of them survived. Palmer would not take sides in the Civil War and thus gained the enmity of both parties [Ancestry; Census].

Peck, William (1797). gunsmith. Madison County. William was born in 1797 in Mossy Creek Twp., Jefferson County, TN, a son of Adam and Elizabeth Sharkey Peck. On 22 June 1824 he married Ann Rivers in Madison County [Ancestry]. Dan Wallace found an advertisement from 1823 in which Peck indicated he repairs guns and restocks them.

Perkins, William P. (1827). gunsmith. 1860, Mobile County. William, age 33, gunsmith, value $3000 real estate; $1000 personal value, born in AL; Sarah, 25, born in LA; Mary, 6; William H., 5; Sarah, 3; Francis, 7 months, all born in AL [Census].

Perry, James G. (1808). gunsmith. Athens, Limestone County. 1850, James S. Perry, gunsmith, 40; Elizabeth, wife, 35; Richard, 20; Nancy, 17; Mary, 10; Eliza, 6; James, 4; Elizabeth, 2, all born in TN.1860, Athens: James S. Perry, gunsmith, 50; Elizabeth, wife, 45; Mary, 20; Eliza J, all born in TN; James, 14; Sarah, 11; William, 10; Columbus, 6; Phoebe, 3; Oliver, 1, all born in AL. 1870, Athens, James E. Perry, 61, born in TN, farmer; Eliza, 27; Sarah, 22; Columbus, 16; Elizabeth, 14; Oliver, 11; James S. 24, all born in AL. His rifles show strong influences from TN. Jerry Noble listed a sniper rifle and a flintlock rifle signed *J G P*. [Census; Wallace]. *One rifle is shown in the Photo section.*

Person, William Davis (1818). plantation owner and gunsmith. Person was born in Limestone County. 1850, Kemper County, MS: William D. Person, blacksmith, 32; Judy, wife. 30, both born in MS; Franklin, 13; Redford, 12; Martha, 8; William, 6; Elizabeth, 4, all born in MS. 1860, South Bend, Duncan County, AR: William D. Person, born in AL, 42, farmer; Judith C, wife, 42, born in AL; Franklin, 22; Radford, 20; William D. 22; Martha Ann, 18; Elizabeth, 14; Sarah E., 10; Ellen, 8, all born in MS; Susan, 4; Emma, 2, both born in AR. Ancestry shows that Person died in Lincoln County, AR, but does not give a date [Census; Ancestry].

Pessou, L. (1790). gunsmith. 1850, Mobile. There was a man named L. Pessou in New Orleans in 1861, shop at 369 St. Claude [Census; *Dir*.].

Peterson, George W (1818) gun and blacksmith. He was born in Sampson County, NC. George married Sarah J Tatum also born NC. They sold land as late as 1842 in NC, and appeared in 1850 Benton County, AL: G W, age 31, gunsmith; S J 32, his wife; M A, 8 female, all born in AL. 1860, Calhoun County, George W 42, farmer; Sarah J 43; Margaret 19; 1870 Calhoun County: George, 50, blacksmith; Sarah 45; Sallie 12; George, 8. 1880 Maddox Twp., Calhoun County, G W, 62, farmer NC, Sarah Jane 68 both born in NC [Census]. He served in the Glorious Cause in Company D, Hardies Alabama Cavalry, as a Private.

Peterson, Karsten gunsmith. In 1804 Indian agent Benjamin Hawkins and a few Creek leaders proposed to the Salem Moravians the establishment of a mission at the old Indian agency, Fort Lawrence, just west of the Flint River, near Reynolds. Both Hawkins and the Creeks opposed the teaching of Christianity but agreed that they should become acquainted with craftsmen's skills and English. Acquiescing to their demands, the Moravians in 1807 sent Christian Burkhardt, a weaver, and Karsten Petersen, a turner, joiner, and gunsmith, to the Creek Nation. While teaching the "arts of civilization," the Brethren also taught the Gospel, taking extended forays beyond the Chattahoochee River into Alabama, where more Creeks lived. The Moravians were unsuccessful on all fronts; the Creeks and Hawkins disliked the pietistic religion. The mission closed in August 1813, after Creeks attacked Fort Mims (above Mobile on the Alabama River), and warlike hostilities developed. Burkhardt and Petersen returned to North Carolina. The War of 1812 prevented further evangelization [*New Georgia Encyclopedia*].

Pettis, William R. (1815-1887). gunsmith. 1881-85, Troy, Pike County. Pettis was born on 17 April 1815 in NC. 1850, beat 6, Russell County: William Pittis [*sic*], mechanic, 35; Mary, wife, 27, both born in NC; Mary, 12; Susan, 10; Stephen, 8; Sarah, 6; George 2, all born in AL. 1870, Troy, Pike County: Sallie Higgins, 80, born in VA; William R. Pettis, born in NC, 55, mechanic; Martha, 35; David, 17; Martin, 4; Andrew, 2; Martha, 16, all born in AL. 1880, Troy: William, carpenter, 65; Martha, wife, 36; Martin, 13; Andrew 12; Albert, 7; Lula, 3. He died on 25 September 1887 [Census; Ancestry; *Dirs*].

Phillips, Elisha L. (1836-1911). armorer and gunsmith. Dadeville, Tallapoosa County. He was born on 3 July 1836, in Anson County, NC [another source gives 1829], a son of Clement Phillips and his wife née Little. On 25 December 1850 he married Frances Saxon. Entered as private and gunsmith 28 July 1864, at Davis and Baseman's Gun shop in Coosa County, and continued until 9 April 1865. Phillips died on 7 March 1911 in Tallapoosa County. He filed for his pension in Tallapoosa County. His widow later filed for his pension in Tallapoosa County [Ancestry].

Pinkston, Rid (1819-1894). gunsmith. 1880, Jefferson County. Rid Pinkston, gunsmith, 62, born in NC, living in a boarding house. Pinkston was born on 22 January 1819 and died on 17 March 1894 and was buried in Jefferson County [Census].

Pisson L., Sr (1790) gunsmith. 1850, Mobile County. L. Pisson, 60, gunsmith; L. Pisson, 21, gunsmith, both born in LA; H. Cowen, 31, born in NY. All living with J. B. Fellows, merchant [Census]. There was a gunsmith, born in Santa Domingo, mulatto, in New Orleans, Joseph Alphonse Pesson (1795-1875) [which is probably how the name should be spelled].

Pisson, L., Jr. (1829) gunsmith. 1850, Mobile County. L. Pisson, 60, gunsmith; L. Pisson, 21, gunsmith, both born in LA; H. Cowen, 31, born in NY. All living with J. B. Fellows, merchant [Census].

Poyas, Francis Delisseline (1802-1879). gunsmith. Francis was born July 1802 in Charleston, Dorchester County, SC, and died January 11, 1879 in Pickens County, AL. 1819-31, 17 Meeting St., Charleston. Poyas noted in one advertisement that he had served a "regular apprenticeship" with John Schirer so he may well have been a Charleston native, here long before the 1819 date. On 26 August 1819 George Row placed his son Andrew C. in an apprenticeship with Poyas [Indenture Book for Boys and Girls, 1818-1820: 45]. In 1825-26 Poyas got involved in a nasty exchange with his former master. It seems that Schirer discovered and eventually patented a method of changing the cast ["crook"] of gunstocks using steam. Poyas also advertised this service and Schirer belittled him. Poyas responded that when apprenticed to Schirer, Poyas was to be taught all Schirer knew; besides Schirer had sought the patent after Poyas had completed Poyas's apprenticeship [*Charleston Gazette*, 7 April 1825; 28 April 1826; *Charleston Courier*, 21 April 1825; 28 April 1832]. There is some reason to believe that Poyas assisted in a slave revolt; this matter could be the subject of future research. He married Martha Standford Stent on February 18, 1824 in Charleston, daughter of John and Ann Alexander Stent (1808-1882); she also died in Pickens County, AL. In Charleston he was a gunsmith who became a Methodist Minister. Both were buried at Union Chapel Cemetery [Ancestry].

Poyas, James Osgood (1841-1905). gunsmith. 1881-85, Carrollton, Pickens County. James was born on 28 May 1841 in Tuscaloosa, a son of Francis D. and Martha Standford Poyas. After Joseph King was killed in battle during the Civil War, the widow, Annie Jane King then married James Poyas, a gunsmith, who also served in the Confederacy. They moved to Waco, McLennan County, Texas. James died on 7 October 1905 in Waco. Annie died a widow in Glendale, California and is buried at Forest Lawn Memorial Park, Glendale, California [*Dirs.*; Ancestry].

Price, Isaac (1822-1897) gunsmith. Isaac was born on 5 July 1822, a son of William and Nancy Baldridge Price. He married moved to Nashville, then in 1810 to Giles County, TN, and then in 1823 to Lauderdale County, AL. 1880, Lauderdale County: Isaac, blacksmith, 58, born in TN; Sarah, 27; Mary, 35; William, 32; Charles, 22; Annie, 18; Randolph, 15; Una, 10; Felix, 6, all born in AL. He died in Florence, Lauderdale County on 8 February 1897 [Wallace; Ancestry; Census].

Price, William (1776-1857) gunsmith. Price was born in Mecklenburg County, NC, on May 24, 1776; and died in Lauderdale County, AL, on March 5, 1857. His son, Isaac Price, was a gunsmith. He died on 5 March 1857.[family].

Prickett, William Parks (1832-1895) armorer. Prickett, private of Captain Bowie's Company, AL Cavalry. Confederate States Army enlisted 13 August 1861 at Decatur, AL, age 28 years. Union prisoner of war records show that he was captured 31 January 1863 at Rover, TN, and imprisoned at Fort McHenry, MD; Fortress Monroe, VA; and City Point, VA, from where he was paroled and exchanged 18 February 1863. He then worked in C.S.A. Ordnance as a gunsmith. After the war he was paroled at Hillsboro, NC [Ancestry].

Pruett, T. L. blacksmith, cutler. Prattville, Autauga County. During the Civil War Pruett was a private in 15th Battalion, Alabama Partisan Rangers, noted as a blacksmith. Pruett made D-guard Bowie knives for the Confederacy.

Pugh, Isaac (1785-1839). gunmaker. Isaac was born on March 9, 1785 in Wilkes County, and died September 8, 1839 in Grove Hill, Clark County, Alabama. He married Hannah Baskin on December 5, 1809. Isaac grew up in Wilkes and Washington Counties, Georgia. As a young man he came in 1810 to the Indian Wilds of the Choctaw Purchase, a part of the Mississippi Territory. He located in what is now central Clarke County, Alabama. Isaac lived for a year with the Choctaw Indians and became a friend of Push-mattaha, the a young man and not yet chief. Isaac was a gun maker. Isaac then returned home in Georgia and remained there until 1812 when he went back to Alabama, and took his wife with him, along with his parents, brothers, and sisters. They all settled a few miles west of what is now Grove Hill, Alabama [Ancestry; Family Genealogy].

Pugh, Stephen (1805-1883) gunsmith and plantation owner. 1860, Grove Hill, Clarke County. Stephen was born on 10 January 1805, the fourth son of Elijah Pugh, and his wife née Ruth Julian .He never married. He learned the trade of a gunsmith. "He is yet living about four miles from Grove Hill, now, in 1877, seventy-one years of age. He is still active, attends to his plantation, and is an intelligent, worthy citizen." Pugh died on 6 September 1883 in Clarke County [Ancestry; *Revolutionary War Soldiers in Alabama*].

Q

No Names

R

Raynolds, D. H. gunsmith. Mobile. There is a flintlock rifle signed Dade & Raynolds [Noble]. Also listed by Sellers. Neither Dade nor Raynolds/ Reynolds located.

Read, John B. (1816) inventor, physician. Tuscaloosa, Tuscaloosa County. 1850, district 1, Tuscaloosa County: John B. Read, physician, 34; Susan W., 33. On 28 October 1856 Read obtained U.S. patent 15,999 for a projectile; on 5 May 1857 he obtained U.S. patent number 17,233 for a breech-loading firearm; and on 24 November 1857 he was issued patent number 18,707 for a projectile. 1870, John B. Read, physician, 54, born in AL; Susan, wife, 52, born in NC; Susan, 15, born in AL [Census].

Reedy, Logan B. (1845). gunsmith. 1850-70, Huntsville, Madison County. 1872-82, Mexia, Limestone County, TX. 1870, Huntsville: The household was headed by Jane Reedy, 53, widow and Logan's mother. Logan was unmarried and the other men were clerks, grocers, etc., all born in AL. 1880, Mexia: Logan B. Reedy, gunsmith, 36; Catharine B., 35, wife, both born in AL; Hugh W, 2; Frank M., 1, both born in TX [Census].

Respess, A. (1843). gunsmith. 1880, Branchville, St. Clair County. A. Respess, gunsmith, 37; S. E., wife, 21; A. L., 4; E., 3; A. R., infant, all born in AL [Census].

Rews, B. B. (1828) gunsmith. 1860, Covington County; born in VA; lived in a hotel, single [Census].

Reynolds, H. L. (1818) merchant. Mobile. 1850, H. L. Reynolds, 32, born in OH, merchant; Martha, 23 [Census]. Jerry Noble listed him as a arms merchant. There is a signed Dade & Reynolds rifle known.

Asa Richardson

Richardson, Asa (1820). arms maker. Asa was a son of Isham and Judith Garner Richardson, born in Moore County, NC, on 4 May 1820. He married Flora Smith. 1850, Division 2 East of the Military Road, Lauderdale County: Aas Richardson, born in NC, 30, blacksmith, value $200; Flora, 28; Nancy, 8; Mary, 6; Juda, 3; Sarah, infant, all born in AL. 1860, Florence, Lauderdale County: Asa Richardson, born in NC, 40, works in factory; Flora, wife, 37; Lucinda, 18; Nancy, 18; Mary, 16; Luda [?], 13; Sally, 9; John, 7, all born in AL. One long rifle marked *A R* is attributed to him. He reportedly worked at the Kennedy gun factory at Greenhill. A Confederate D-guard Bowie knife is known, marked *A. Richardson & Co*. He reportedly died in Lauderdale County in 1868 or 1869 [Ancestry; Family; Wallace].

Richardson, David, Jr. (1809-1844). farmer & gunsmith. Lauderdale County. David Richardson, Jr., was born on 2 May 1809 in Moore County, NC, a son of John David and Catherine Stutts Richardson. Reportedly he worked at the Kennedy gun factory at Green Hill. David died on 11 March 1844 and was buried at Green Hill [Ancestry; Wallace].

Richardson, Isham (1793-1864) gun and blacksmith & farmer. Isham was born in Moore County, NC on 22 December 1793. He married Judith Garner on 16 December 1816 in Moore County. 1830, census in Lauderdale County. On 1 April 1852 and 1 March 1858 he purchased each time 40 acres in Lauderdale County. 1860, Green Hill: Isam [*sic*] Richardson, born in NC, 64, farmer; Judea, 64, wife, born in NC; Henry, 26; William, 22; James, 20, all born in AL. Isham died on 22 November 1864 and was buried at Green Hill [Ancestry; Wallace; Census].

Richardson, John David (1776-1857) farmer and blacksmith. Lauderdale County. John was born on 21 September 1776 in Moore County, NC, a son of William Stephen and Elizabeth Townsend Richardson. He migrated to Lauderdale County sometime around 1815-1820. John married Catherine Ann Stutts in 1796 in NC. Family legend has it that they were headed to the MS Territory and when they got to Lauderdale County, they stopped to rest their stock but liked it so much that they decided to stay. Later other family members joined them here. Among other families from Moore County were the Stutts, Kennedys, Ritters, McGees, and Moores. John owned and operated a water-powered mill. John died on 12 February 1857 and was buried at Richardson's Chapel about 20 miles east on Blue Water Creek. [Ancestry].

Richardson, Wiley (1791-1839). farmer & gunsmith. On 2 September 1828 Wiley Richardson married Jane Trousdale in Lauderdale County. On 16 September 1831 Wiley Richardson married Elizabeth M. Phillips in Lauderdale County. On 12 August 1833 Wiley G. Richardson purchased 75 acres and on 10 September 1834 he purchased 39.5 acres both in Lauderdale County. Wiley reportedly worked at the Kennedy gun factory in Green Hill [Ancestry].

Ricketts, William A. (1836-1893) gunsmith. William was born on 12 August 1836, a son of John W. and Mary W. Ricketts. 1870, Wetumpka, Elmore County. born in TN; Mary E. née Parker, wife, 1843, born in AL. Ricketts died on 24 November 1893 in Jefferson County, AL [Census; Ancestry].

Rider David. gunsmith. 1916, Ft. Gibson, Muskogee County; wife Sarah [Ancestry].

Riley, John Frederick (1815-1866), Riley was the first gunsmith in Huntsville. He was one of Abraham and Mary Riley's sons, born 13 January 1815 and died 18 September 1866. John married (1) Elizabeth Ann Patton, daughter of Thomas Patton and Winnefred (?) and (2) Mary Elizabeth Samuel. "Mollie" Riley was the eldest of John Frederick and Elizabeth's daughters [Ancestry; Family].

Rison, Archibald (1803) gunsmith. On 7 April 1836 in Huntsville Rison married Martha Ann Bibb. 1850, Huntsville: Archibald Rison, gun maker, 47, born in TN; Martha Ann, wife, 33; William R., 13; John L., 11; Wilson B., 9, all born in AL. IN 1860, Archibald Rison was listed as a *gin* maker so the entry for 1850 is probably *gin* maker also[Census].

Roberts, Colbert (1831) gunsmith. 1850, Baldwin County; born in AL. There were 10 people in this household in addition to Roberts, including Lewey Sensiar, 32, a carpenter, and Henry Sensiar, 22, a blacksmith [Census].

Robinson, William (1821). gunsmith. 1850, Rusk division, Rusk County, Texas. 1850, Andrew Robinson, 49, blacksmith, born in TN, value $2500; Elizabeth, 53; William, 29, gunsmith; Henry, 23, blacksmith; Caroline, 20; James, 18, farmer; Harris, 17, farmer, all born in TN; Thomas, 15, farmer; Azariah, 13, both born in AL [Census].

Rogers, George W. (1805) gunmaker. 1850, Morgan County. Rogers, age 45, gunmaker, value $700; Elizabeth, age 30, both born in VA [Census].

Rogers, J. B. gunsmith Limestone County. A Southern, iron-mounted percussion signed in script J. B. Rogers [Wallace].

Rose, Tom (1885-1970). gunsmith. Athens, Limestone County. Tom was the 12th of 14 surviving siblings out of a total of 17 children to Samuel Adam Burney and Elmira Almeda (Hargrove) Rose, born on 21 August 1885. He died on 3 January 1970 in Kerens, Navarro County, Texas. He worked c.1901-11 in Mexico [Ancestry; Family].

Ryan, William T. (1851). gunsmith. 1880, township 8, Morgan County. William T. Ryan, gunsmith, 29; Polly A., wife, 17; William T. J., infant [Census].

Ryburn, Hyrum W. (1801-1859). gunsmith. Huntsville, Madison County. Hyrum was born in Montgomery County, TN. According to Dan Wallace, Hyrum purchased William Keesee's gun shop in 1828. 1846, TX census, Grayson County. On 20 December 1847 Ryburn acquired 640 acres in Fannin district, Grayson County. 1850, Sherman, Grayson County, TX: H. W, Ryburn, farmer, 49; H., wife, both born in TN; S., 3; N, infant, both born in TX. Wallace reported 1 signed rifle. He also believed that Ryburn was the brother-in-law of William Keesee [Ancestry; Census; Wallace]. *One rifle is shown in the Photo section.*

S

Saltsman, Daniel (1817). gunsmith. 1850, Conecuh County. Daniel, 33, born in PA, gun smith; Haney, his wife, 24; Martha, 11; Mary, 7; Elizabeth, 9; Lucy, 1; Fleming, 3, all born in AL [U.S. Census]. He was a river boat worker whose health was jeopardized by that work, plying his trade on the Alabama River on the *Old Mary Swan*. He also worked as a construction engineer. Daniel married, first, Mary Fables; and, second, Haney Kennedy. There is a biography at http://saltsman.org/saltsmanhis2.pdf

Salisbury, William L. (1899) doing business as **Salisbury & Bailey**. gun and locksmiths. Birmingham [*Labor Advocate*, 29 June 1895]

William L. Salisbury, formerly a member of the firm of Salisbury & Bailey, gunsmiths, suicide yesterday at his home in North Birmingham, by shooting himself with a double barrel shotgun, producing almost instant death. Salisbury had been sick for some time, and had recently grown very despondent, and it is thought that his mind became unbalanced. Yesterday morning he took a shotgun, which he kept in the house, seated himself in a chair, and deliberately placed the gun between his legs and pulled the trigger. There was a loud report and when members of the family rushed into the room, they found Salisbury with half of his head blown off, lying prone upon the floor. Salisbury was a blacksmith by trade and has lived in the city for a number of years . . . Salisbury leaves a wife and several children [*Age Herald*, 2 April 1899]

Salter, William Joseph (1856) gunsmith. Short Creek, Jefferson County. William was born on 8 April 1856 in Jefferson County, a son of Silas and Patsy Prescott Salter. Noted as age 84, widower of Caroline, in 1940 census of Birmingport, Jefferson County. William died on 26 February 1941 in Powhatan, Jefferson County, age 84, and buried at the Salters Cemetery. Jerry Noble reported one signed flintlock rifle [Noble; Wallace; Census; Ancestry].

Sanders, Benjamin (c.1766-c.1849) black and gunsmith, farmer. Jackson County. Sanders owned several hundred acres of land. Based on census records from 1800, 1810, 1830 and 1840, Benjamin was probably born between 1766 and 1770. He doesn't appear on the 1850 Jackson County census, and because of family tradition about his having lived to an advanced old age we may assume he died closer to the year 1850 than to 1840. If he died in 1849 and was born about 1766, he would have been about eighty-three when he died. Because many people in those days lost track of the exact year they were born, it's very possible Benjamin and his family were genuinely convinced he was at least a decade older than his real age at the time of his death. 1840 census of Jackson County, Alabama. Even though actual names other than the head of household are still not listed in 1840, we can identify the following people in the household: Benjamin (70-80 years old), Mary (60-70), John (15-20), Alfred (10-15). Also in the household are one unidentified female, and three unidentified females. Isaac, one of Benjamin's sons, is listed as living next door. Isaac was my great grandfather. I have been able to obtain much information about Isaac from census and other records, but much of what I have came from family tradition that was passed down from my grandfather to my father. Within a couple of years after the 1840s census, Isaac would move from Jackson County and move west to Mississippi and eventually to Arkansas. One of the traditions about old Ben's last days is that he converted from the Roman

Catholic to Protestantism at a camp meeting in Jackson County when he was ninety-six years old, dying two years later. A 1917 newspaper article in Van Zandt County, Texas, gives information that probably came from the recollections of Benjamin's grandson: "Levi Lindsey Sanders was born in Jackson County, AL . . . . He was a son of Buck Ben Sanders, a gunsmith, and came of Irish Catholic ancestors, his people settling in North Carolina. Uncle Levi's paternal grandfather, Ben Saunders, as the name was originally spelled, was converted from the Catholic faith at a camp meeting in Jackson County, Ala., at the age of 96 years." [Ancestry].

Sanders, Levi Lindsey (1837-1917) gunsmith. Jackson County. Sanders died in TX.

"L. L. Sanders, one of the oldest and most highly respected citizens of Van Zandt County, died at his late home at Ben Wheeler, Thursday, Jan. 4, at 3:30 p.m. Levi Lindsey Sanders was born in Jackson County, Ala., February 21, 1837, his age being 79 years, 10 months and 17 days. He was a son of Buck Ben Sanders, a gunsmith, and came of Irish Catholic ancestry, his people settling in North Carolina. Levi was one of nine children and left home at the age of 16, working on a steamboat on the Mississippi for some time. Later, he settled in Arkansas, following his trade as a blacksmith. He came to Texas in 1857 and married Miss Susan Collins in 1858, the marriage occurring in Dallas when that city was a mere village."[Canton, Texas *Herald,* January 12, 1917]

Saunders, C. W. (1876-1913). gunsmith. Anniston, Calhoun County. Saunders, a married gunsmith, died on 24 June 1913 at Anniston and was buried there [Ancestry death certificate].

Schley, William (1815) blacksmith. 1850, Chambers County. William Scley, blacksmith, 35; Mary, wife, 30, both born in SC; Amanda, 5; John, 4; William A., 2; Elizabeth, infant, all born in AL [Census].

Sellers, Young (1792). gunsmith. 1850-60, Jackson County; 1850, called a blacksmith; 1860, Young, gunsmith, age 68, $200 land; Sallie, 56, his wife, both born in N.C.; Salina, 9; Young, 18; Aran [m], also 18; Crawford, 12, all born in AL. 1860, division 1: Young Sellers, gunsmith, 68, born in NC; Sallie, wife, 56, born in TN; Salina, 9; Fanny, 18; Aran, 18; Crawford, 12, all born in AL. Living next door was Fineas Freeman, 37, gunsmith [Census; Ancestry]. Young despite his age, served in the 6th Regiment, Alabama Infantry as did his son.

Senn, James (1825-1892) gunsmith 1870, Pike County. James Senn was born 24 August 1825. 1870 John T. age 33 gunsmith born in SC; Josephine age 31 keeping house born in GA; John, 10; George, 8; Charter, 7; :aura, 5; another child, 2. He died on 17 July 1892 and was buried in Shady Grove Baptist Church Cemetery, Pike County [Census].

Sewall, A. F. (1807) gunsmith. 1850, district 19, Jackson County. A. F. Sewall, gun smith, 43. born in KY; Susan, his wife, 37, born in VA; Sarah, 13; Mary, 10; Emily, 7, all born in AL [Census]. Also seen as Sewell.

Shipp, William (1810) gunsmith 1860, Lauderdale County; born in NC [Census].

Short, Samuel Andrew (1836-1904) gunsmith Sam was born on 19 November 1836 in Polk County, TN and died on 5 March 1904 in Elkmont, Morgan County, Alabama. Sam was a son of

John Bunyan and Matila (Whitten) Short. On 1 September 1859 he married Elizabeth Jane Kile in Murray County, Georgia [Ancestry; Census].
[http://www.rushings.info/d0006/g0000028.html]

Shotts, David Hilliard (c.1790-c.1830) gunsmith Cahaba, at the confluence of the Alabama and Cahaba Rivers, Dallas County. He was a son of Daniel Shotts. The family legend of the Alabama Shotts is that David Shotts and his wife, Nancy Clark, with their sons, settled at Cahaba, then the capitol of Alabama, and that he became the first blacksmith, gunsmith, cabinet maker and general handy repair man for that new town. Cahaba was the capitol from 1820 until 1825 and is now an abandoned town. Three other children were born after the family moved to Alabama, David Hilliard, Harriet and Jake. Soon thereafter David Shotts died, perhaps in the early 1830's. [J. E. Shotts, *Shotts Family of Marion County, Alabama*].

Singer, Edgar C. gunsmith. Singer was originally from Ohio, but fought on the side of the Confederacy. He was the nephew of Isaac Merritt Singer the inventor of the first commercially successful sewing machine, was the man who invented the underwater mines used by the Confederacy. He got help from the local Masonic Lodge he had joined when he arrived in Texas in 1840 to perfect his design and successfully demonstrated it to General John Magruder in Houston by blowing up an old scow in a near by bayou. Singer's under water torpedo was eventually recommended to the war department in Richmond and used throughout the Confederacy. Singer recruited more help from his Masonic lodge to mine the bays and rivers around the South. They eventually became known as Singer's Submarine Corps. One of Singer's mines sunk the *USS Tecumseh* and prompted Admiral David Farragut's famous words "Damn the torpedoes; full speed ahead. While mining the port in Mobile, Alabama, Singer meet Horace Hunley who had lost two experimental submarines in the past two years. Singer and his fellow Masons went together to help Hunley finance his boat and the CSS Hunley became a reality.

Skates & Company. Mobile. This firm rifled a number of heavy pieces and produced field calibers. Skates & Company, also known as the Mobile Foundry, was located at the corner of Magnolia and State Streets. Prior to the war the firm manufactured steam engines, boilers, gin gearings, and iron machinery. during the war the Skates firm engaged primarily in rifling and banding of heavy guns and the casting of artillery projectiles. [*Memphis Appeal,* September 28, 1861]. In September, 1861, a contract was signed with the firm for four field batteries complete with harness [O.R., VI. 726, 729] "...These guns should unquestionably be reinforced with wrought-iron bands, so as to make up one an inch and a half thick and 8 or 10 inches wide. The gun should be perfectly clean, and the band be shrunk on at a light heat. The preponderance of the breech does no great harm. The shells ought not to be longer than two calibers probably, nor to weigh more than 40 or 45 pounds. The charge of powder will not exceed 5 pounds. I will send to Messrs. Skates a sketch showing the mode of rifling adopted here and the form of the shell most approved. There are many varieties. The heavy guns bored with small calibers carry heavier shot and higher charges. There are some old guns lying at Forts Morgan and Gaines. You are authorized to have them rebored, and to build carriages for them if found fit for service, such a firing round or grape shot for the defense of redoubts or of the city. I have prevailed on the Ordnance Bureau to order of Messrs. Skates & Co. four batteries of field guns, with harness . . . ." Company vouchers give evidence that only two cannon were delivered - a rifled bronze gun caliber 3.67 with carriage complete delivered October 29, 1861, at $1000 and a bronze 12-pounder howitzer with carriage complete delivered December 14, 1861, at $900. ("Citizens File") The

Charleston Mercury of April 2, 1862, reported: "The Government has copper enough in Mobile to make four or five brass cannon, but it cannot for the want of tin, which cannot be had or at least is very scarce. . . . The foundries at Mobile can make no brass cannon at present. Their whole time is devoted to making more useful articles namely iron cannon and shot and shells and rifling cannon." On March 21, 1862, Skates and Company addressed Colonel H. Oladowski of the Ordnance Department that "we have completed the iron Parrott guns and disposed of them to the State [of Alabama]. We have done some excellent shooting with 8 ounces of powder with a range of 2 3/4 miles at all the elevation we could get." [Citizens File] It is uncertain whether or not this was a reference to guns actually having been cast at the foundry.

Sloat, L. W. arms importer. c.1839, Mobile [Noble].

Smith, Edmund Cape (1818). gunsmith. Jefferson County. 1850, Mud Creek Twp., Jefferson County: Edmond C. Smith, 29, son of Jacob and Margaret Smith. Ed married Sarah Franklin. Smith was a gunsmith and postmaster in the community of Toadvine in the western part of Jefferson County. 1860, Freelands: Edmund C. Smith, born in GA, 41, farmer; Sarah E., 23; Louisa, 17; Nancy, 14; Mary, 13; Filander, 8; Salina, 6; Leander, 5; Lucinda, 3; Corley, infant.1880, Edmond, age 62, gunsmith, born in GA; Sarah, 45, his wife; Sirena, 8; Flavius, 6; Centennial, 4 [Census].

Smith, Henry (1795-1858). gun maker. 1850, district 4, Limestone County. Henry, age 55, gun maker, born in TN; Mary, his wife, 55, born in NC; Franklin, 25, blacksmith; Joseph A. P., farmer, 18; Martha, 21; Mary, 14, all born in AL; James Leott, 58, born in TN. On 8 June 1833 Henry Smith obtained 81 acres in Limestone County. There is a tombstone in Elkmont, Limestone County with this inscription "In Memory of Henry Smith, died Jan 27 1858 aged about 55 years" [Ancestry; Census].

Smith, Robert W. (1810-). gunsmith. 1860, Louina, southern division, Randolph County; Robert, age 50, gun smith, value $400 real estate, $500 personal value; Elizabeth, 40, his wife, both born in NC; Mary, 12, born in TN; Elizabeth, 9; Nancy G., 7; Sarah, 5; Martha 15 days, all born in AL. In 1880 there was a retired farmer Robert W. Smith, born in NC in Brownville, Lee County [Census].

Southerland, Samuel S. (1830-). gunsmith. 1850, Randolph County. Samuel, age 20; Mary, 18, his wife, both born in GA. The following households of gunsmiths were enumerated one after another: Foster, Ivy, Southerland, Nunis, Thompson, and Walls.

Starkey, Calvin (1827-). gunsmith. 1850, Jackson County. Calvin, age 23, gunsmith, value $200, born in Maury County, Tennessee; Betty Ann, 23, born in MO, his wife; Mary J., 3; Elisha, 1 month, both born in AL [Census]. Calvin's father Elijah was born in 1776 and in Maury County by 1817 [Noble].

Stover, Nathan. gunsmith. 1866, home on Connor, Mobile. In 1880 there was a Nathan Stover, blacksmith, born about 1827 in GA, in Yonah, White County, GA; wife Elizabeth, 42, with 9 children, ages 3 to 17, all born in GA [Census; Dirs.].

Sturdivant, Lewis G. military rifle maker. 1861-63, Talladega County; 1863, Selma, Dallas County. He supplied arms to the Glorious Cause, mostly of the U.S. Model 1841 Mississippi pattern.

Stutts, George (1800-1869). gunsmith. 1850, Lauderdale County, MS. George is listed in Lauderdale County, AL; later living in Lauderdale County, MS.

Stutts, Jacob. (1797-1881). gunsmith. Lauderdale County. Stutts was born in NC. Living with them in 1850 was Calvin Key. According to Dan Wallace, Stutts was a skilled blacksmith from NC who did not learn the gunsmith's trade until he came to AL and apprenticed with John V. Bull. 1850, Lauderdale County. Jacob, 53, gunsmith; Nancy, 49, his wife, both born in N.C.; Wesley, 23, blacksmith; Elizabeth, 21; Asa, 18, laborer; John, 16, laborer; James, 12; Mary, 10; Nancy, 8, all born in AL. Also Calvin Key, 20, gunsmith, born in NC. 1870, Green Hill: Jacob Stutts, 73; Nancy, wife, 68; Sallie, 34; Nancy, 27; Mary, 19. Stutts operated a gun factory on Cowpen Creek. Jacob "Gunner Jake" Stutts of Green Hill utilized iron ore mined and refined in Iron City TN, just a few miles away and shipped down Shoals Creek. He shipped his long rifles by boat on the Tennessee River to other markets in the South. Stutts died on 26 April 1881 and was buried in the Kennedy Cemetery, Green Hill [Ancestry; Wallace; Census].

The Kennedys and the Stutts came to Moore County, NC from Philadelphia, Pennsylvania during the Revolutionary War. At the time the British invaded Philadelphia, they all moved their factories to Orange County, North Carolina. They later moved to Moore County, North Carolina. In 1823, David Kennedy, son of Alexander Kennedy, left for Lauderdale County, AL and built a gun factory at Green Hill, AL about 15 miles northeast of Florence on the Jackson Military Road, (US Route 43 today). The road was a major connection from Nashville to New Orleans and was obviously an optimum place for a gun factory due to the use by the military and travelers moving to the west and south. In addition, several other major frontier roads intersected in the immediate area including the Natchez Trace, the Columbia Pike, the Pulaski Pike, Doublehead's Trial, Bryer's Road, Gaines Road, and the Huntsville Road. There was an abundance of military trade and migrating families in need of long rifles and pistols for the AL frontier. The Stutts family and the Kennedy family lived within 5 miles of each other in the same area. Leonard Stutts daughter, Catherine, married James Hill in Moore County and they had four children while living there before moving to Lauderdale in approximately 1832. The rest of their children were born in Lauderdale County. The Kennedys and the Stutts were primarily engaged in gun manufacturing and blacksmithing. [Ancestry]. *One rilfe is shown in the Photo section and discussed in the Additional Photo Information section.*

Summersett, James Monroe (1828-1918). gunsmith. Enlisted on 29 July 1861 at Troy, AL, in the 18th Regiment, AL Infantry. He served in Stewart's Division, Hardee's Corps, as regimental blacksmith and gunsmith. He was captured near Atlanta on 5 August 1864 and held at Military Prison, Louisville; transferred to Camp Chase, OH, 14 August 1864; transferred to Point Lookout, MD 18 March 1865. Signed parole, 6 June 1865. His physical description: height: 6' 0"; hair: light; eyes: grey; complexion: fair [Ancestry].

Suter, Casper (1796-). gunsmith and salesman. 1850-66, Selma, Dallas County. 1860-64, C. Suter & Co. with Peter Jessel. Suter and Jessel made Model 1841 "Mississippi" style rifles for the C.S.A. They also made derringer type pistols and sporting arms before the Civil War. During the Civil War Suter and Jessel also converted rifles for the Confederate government. 1860, C. Suter, gunsmith, $6000 real estate, $2500 personal value; L. Suter, wife, 64, both born in Switzerland; Peter Jessel, 34, born in France, gunsmith. For reasons best to known to him, Sellers listed Jessel as Lessier [Census; Gardner, 190]. *One Derringer pistol is shown in the Photo section.*

Suttle, William, Jr. (1780-1863). gunsmith. Elbert County. Son of William Suttle, Sr. (1731-1839) and Margaret Harbin (ca. 1735-1839) married 1800 Elbert Co., GA to Elizabeth White had a child born in 1801 in Richmond Co, GA and others 1804-1811 in Elbert Co., GA in 1830 he is in Laurens Co., GA in 1840 he is in Pike Co., AL [Census]

In 1863 William died in Perry Co., Alabama. He may well have worked as a gunsmith in Georgia from about 1800 until° he moved to Alabama sometime between 1830 an 1840. It appears he was born in 1780 in North Carolina and died in 1863 in Perry, Alabama. The birth of his children indicate he was in Georgia by at least 1801. So it looks like there were father and son gunsmiths named William Suttle, both of whom who worked in Georgia. From the birth of the elder William's children, it appears he had a child born in South Carolina in 1790 and in Elbert Co., GA in 1791. If those genealogical entries are correct, it would appear that the Suttles left Virginia during the War, moved to North Carolina, then South Carolina, and then cam into Georgia about 1791. The elder William Suttle was a gunsmith who lived until age 108. The younger William Suttle was also a gunsmith who probably worked in Georgia for many years before moving to Alabama. The following incident took place about 1822, at which time the elder Suttle was age 91.

". . . his rifle and, with coolest deliberation, shot the gesturing brave through the body. Instantly the entire camp was in turmoil, in consequence no doubt, of what they supposed to be a surprise attack by a large force of angry and determined whites. The child, with rare presence of mind, rushed to the spot from which the gun had been fired and Suttle taking her in his arms ran to the place where his horse was concealed and safely carried her to his home." [MacIntosh, *History of Elbert County*] " . . . a band of roving Cherokees made an attack upon the inhabitants a short distance above the spot where Edinburg once stood and several persons were scalped and murdered. A beautiful 14 year old girl, whose name has long since been forgotten, was spared in the massacre and taken captive. William Suttle, a gunsmith and lay preacher of Edinburg, heard of the raid and determined to rescue the child. Arming himself with an excellent rifle he at once set out alone on his dangerous mission. About midnight he came in sight of the Indian camp fire. In true frontier fashion he made his way to within 30 yards of the encampment and saw the terror stricken little girl being forcibly held upon the lap of a stalwart brave. In a few moments this brave arose and began talking in a loud voice with the accompaniment of many gestures. Suttle from his ambush, raised . . ."

Swain, Charles (1869-). gunsmith. Third Ave., Birmingham. 1910, ward 12: Charles Swain, machinist and mechanic, 41, born in TN; wife Christiana, 37; James, 8 [*Age Herald*, 18 January 1898; Census]

T

Thomas, N. (1810-). gunsmith. 1850, Clarke County. Thomas, age 40, born in GA, value $250, gun smith; Nancy, 36, his wife; Ben, 18; Richard, 16; Betty, 12; Nancy, 10; Edward, 6; Jane, 4, all born in AL [Census].

Thomas, William B. (1798-). gun- and blacksmith. Pickens County. 1850, William Thomas, blacksmith, 52; Jane A., 17, both born in NC; Thomas, 14; Charlotte, 13; Frances, 9; William, 8, all born in AL. 1860, William B. Thomas, 62, born in NC. His son William, 24, is also a gunsmith. The only other child is Mary, age 7. In household 522 is John Thomas with wife Lydia and three daughters, Martha, Mary and Ann ages 9 to 9 months; and in household 524 is Thomas, Jr., 24, with wife Sarah, 18 [Census].

Thomas, William (1842-). gunsmith. 1860, Pickens County; born in AL; son of William B. Thomas. 1870, Speeds Mill, Pickens County, William Thomas, farmer, 27, single. 1880, Pleasant Grove, Pickens County: William Thomas, 38, farmer [Census].

Thompson, J. (1855-). gunsmith. 1880, Opelika, Lee County. J. Thompson, 25, gunsmith, single, living in a boarding house. J. was a son of M. J. and S. Thompson of Beulah, Lee County [Census].

Thompson, James O. (1888-1934). gunsmith. 1029 S. 10th Ave., Birmingham. James was born on 21 September 1888 at Troy, a son of James H. and Elizabeth Flowers Thompson. He was married to Ruth Hunt. He died at Birmingham on 19 September 1934 at age 45, noted as a gunsmith on his death certificate [Ancestry].

Thompson, Seth (1825-). gunsmith. Randolph County. 1850, Seth Thompson, 25; Nancy, wife, 23, both born in GA; Nancy, 1, born in AL. The following households of gunsmiths were enumerated one after another: Foster, Ivy, Southerland, Nunis, Thompson, and Walls. 1860, Rockdale, Randolph County: Seth Thompson, miller, 38; Nancy, wife, 36, both born in GA; N. E., 11; Shady, 10; M. J., 8; B. T., 4; Sam, 1, all born in AL [Census]. He was probably the Seth Thompson, born about 1825, who died on 31 December 1879 and was buried in Lynnville Cemetery Lynnville Warrick County IN [Ancestry].

Thompson, W. P. gunsmith. Opelika, Lee County [*Age Herald*, 11 April 1897]

Thoss, Eugene (1858-1928). gunsmith. 1887-1908, Mobile. "Thoss-Tompkins Sporting Goods Co. Wholesale & Retail Firearms, Ammunition, Fishing Tackle Sporting Goods. Bicycles & Sundries. Repairing Done at Short Notice No. 76 Dauphin Street Mobile, Alabama " [*Confederate Gray Book* 1912]. "The store of Eugene Thoss, gunsmith, was broken into last night, the thief securing quite a number of pistols, cartridges, etc." [*Times Picayune*, 31 January 1883]. A robbery occurred at his gunshop on Dauphin St., near Water St. [*Montgomery Advertiser*, 12 March 1907]. 1889, cutlery, guns, sporting goods at 14 Dauphin; home west side Jackson south of Conti St. [*Dirs*.]. Thoss was born on 21 July 1858 in Germany. On 2 December 1889 he married Eugenia Lohr. He died on 1 May 1929 and was buried in Mobile [Ancestry].

Tissier, Charles George (1861-1948). gunsmith. Selma, Dallas County. Tissier received U.S. patent number 289,787 on 4 December 1883 for an extractor with Peter Tissier. Charles was a son of Pierre [Peter] Tissier and his wife née Emily Kuhne. He married Houston Cole. Charles died on 27 May 1948, aged 87 years, at Selma. Known percussion pistols. [*Selma Times Journal*, November 2, 1927; Ancestry]

Tissier, Peter (1824-). gunsmiths. Selma, Dallas County. Peter was born in November 1824 in France and arrived in America in 1845. 1870, Peter Tissier, born in France, 48, gunsmith, $3500 real estate, $1000 personal value; Emma, born in Prussia, 28; Charles, 8; Henry, 1; Eliza, domestic servant, 14, all born in AL. 1880, ward 2, P. Tissier, gunsmith, 55, born in France; Emma, wife, 40, born in Germany; Charles, 19, clerk; Henry, 14, both born in AL. 1871-85, Peter Tissier & Company [*Dirs*].

Todd, David (1877-1952). gunsmith. 1894-1904, Montgomery. Son and apprentice of George Todd, took over his gunshop. He died on 6 June 1952 [Ancestry; *Montgomery Advertiser*, 4 December 1904; 21 June 1914].

Todd, George H., Sr. (1837-1912). gunsmith. 1890-1900, Montgomery. 1893, shop at 115 Jefferson Davis Ave. George was born on 24 November 1837, in Duchess County, NY, a son of David and Catharine Stoutenberg. They were the parents of of David Todd. Third generation included Walter J. Todd and Henry P. Todd at the same address. George married Henrietta A. Metz in Austin in 1860. George died and was buried in 1912 at Montgomery [Ancestry; *Dirs*.].

Todd, John Norton (1873-1938). gunsmith. 1893-1914, Montgomery St., Montgomery. 1893, shop at 115 Jefferson Davis Ave. John was a son of George H. and Henrietta Metz Todd, born on 29 December 1873 at Montgomery. Fire at his gunshop [*Montgomery Advertiser*, 7 December 1901]. John married Libbie C. [?], but was noted in the 1930 census with a wife named Ruth. He died at Montgomery in October 1938 [Ancestry; *Montgomery* Advertiser, 7 December 1901; 21 June 1914; *Dirs*.]

". . . when the founder's daughter married George H. Todd, Sr., who took over the business. George Todd's grandson, David Todd was the last family man to own the business. He died in 1952. The ownership then passed to Samuel Audrey Beaird, who worked in the store since 1918. Campbell, Beaird's son-in-law, purchased Todd's Gun Store from Beaird in 1970, a year after [it] moved to North Court Street. When he started working at Todd's in 1954 Camp said Remington shotguns were the store's biggest seller. The price for a Browning A-5 semi-automatic rifle [shotgun] sold for about $135, compared with today's price of $600 to $700 he said. But even from the store's earlier days the repair of fishing and hunting equipment has remained the store's main source of income said Campbell, a gunsmith by profession. Although the store never made a lot of money, Campbell said he has been able to comfortably raise a family on the store's profit." [*Montgomery Advertiser*, 27 August 1997]. *Todd's Gun Store to close*. In 175 years time failed to bring much change inside Todd's Gun Store. But on Tuesday the cash register sat silently at the end of one display counter, while the Remington shell boxes were piled low in front of the counter windows. Store owner Kenneth Campbell sat is his office chatting on the phone, explaining to several customers that the building he had rented at 245 N. Court Street since 1969 had been sold. As far as he knows, Campbell said the attorneys who own the property sold it for an undisclosed amount to a lobbyist who is expected to use it as office space. Friday will be the last sales day in the store that Campbell said is the city's oldest continually run business. Campbell, 72, was clearing out the guns, ammunition, fishing tackle, and related items Tuesday that have been part of the inventory for most of the store's history. That morning the huge tin gun that was displayed on the store front was removed and taken to Campbell's house. "The basic lines of merchandise haven't changed," Campbell said. "We still operate the same way we have for years." Todd's gun store was established in 1822 (1842?) when a Prussian gunsmith named Nicholas Becker founded the business on Commerce Street. The store was named the Little Gun Store, but was renamed Todd's in 1848 (1868?)

Todd, Joseph (1828-). gunsmith. 1850, Montgomery City. Nicholas Becker [Beekan], age 35, born in Prussia, gunsmith; Caroline, 24, his wife, born in NY; Alice, 2, born in AL; Joseph Todd, 22, gunsmith, and George Todd, 11, both born in NY [Census].

Tolbert, Edward (1836-). shoemaker, gun- and blacksmith. Tolbert was born in Chesterfield District, SC, on September 5, 1836, a son of Sam and Christian (Norris) Tolbert.. Edward Tolbert grew to manhood in Calhoun County. In 1862 he enlisted in the 31st Alabama Regiment, and served until wounded at Fort Gibson on May 1, 1863. He was paroled, and upon his arrival home found four of his brothers badly wounded. He provided what care he could for his extended family. In 1871 he moved to Arkansas where he was engaged primarily as a shoemaker [Family Genealogy; *Franklin County Arkansas Biographies*].

Tolbert, Samuel (1802-1867). gun- and blacksmith. Jacksonville, Calhoun County. Sam was a native of Virginia, but in early life moved to SC, where he followed farming and blacksmithing. Sam Tolbert was reared in SC, and subsequently removed to Calhoun County, AL. On 17 August 1838 he obtained 80 acres in Calhoun County. He was severely handicapped for the greater part of his life, and was a blacksmith, farmer, and gunsmith by trade. Tolbert married Christian Norris. His death occurred in 1867. 1860, Samuel Tolbert, blacksmith, 55; Christian, wife, 48; Lucinda, 24; Edward, 22; James J W, 18, all born in SC. [Census; Ancestry; *Franklin County Arkansas Biographies*].

Toomer, F. C. gunsmith. 1880-93, Montgomery; worked for George Todd, resides in the country [*Dirs.*].

Traylor, William P. armorer. Private, enlisted on 29 June 1861 at Little Rock, AR. Detailed as brigade carpenter 23 June 1862. Detailed as a gunsmith 28 November 1862 through 29 February 1864 at Selma, AL [Ancestry].

Turner, Frank (1843-). gunsmith. 1870, ward 1, Montgomery. Mattie Seed, 35, servant; Frank Turner, 27, gunsmith; Eliza Seed, 24, servant; Julia, 2, Leon, 8; Georgiana, 14, all listed as mulattoes, born in AL. 1880, William Turner, 43; Fannie, 24; Frank Turner, born in SC, 40, single, gunsmith, brother of William, all mulattoes [Census].

Tyrey, Jesse (1811-1860). gunsmith. Marion County. Jesse was born in VA, a gunsmith, age 49, who died in February 1860 of pneumonia [Federal Mortality Schedule].

U

No Names

V

Vaughan, George (1805-). gunsmith. 1860, Summit, Blount County. George, 55, gunsmith, value $300/ 500, born in NC; Lucy, 52, born in SC [Census].

Vincent, David, Sr. (1785-c.1858). gunsmith. 1850, district 27, Cherokee County. Vincent was born in Franklin County, NC. Vincent married Elizabeth Poore. On 10 April 1848 Vincent purchased 38.5 acres, and on 10 August 1849 he purchased 40 acres, in Cherokee. 1850, David Vincent, gunsmith, 62; Elizabeth, wife, 58. David died at age 72 in Cherokee County [Census].

W

Walls, Ellis, Jr. (1827-). gunsmith. 1850, Randolph County. The following households of gun-smiths were enumerated one after another: Foster, Ivy, Southerland, Nunis, Thompson, and Walls. 1850, Ellis, age 23, gunsmith; Mary, 27, both born in GA; Sarah, 7; Martha, 1, both born in AL [Census].

Ware, Jeptha M. (1816-1901). gun- and blacksmith. Jefferson County. Jeptha was born in 1816 in Jefferson County, a son of George and Ruth Ware. On 21 September 1843 Jeptha married Adeline A. Rockett On 15 July 1884 Jeptha purchased 40 acres in Jefferson County. On 1 June 1858 he purchased an additional 80 acres [Ancestry]. The estate of Jeptha M. Ware, deceased, taken on July 9, 1901, and included

1 rifle
1 shot gun
4 hammers
1 iron shoe last
1 hand axe
1 saw set
2 augers
1 pr. sharp shears & 1 pr scales
4 axes
3 shovels
1 iron wedge
1 set black smith tools
2 grubbing hoes
2 grindstones
2 bibles.

Washburn, B. M. armorer. Montgomery. Armorer to the Blues [*Daily Confederation*, 11 January 1860].

Weeks, Oscar (1833-1868). gunsmith. Mobile. Oscar was born on 20 September 1833 in Baldwin County, a son of William E. Weeks and his wife Redigond Price. His full name was Etienne Oscar Weeks. On 30 December 1862 Weeks married Mary Catharine Barnard. born in AL. Weeks worked for J. F. Dittrich; lives on Conti, 1866. He died on 7 October 1868 in Mobile [*Dirs.*; Census; Ancestry].

Weidman, Felix (1845-). gunsmith. Mobile. Felix arrived in AL in 1868. 1885, 12 Dauphin St., Mobile. Home west side Franklin, south of Madison. 1866, gunsmith at Danne & Zepernick. 1870, 130 St. Francis St. 1876, residence at 64 Claiborne. 1883, west side of Franklin near Madison. 1900, 58 N. Broad St. [Ancestry; *Dirs.*]. Also seen as Wheidman. Not located in censuses.

West, George W. (1811-1887). gunsmith. Limestone County. West was born on 1 October 1811 in Limestone County. 1850, district 3: Jane P. West, 68; George P. West, 38, carpenter; Catharine, wife, 31; John P. West, 25. 1860, Shoalford, Limestone County: George W. West, 48, machinist; Catharine, wife, 42, both born in TN; Jane P. West, 78, born in VA. 1880, Limestone County. The senior West was working as a gunsmith in New Liberty, Owen County, KY, in 1840, and was in North Liberty in Owen County in 1870. 1880, George W. West, gunsmith, 68, born in TN; Sarah B., wife, 41, born in AL. West died on 30 March 1887 and was buried at Athens, Limestone County [Ancestry; Census].

West, George Jr. (1831-). gunsmith. 1870, Limestone County. William F. Cole was born in TN, a gunsmith, living in household of John West, 45, farmer, and with George West, 39, born in TN, gunsmith [Census].

Wettman, ---. gunsmith. Mobile. Wettman was employed by Gelbke's on Dauphin St., while examining a gun, accidentally shot himself through the hand. While the wound is not life threatening it is painful [*Mobile Register*, 26 February 1869].

White, John, Jr. inventor. Col. Gardner listed White in Citronville, AL. It may be Citronelle, Mobile County. White received Confederate patent number 54 on 7 December 1861 for a breech-loading firearm [Gardner, 208]. There were at least 5 men named John White in Mobile in 1860, including an engineer and a carpenter.

Wilcox, T. D. (1826-1900). gunsmith. Talladega, Talladega County. 1850, Thomas D. Wilcox, farmer, 24, born in TN; Nancy, 3. On 22 May 1852 he married Palura Jane Moore in Talladega. On 1 January 1859 T. D. purchased 40 acres of land in Talladega County. 1860, T. D. Wilcox, gunsmith. T. D. Wilcox served in the 31st AL Infantry during the Civil War. 1870, Hernando, DeSoto County, MS: T. D. Wilcox, farmer, 45, born in TN; Mary, wife, 25, born in Ireland; Thomas, 8; Sarah, 4; Mary, 2, all born in MS. 1880, precinct 2, Red River County, TX: T. D. Wilcox, farmer, 55, born in TN; P. J., wife, 46, born in MS. Only in 1860 was he noted as a gunsmith [Census; Ancestry].

Williams, David (1825-). gunsmith. 1850, Tuscaloosa County; born in SC. There is a D. D. Williams, same age and origin, gunsmith, in Union, Greene County in 1850 [Census].

Williams, Job (1820-1899). gunsmith and armorer. Job was born on January 13, 1820, he died on January 2, 1899. He enlisted in February 1862 at Stone's Crossroads MS, as a private. He was the gunsmith in Company H, 28th Mississippi Cavalry. He is buried Antioch Fayette County, AL [*Fayette County CSA Records*].

Williams, William F. (1824-). gunsmith. 1860, Randolph County; born in GA. Armorer to Montgomery True Blues [Census; *Daily Confederation*, 13 January 1859]

Williamson, Robert (1790-1847). gunsmith. Montgomery County. King was born in 1790, a son of Thomas and Elizabeth Hinds Williamson, in Cheraw, a town on the Pee Dee River in Chesterfield County, SC. On 4 December 1811 in Darlington, SC, Robert married Abigail King. He died in Luverne, Crenshaw County, AL, on 2 May 1847. Noted as a gunsmith in 1838 [Ancestry].

Willis, John 1812-). gunsmith & wagon maker. Wills married Sarah Davis in Meriwether County, GA on March 25, 1831. Wills was in Russell County, AL in the 1840 Census. 1850, Goodman's district, Harris County. John, 38, gunsmith, born in SC; Sarah, 35, and James, 19, gunsmith, born in Georgia; Children 8 months to 13 years all born in AL. Henry, 16; Thomas, 13; Sarah, 10; Eliza, 9; William, 6; Leonidus, 8 months. 1860, Harris County, John, gunsmith; 1870 White Plains Twp., Calhoun County. J.W. Willis, age 56, wagon maker; Elizabeth, his wife, age 20; Martha, his daughter, age 18, all born in GA. He and several of his sons served in the Glorious Cause. John's first wife was Sarah Davis, married in Meriwether County, on 25 March 1831. Wills was a private in company G, 20th Regiment, Georgia Infantry. He enlisted on 15 July 1861 and was detailed to the Artillery Workshop in Richmond in November 1862 until 4 March 1864. Wills was last noted on 1 February 1865 on detached service as gunsmith at Columbus, Georgia. No prisoner of war record found. Noted in Harris County in Census of 1860, gunsmith, age 46, wife Mary [Ancestry; Census].

Wing, M. locksmith. 168 Dauphin St., Mobile. also bell hanging [*Mobile Register*, 27 June 1868; 15 November 1868]. There was a J.B. Wing, locksmith in 1901, Perry St., Montgomery, who advertised for an apprentice about 13 or 14 and for an electrician [*Montgomery Advertiser*, 9 July 1901].

Wise, I. A. gunsmith. Selma. Jerry Noble reported a half-stock rifle marked *I A Wise Selma, Alabama*. The closet match I have located is Amricon Wise, tinner, 44, born in PA, in Selma in the 1870 census.

Wooten, Isaiah (1816-). gunsmith. 1850, district 21, Heard County: Isaiah Wooten, born in SC, 36, [occupation unreadable]; Elizabeth, wife, 28, born in GA. No state of birth given for children ages 3 to 12, but probably GA. On 1 February 1860 Wooten purchased 80 acres in Tallapoosa County. 1880, Coppers, Chilton County. Wooten, born in SC, 64, gunsmith, married [?] but living alone. Find a Grave lists his grave site as Eclectic, Elmore County, but gives no dates [Ancestry; Census].

Wooten, Jonathan (1810-1860). founder. Lauderdale County. Jonathan was a son of John and Peggy Wooten, born inTN. On 9 June 1843 before a justice of the peace Wooten married Martha Whitten. Dan Wallace reported that Wooten worked for the Kennedy family at their gun factory in Green Hill. Jonathan died in 1860 in Lauderdale County [Ancestry; Wallace; Census].

Wright, James A. (1815-1891). gunsmith. Marshall County. James was born in KY on 19 March 1815. 1850, subdivision 23: James Wright, born in KY, 37, gun smith; Hariett, 38, wife; Susannah, 18; Rachel, 17; Charlotte, 16; Levi, 13; Nancy, 12; Isham, 11; Jane, 10; James, 8; John, 6; Martha, 5; Abraham, 4; Mary, 4; Sophia, 3; William, 2; Eliza, infant, all born in AL. James was born in Marshall County, a son of Isham and Rachel Wright. He married Harriet Hill. James died on 18 January 1891 [Ancestry; Census].

Wright, William (1819-). gunsmith. Montgomery. 1850, Wright, single, gunsmith, 31, born in England. 1880, William Wright, machinist, 61, single, born in England [Census].

X

No names.

Y

Youngblood, R. C. (1848-). gunsmith. 1880, Ridgeway, Bullock County. 1880, R. C., age 32, gunsmith, born in GA; Sarah, 25 [Census].

Z

Zeperick, Charles. gunsmith. Mobile. Charles was a first sergeant in the 12th AL Infantry during the Civil War. The AL state census of 1866 listed Charles in Mobile. Charles was in partnership, doing business as Danne & Zeperick with John W. Danne. The city directories of 1890 and 1892 list Emily, widow of Charles Zepernick, Conception St. near Conti. Jerry Noble listed a signed percussion pistol [Ancestry].

Confederate Arms in Alabama

Cook & Brother. gun manufactory. New Orleans, 1861-62; Athens, Georgia, 1863-64. The firm manufactured carbines, rifles, musketoons, and swords. Englishman Ferdinand W. Cook, an engineer and architect, and his brother Francis Cook started their arms company in June 1861. While in New Orleans, their production was sold to the state of Alabama. Just before the move from New Orleans on April 1, they accepted a large contract with the confederacy for 30,000 arms. In April 1862, the Cook brothers loaded machinery on to two ships to avoid possible capture by Farragut's fleet. They went from New Orleans to Vicksburg, Miss. And then to Selma, Ala. The brothers than traveled from Selma to Athens, Ga. where they purchased the grits mill from the Hodgsons family. Production was reported to be about 300 to 600 arms per month. The markings on the lockplate for the rifles, carbines, and musketoons were "Cook & Brother, N.D." or "Cook & Brother, Athens, Ga." and next to this is stamped the serial number and the date. A confederate flag is stamped on the lockplate behind the hammer. The serial number appears on most parts including the screw heads. The breech of the barrel is stamped "proved" (upside down). The barrels on the arms made in New Orleans were stamped, "Cook & Brother N.O.". The Cook arms were well made and were very serviceable. The inspector's cartouche is F.W.C which stands for Ferdinand W.C. Cook. The first arms made in 1861 and early 1862 were for the sword bayonet, and later in 1862 , almost all were made for the socket bayonet. Early guns had two-piece trigger guards and later arms went to the more simple serviceable one-piece trigger guards. They used both walnut and cherry wood with good inletting finish.   All of the arms examined dated 1862, 1863, and 1864. There were no 39" shot riffle, 24" artillery carbine, and 21" cavalry carbine. The barrels were brown and Damascus. The twisted iron barrel is a visible characteristics of all Cook arms. The source of iron for the Cook arms was the Shelby Iron Works.

Greenwood & Gray. Columbus, GA. Before the Civil War, John P. Murray, an English man, was a well-known gunsmith in Columbus. When the war started, he converted flintlock muskets to percussion for the state of Georgia. Eldridge S. Greenwood and William C. Gray (1818-1883) operated a cotton warehouse business in Columbus. On 17 January 1862, they purchased a sword factory from A. H. Dewitt to start their riffle, carbine, and saber armory. J. P. Murray was master armorer at the new Greenwood and Gray factory. Columbus, Ga. This was the site of much ordnance activity during the war. In addition the arms from Greenwood and Gray, the firm of L. Haiman & Brother was located there, as well as a large Confederate arsenal and depot. All of this activity of the Columbus Ordnance Department was under the command of Major F. C. Humphreys. Major Humphereys' initials appear on the barrels of the rifles and carbines made at Greenwood and Gray. Greenwood and Gray sold part of their production to the state of Alabama. Shipments of arms against this contract from October 1, 1863 to November 1864 show that a total of 262 Mississippi rifles and 73 carbines were invoiced to Alabama at $18,335. The barrels are marked "Ala." with the date and inspector's mark.

Montgomery Naval Facility. The C. S. Navy contracted to have a large side-wheel iron-clad manufactured at Montgomery. For a river craft, *Nashville* was a monster with a 63 foot beam and 271 foot length. The paddle wheels spanner over 95 feet from end to end. It drew 10 feet, 9 inches of water when loaded. The armory at Montgomery was commanded by Major C. G. Wagner.

Mount Vernon Arsenal. Located at Mount Vernon, Alabama, this facility had existed primarily as a storage and distribution center before the war. When independence was proclaimed, it undertook repairs of small arms and shot and shell.

Selma Arsenal. During the Civil War, Selma had a number of separate and adjunct facilities, including.

1. **Government Naval Foundry**, consisting of five large buildings powered by 3 fine engines and furnaces with complete machinery. The naval facility was commanded by Captain Catesby Jones, made naval and siege guns, and employed 3000 men at the peak.

2. **Selma Arsenal**, consisting of 24 buildings, commanded by Colonel J. L. White, made knapsacks and cartridges and converted flintlock muskets to the percussion system and repaired arms. Its staff included Captain DeHaven, Major C. E. Thames, and Captain John C. Graham. Among the lock- and gunsmiths employed at Selma were B. Jacob, P. Tissier, A. Bourdin, and I. Fettback. When Union General Edward P. Winslow was ordered to destroy "everything which could be of benefit to the enemy" he found it contained "an immense amount of war material and machinery for manufacturing the same." Much of the machinery had been packed and was ready for shipment to Macon and Columbus, Georgia. Winslow's report gave a list of supplies destroyed:

   15 siege guns and 10 heavy carriages
   10 field pieces, 60 field carriages and 10 caissons
   60,000 rounds of artillery projectiles
   1 million rounds of small arms ammunition
   3 million feet of lumber
   10,000 bushels of coal
   300 barrels of resin
   3 large engines and boilers

3. The **Central City Iron Works**, also called Pierce's Foundries 1 and 2, was commanded by Captain Henry W. Ware. The foundry was operated by M. Meyer, W. S. Knox, W. R. Bill, and S. C. Pierce. Each foundry contained an engine, extensive machinery, and a large lot of tools.

4. Pig iron came from the **Alabama Foundry** operated by Thomas B. Pierce.

5. **Brooks & Gainner** made harness and canteens.

6. **Phelan & McBridge** made iron shells for cannon.

7. **Nitre Works**. Jonathan Haralson operated the saltpeter works, which consisted of 18 buildings, 5 furnaces, 16 leaches, and 90 nitre banks.

8. The **Powder Mills and Magazine** consisted of 7 buildings, and upon General Winslow's arrival, had 6,000 rounds of artillery and 70,000 rounds of small arms ammunition. It had full equipment to produce approximately one ton of gunpowder a day at peak capacity.

Captain Jones eventually cast Brooke guns as large as ten inches and these were considered to be of superior quality. General Maury once observed that "It must be the best gun metal in the world" because he never saw one of Selma's guns strained or burst even under continuous firing with heavy charges of gunpowder.

Colin McRae was a Selma businessman with substantial holdings in local real estate who undertook the development of an arms manufactory at Selma as a profit-making venture. He was also a member of the C. S. Congress. In March 1862 he reported to the Ordnance Department that substantial deposits of iron north of Selma made it a perfect place to build an armory and foundry to cast cannon. McRae proposed the construction of a large foundry and soon received a substantial government contract to assist in building his manufactory. Lack of technical expertise and serious miscalculations about how to build a cannon factory delayed completion. McRae purchased the Selma Manufacturing Company for $15,000. Using the older casting pits to cast parts for the new plant. The original facility was insufficiently large to cast cannon. McRae envisioned a large facility having a capitalization of $500,000. When he was unable to raise that sum, he settled on $210,000, with $50,000 from investors and $160,000 from government contracts. Ordnance offered $75,000 maximum. McRae was to supply guns, mortars, bolts, boiler plate and shot. At one point, C. S. Commissary ordered him to cast 100 kettles to boil salt water to help relieve a critical shortage of salt in Alabama. The boiler plate was to be used on ships as armor. He obtained workers from as far away as Tennessee, but operated primarily with slaves whose services he rented from their masters.

In February 1862 a contract was signed between representatives of the naval and army ordnance departments and Colin J. McRae, then a member of the C. S. Congress and serving on the naval affairs committee. President Jefferson Davis allowed Congress a free hand in naval affairs since he seemed to have little interest in this aspect of the war. The contract stipulated that the first cannon were to be cast by 1 September and plate by 1 December. McRae thereafter assumed control of all aspects of operation, from hiring workers to purchasing machinery and tools.

By January 1863, McRae and his investors were seeking a way to bail out of the enterprise by selling out to the government. Labor shortages and excessive wages had obviated any chance of profit. The C. S. Navy had begun to pay skilled labor $4 to $6 a day while McRae had been losing money paying $3 to $3.50 a day. McRae was to obtain iron from the Shelby Iron Company on a contract which paid $40 a ton. Shelby was losing money at that price and iron was selling throughout the Confederacy at prices of $50 to $75. Naturally, Shelby sold most of its iron to other facilities. Gorgas and Ordnance recommended paying Shelby a higher price, but McRae refused. The Selma Manufacturing Company was virtually bankrupt, but McRae sought $40,000 for the plant. Two factors were important in the government's decision to buy. First, the government wished to send McRae to Europe to assist in straightening out C. S. finances. Second, the government had come to the conclusion that Selma was a relatively secure location with the iron ore deposits a cannon factory required. Mitigating against the purchase were the facts that it was distant from the battlefields and poorly served by railroads.

Early in 1863, the C. S. government wanted to send McRae to Europe so badly that it was willing to buy McRae's interests at Selma. McRae, for his part, was happy to get out "without pecuniary loss to himself." By the middle of February, the army and navy ordnance departments assumed joint control of the foundry. On 1 June 1863, the C. S. Navy assumed exclusive operation under Lieutenant Catesby Jones.

The facility was not completed and ready for casting until January 1864. By November 1864, 59 large caliber guns had been cast, most of which went to the defense of Mobile, with another 12 having been used at Charleston. Eventually, the C. S. Navy took over operations at Selma under the direction of Captain Catesby Jones. The Brooke gun, developed by John M. Brooke of the Ordnance and Hydrography Department, had been made at Tredegar Iron Works since late 1861 and was considered superior to the Union Parrott rifled gun. Both rifled and smooth-bore versions were made of cast iron banded by an iron external ring. About 102 Brooke guns were made at Selma and 75 delivered to C. S. Ordnance. Selma also made 20 experimental 6 pounders, 20 coehorn mortars, and a small quantity of Parrott rifles.

On 1 May 1862 Henry Bassett, a shipbuilder from Mobile, proposed making two identical floating, iron-clad batteries, for $100,000 each. When the C. S. government agreed, Bassett chose Selma as the site. Located 160 miles up the winding Alabama River, it was secure from Union raids, yet situated on the river while it was still deep enough to float the boats down to Mobile for final finishing. He established his facility on a steep bank one hundred feet above the river. At this point, McRae offered to provide iron plate, boilers, and guns. As the war continued and the government tightened its control over private manufactories, the navy sent Cateby Jones from Charlotte Ordnance works to assist. The navy hoped to construct eight floating iron-clad batteries for the defense of Mobile. This facility also assisted in the construction of the naval rams *Tennessee, Selma, Morgan*, and *Gains*. It manufactured the *Huntsville* and the *Tuscaloosa*, 150 feet in length, mounting a six inch Brooke gun and four 32 pounders, and covered with four inches of iron plate.

Mobile had served as a major port of entry and departure for blockade runners. When it fell to the Union navy under Admiral David Farragut on 3 August 1864, Selma and its naval production were also threatened. When the Union army moved on Selma, all that could be mustered was a mixed force of militia, a small number C. S. regulars, and men from the arsenal. With a force less than half the size of the Union, the brave boys in grey had a final victory, inflicting substantial casualties on the attackers with the loss of about 20 wounded and as many killed. But Selma fell on the same day Richmond capitulated, 2 April 1865. General Winslow was ordered to destroy all facilities and supplies. His report on his fulfillment of his assignment is the primary basis of our knowledge of the extent and lay-out facility.

By March 1864 Selma had slowed production because of the lack of raw materials. The arsenal had depended to some degree upon slave labor from the beginning, but by February 1865, 300 of the 450 men working at the facility were slaves.

Tallassee Arsenal. The Confederate government rented, in late 1863 or early 1864, from the cotton mill in Tallassee, Alabama, a two storey stone building, attached to the main part of the old mill. This factory was supposed to make 6000 cavalry carbines for the CSA, but probably never made over 500. General Lee ordered these to be made to a pattern approved by him and General J.E. B. Stuart. Some were actually made, issued, and used. There is information that the proper wood for the stocks was hard to procure.

The four story stone building that formed the nucleus of the Tallassee complex was erected by slave labor about 1844 under the direction of Thomas M. Barnett and William M. Marks. In 1847 the two men purchased additional tracts of land on both sides of the Tallapoosa River in what was then Tallapoosa County, Alabama. The partners had incorporated the Tallassee Falls Manufacturing Company on 31 December 1841. They purchased a right of way to construct a dam and raceway above the falls from Barent DuBois. Their intention was to use the water power to clean, spin, weave, bleach, and dye cotton. By the Civil War, the firm was run by Nicholas, son of Thomas M. Barnett, and brothers Benjamin and B. H. Micou. They contracted to manufacture uniforms and other cloth items for the C. S. government.

As the enemy closed in around Richmond in 1864, Ordnance chief Josiah Gorgas ordered James H. Burton, superintendent of armories, and his deputy Captain C. P. Bolles, to leave Macon and to consider the possibility of removing the old Robinson carbine factory from Richmond to Tallassee. Bolles was a master armorer who was then serving at Raleigh Armory. Burton wrote to Gorgas, indicating that he approved the site. Rather than manufacturing the Robinson version of the Sharps carbine, the focus was on a new model .58 caliber muzzle-loading carbine. General Robert E. Lee had recommended it, and General J. E. B. Stuart had tested it and made some recommendations for improvements. The new weapon is reportedly the only official Confederate carbine. It had a 25 inch long barrel and was about 40.5 inches in length overall. It had a swivel ramrod, brass buttplate, folding rear sight, and sling swivels under the stock. The barrel was secured to the stock with 2 bands.

According to Colonel Josiah Gorgas' memory, Tallassee was selected as a good point to manufacture arms because a large building hitherto used for cotton making had been offered to C. S. Ordnance. By the time that the Confederacy had begun to set up its machinery there, the war was ending. Gorgas noted that some machinery for the manufacture of pistols had been set there as well as the necessary equipment to make carbines. We know of no other source of information that sustains Gorgas' opinion that pistols were made at Tallassee or at least that the appropriate equipment was located there.

On 1 June 1864, Burton wrote to Gorgas, describing the facilities at Tallassee following his return from the site. This is the only known description of the town made during the war.

"With reference to the accommodations of the machinery, we found the only buildings adopted to this purpose to consist of 2 cotton mills, an old one and one of recent erection. The former [is] full of machinery in active operation. The choice of selection lay between the possession of the whole of the old building, and the 2 upper floors of the 4 story new building. The latter would afford room sufficient for all the machinery to be removed, except the trip hammers, but the location so high we deemed too inconvenient . . . [and there is] a risk from fire, and too close an association with the operatives of the cotton mill.

We therefore decided in favor of the old building by which complete isolation from the large cotton mill is secured. We have arranged with Messrs. Barnett, Micou & Co. for the possession of the smaller factory building as soon as the machinery now in it can be removed. . . .

As the building secured does not afford sufficient floor room for the . . . Carbine Machinery, it will be necessary to erect a temporary addition to it, about 80 feet long and 40 feet wide, 2 stories high, with plenty of windows to accommodate the requirements of filing operations. . . . . The expense will not be great as stone abounds on the spot of a nature easily quarried. . . . We have arranged with Messrs B., M. & Co. for the exclusive use of these premises on a lease for the war . . . erecting additional buildings as may be necessary . . . the use of the water wheel & gearing now in the mill, with water to propel it . . . .

With reference to the accommodation of the workmen and their families, we found that there was none available for families and but little for the unmarried men, the town of Tallassee consisting entirely of cottages of factory operatives. . . . At the present time, board and lodging for about 30 single men can be provided. . . . [We have arranged] for the lease . . . of a sufficient number of town lots for the erection of 25 double tenements . . . convenient to the factory. . . . Messrs B., M. & Co. have a sawmill on the spot, but its utmost capacity is but 2000 feel of lumber per day. . . . Bricks can be made on the spot. . . . All supplies from a distance will have to be hauled . . . 6 miles, crossing the Tallapoosa River by means of a flat ferry."

Neither Burton nor Bolles was especially interested in seeing an armory erected at Talloosa permanently. Nonetheless, there were certain advantages. There was more than sufficient water power and no record of flooding (as had been the plague of Harper's Ferry). Sites outside the hamlet could be purchased at a reasonable price. Should the government really be interested in creating a permanent facility, it should be done only after a full investigation by an appropriate committee.

Bolles' reward for his candor and investigation was assignment to develop the new armory. He loathed his assignment since he had no tools, equipment, materials, or workmen. Worse still, he had no real money to purchase any of these items or hire men. Housing workmen being reassigned from Richmond was impossible, especially if accompanied by their families. Still, throughout June, July, and August of 1864 workmen in all the necessary trades arrived. Sporadically machinery arrived until a full set of all needed parts were in place. Meanwhile, Gorgas continued to urge testing of the new model carbine. Colonel John W. R. Chamberlain of General Lee's cavalry brigade was chosen to field test modified versions.

The newspapers of Richmond and Charleston reported that all Confederate carbines would henceforth be undertaken at Tallassee and that no other carbine models would be manufactured any longer. Money to buy materials and pay workmen was in short supply. Slave labor was impressed to undertake such tasks as they could accomplish. Some northern deserters were taken in.

In early July, Major-general Lovell H. Rousseau with thousands of "Rousseau's Raiders" swept into the region, cutting a wide swath of destruction as they rode. Apparently, Rousseau was not familiar with the Confederate efforts at Tallassee and no foray was made against the town. Things were going badly as even Burton wrote to Barnett, Micou & Company, asking for cloth to make uniforms for his men. So desperate was the South for able-bodied men that even the most skilled tradesmen were being inducted into actual service.

Bolles repeatedly requested transfer, a decision which his superior, Burton, could appreciate. Burton recommended that Gorgas approve the transfer and appoint Walter E. Hodgkins of Macon, a civilian, to take over work at the arsenal. Hodgkins had worked under Colonel R. M. Cuyler at Macon as superintendent of arms repairs. Gorgas apparently had become preoccupied with other matters and never responded and Bolles languished at Tallassee.

Tallassee Armory under Bolles' direction completed an unknown, but small, number of the carbines. There were apparently many more parts produced than completed guns, and some of the known specimens may have been made up after the war from these parts. Appropriately strong and aged black walnut for gunstocks was the last of the raw materials to arrive so many parts were stored awaiting gunstocks. Bolles continued to inquire about securing more experienced workmen, perhaps from Macon Armory. In November there was the only report of actual production: 100 carbines had been completed.

In early 1865, C. S. Ordnance finally complied with Bolles' repeated requests to be relieved. Major W. V. Taylor came to Tallassee. Ordnance issued conflicting orders, suggesting that Tallassee might do well to repair arms rather than make the new carbines. Certainly, repair work might occupy the workmen who were either idle or making such parts as the supplies of raw materials allowed. There are a few oblique references to quantities of gunstocks, one about 260 and another concerning 500. A report of 3 April 1865 suggested that another 400 carbines had been completed. Steuart and Fuller used 600 as the final figure for completed arms (100 initial production plus 500 noted here). Albaugh and Simmons reported that Major Taylor was notified on 3 April to ship the 500 newly completed carbines to Colonel Cuyler. Surely, the armory did not produce anything like 1500 to 2000 new guns. But the exact quantity manufactured remains unknown and there is nothing in C. S. Ordnance files that suggest that the mystery ever will be solved.

By March 1865, the continued presence of northern troops in the region suggested that it was only a matter of time until a cavalry unit stumbled on to Tallassee, or until intelligence reports about the armory came to the attention of unit commanders. Burton recommended that the machinery be removed, packaged, and repaired for shipment to another, unspecified location. Burton ordered Taylor to Athens, Georgia. Finally, the workmen began to seek transportation to Athens. Some equipment may have been sent to Athens, but on 16 April that armory capitulated following the Battle of West Point, Georgia.

There is no clear record of what happened to the equipment and parts left at Tallassee. The county historian claimed that no shot was ever fired on the armory or town. One local legend says that when walls and new buildings were constructed, the remaining carbines and parts were used as re-inforcing rods and lie buried in solid concrete.

In *The Army of Robert E. Lee*, (Page 141) the author states that "500 carbines were ready for shipment on April 3, 1865, which was a little too late. There is a book about the Tallassee Armory by Olivia Solomon of Tallassee that suggests that stocks could not be made/procured reliably for the carbines. The white wooden building, next to the Armory, in which the stocks were made, attached to the above stone building, fell down in a windstorm about 1995, but the other stone buildings still stand (1998). A great portion of the roof of the main mill building fell in during a violent rain storm.

Wright & Rice Foundry. Florence. Established in 1835, by William P. and Mary Johnson. The land was sold in 1844, to Felix Johnson, who was a blacksmith as well as a preacher and president of La Grange College, a military academy. That same year he founded the Johnson Factory. It was operated by Felix Johnson and his son James. Wright & Rice Foundry was one of the early iron foundries located in an area known as the Mars Hill. Wright & Rice were, iron and brass founders, who created a breech loading cannon that could be fired 10 times a minute. This firm also created a revolver for Reverend Felix Johnson. During the Civil War the foundry produced shells, guns and other items for the Confederacy. By August, 1861, the Confederate Government had undertaken a contract with Wright & Rice for forty 24-pounder siege howitzers with carriages and caissons. On November 4, 1861, John B. Read wrote Brigadier General Withers at this Mobile headquarters concerning the firm. He wrote in part: "Mr. Wright, the ranking shop partner, is very skillful in his line. The firm will take contracts for guns of any size for [which] they want at the average rate paid for such work by the government. They use a blast furnace; but so does the foundry at Huntsville from which Col. Gorgas has ordered a number of guns for Richmond. They use Mr. Kirkman's iron from [the] Cumberland river, and Mr. Wright has great confidence in it. . . . They have patterns now ready for casting eight inch Siege Howitzers if you should want any of that size. They have also drawings for 24-pdr. Siege Howitzers sent them by Col. Gorgas. They have no seasoned timber for gun carriages. None of the desired metals are to be had in Florence." In 1863, the factory was destroyed by the Union Army [Albaugh and Simmons, 277].

J. R. Young & Company. The Madison Iron Foundry of Huntsville, Alabama, was founded about 1855, and operated by J. R. Young. On 11 April 1862, Huntsville fell to Union forces. A few smaller cannon, including at least 7 iron 6 pounders, were delivered before occupation. At the time that the C. S. forces withdrew, Young was preparing to install a rifling machine. Had the city remained free, the Young firm would doubtless have delivered many cannon.

Photos

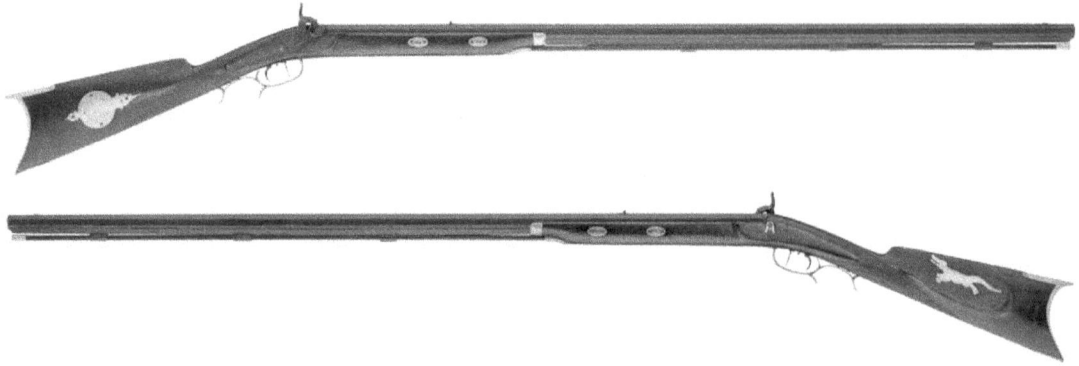

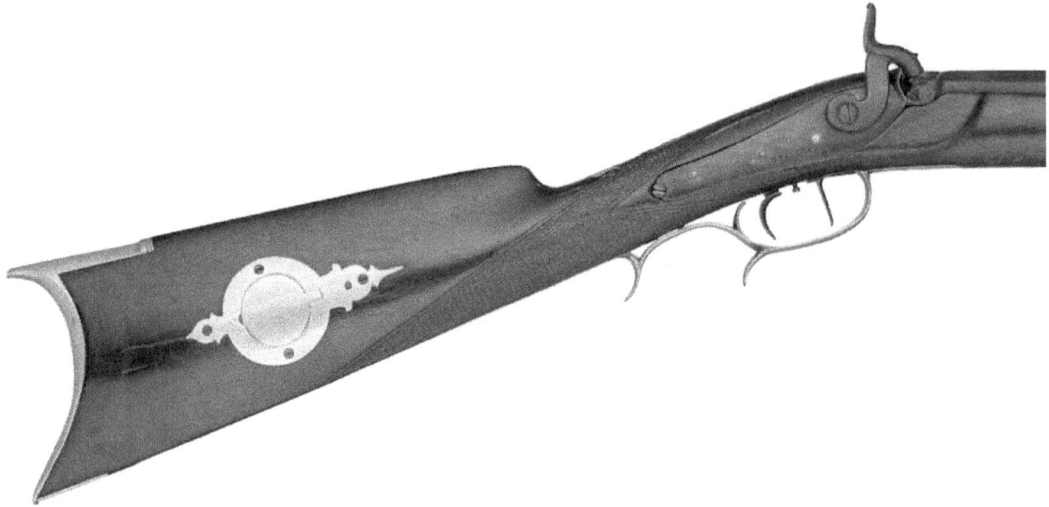

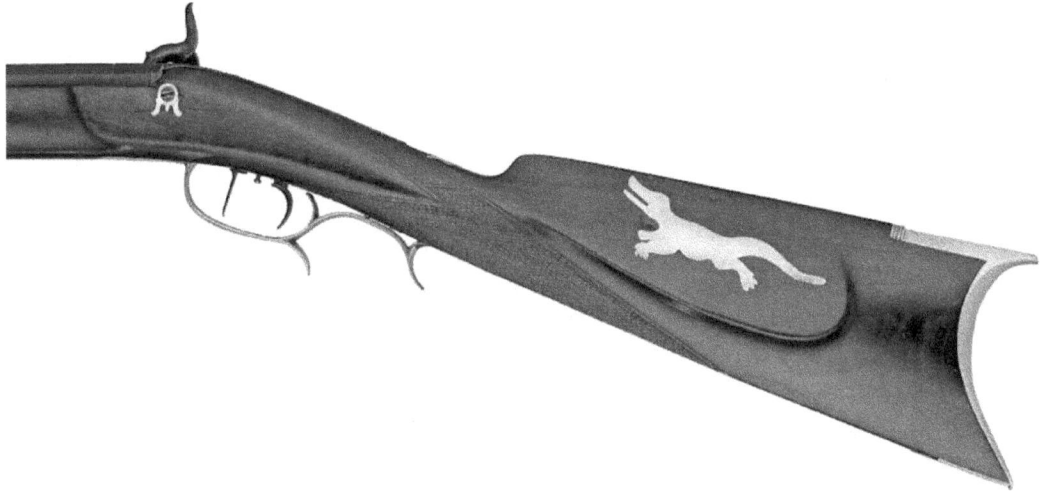

George Balzer, Hayneville, Lowndes County, AL

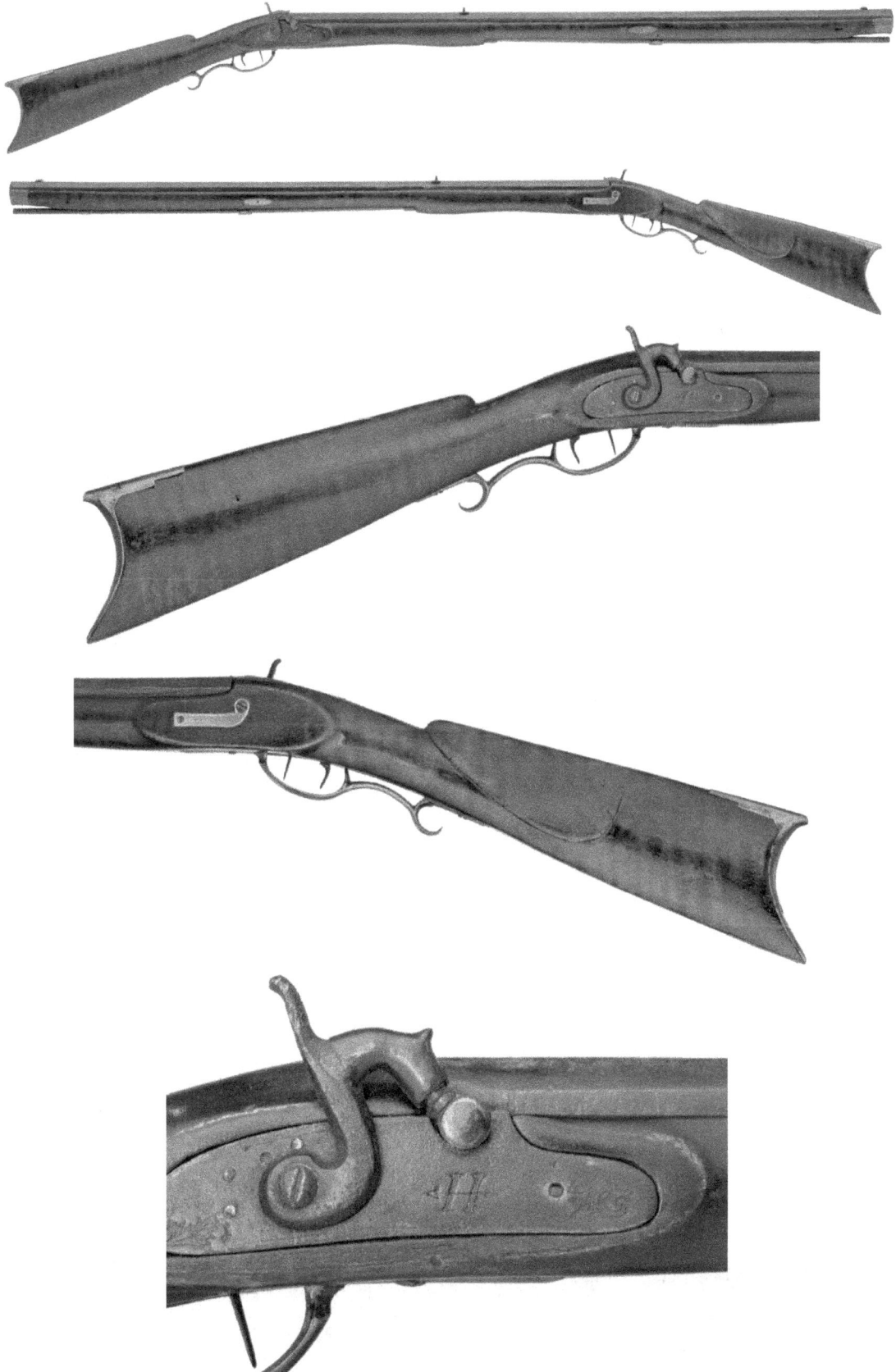

Riley Bates, Logan, -Winston County, later was Cullman County, AL

N. Becker Pistol 1, Belgium Import. Montgomery County, AL.

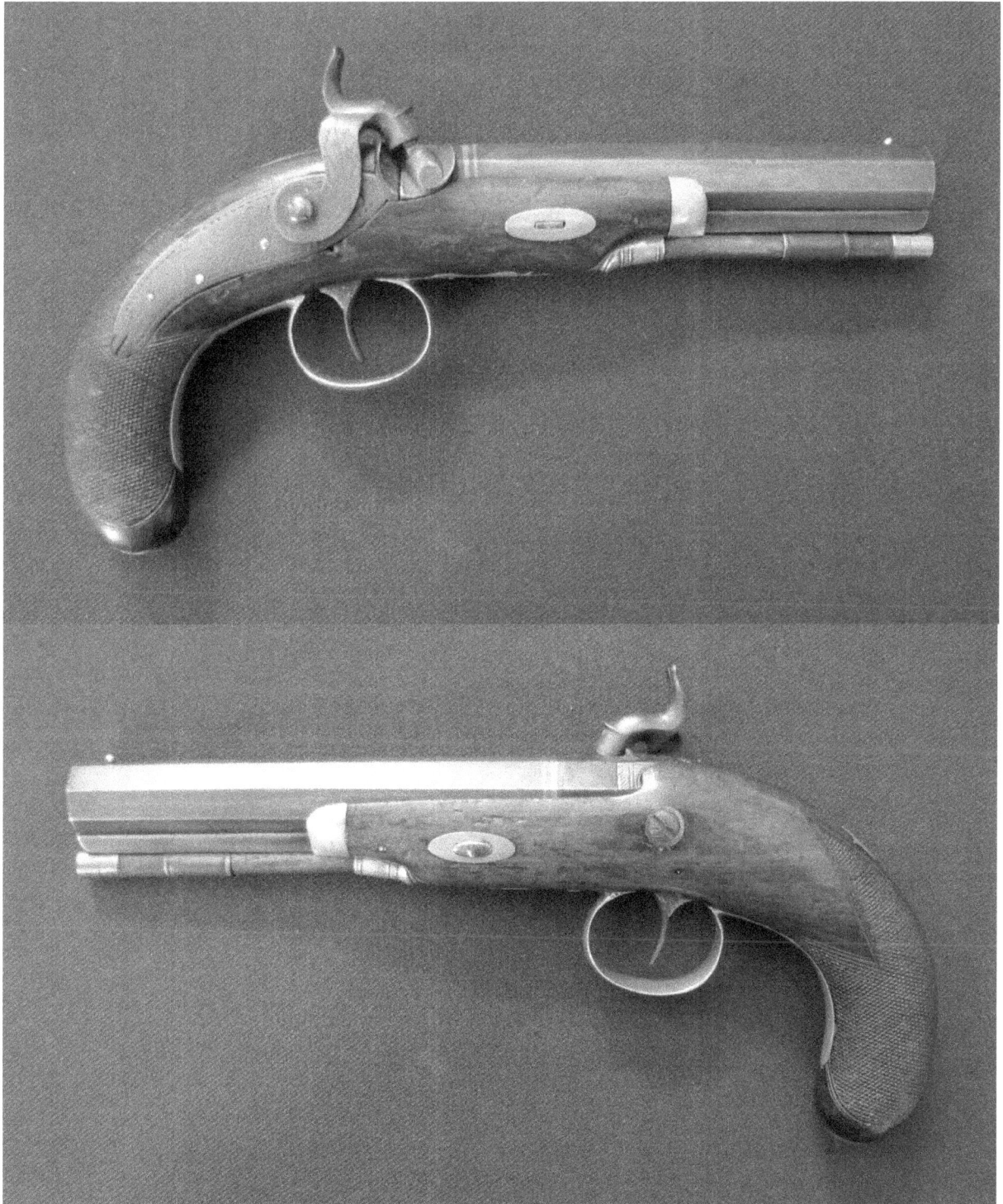

N. Becker Pistol 2, English Import, Montgomery County, AL

N. Becker Pistol 2, English Import, Montgomery County, AL

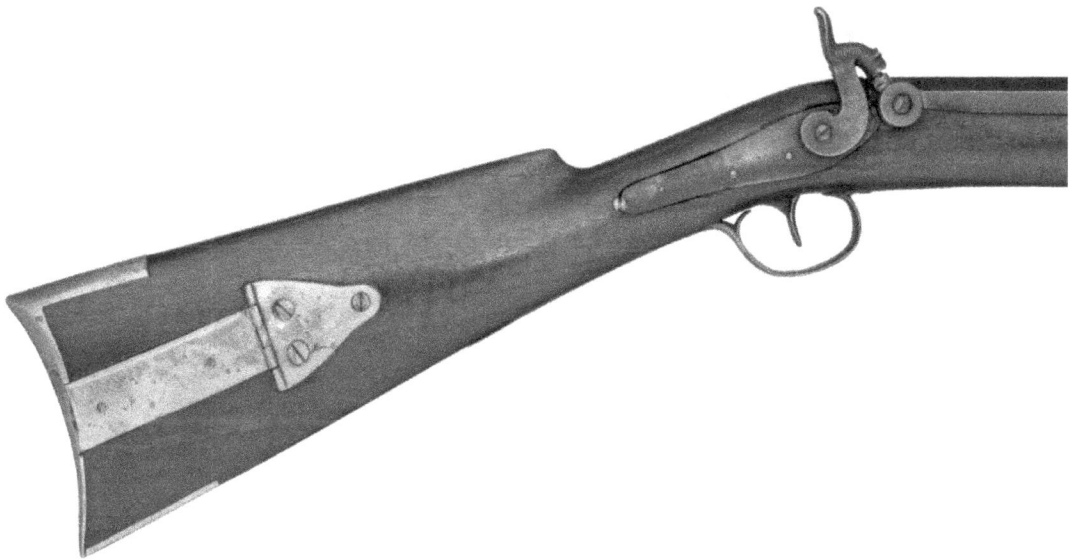

John L. Bender, Mobile County, AL

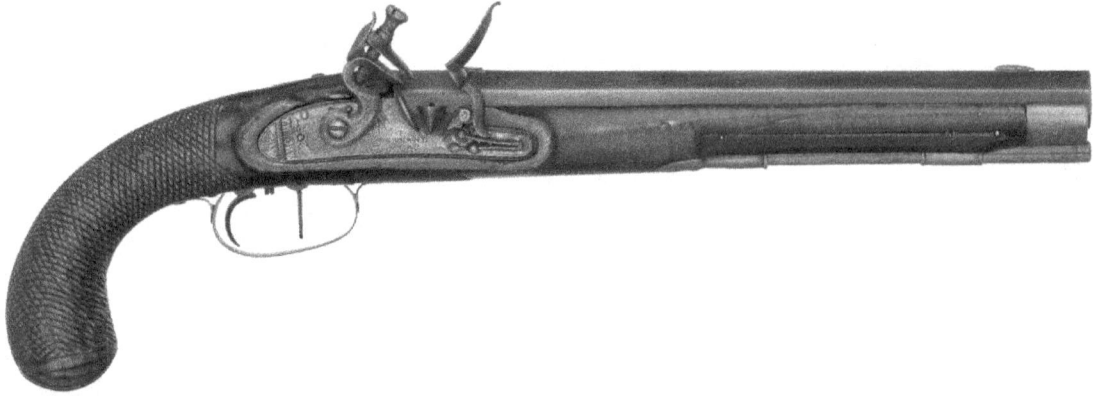

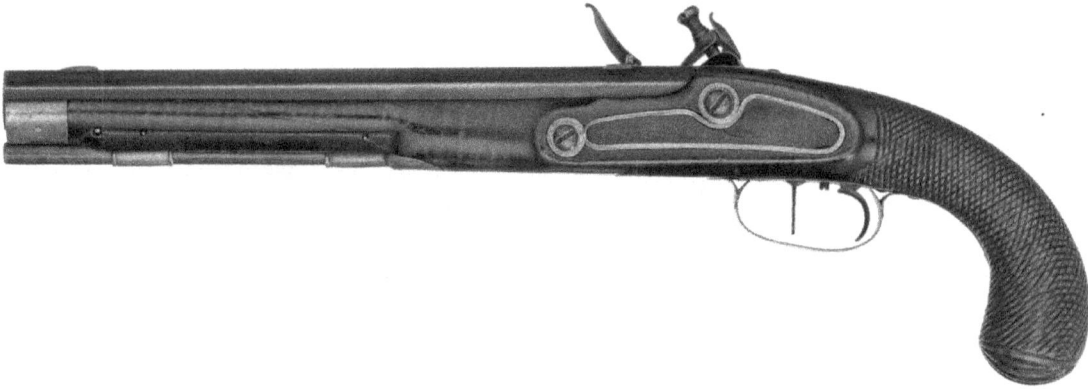

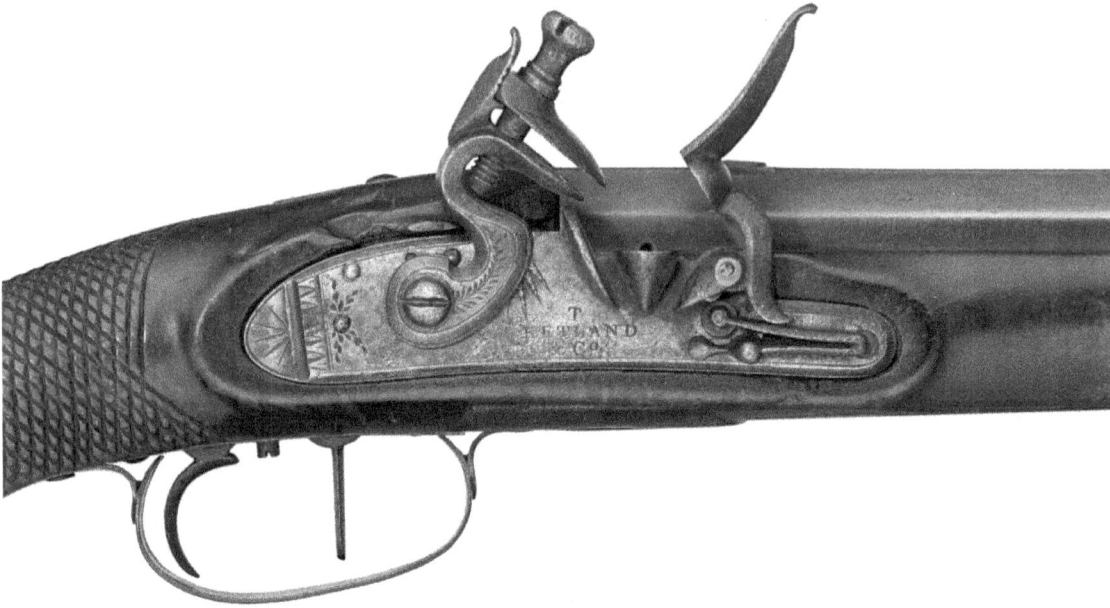

John Valentine Bull Pistol, Marion County, AL

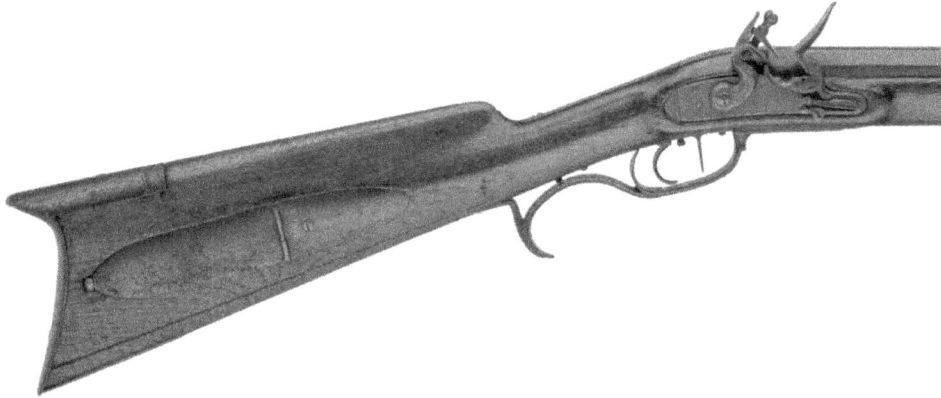

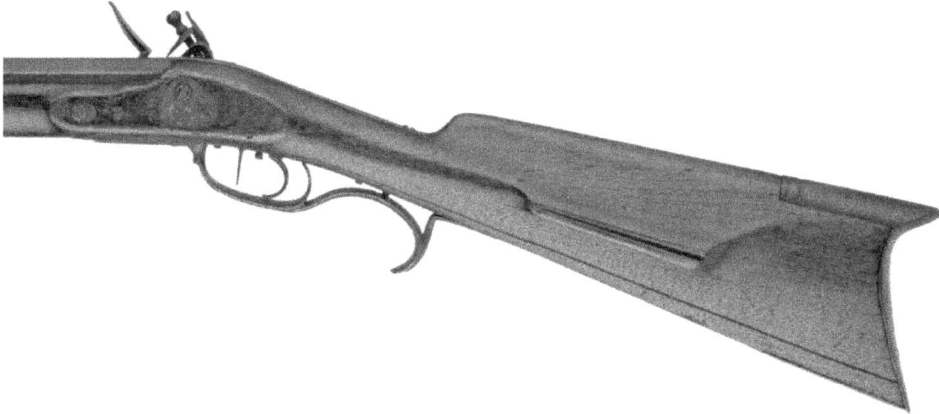

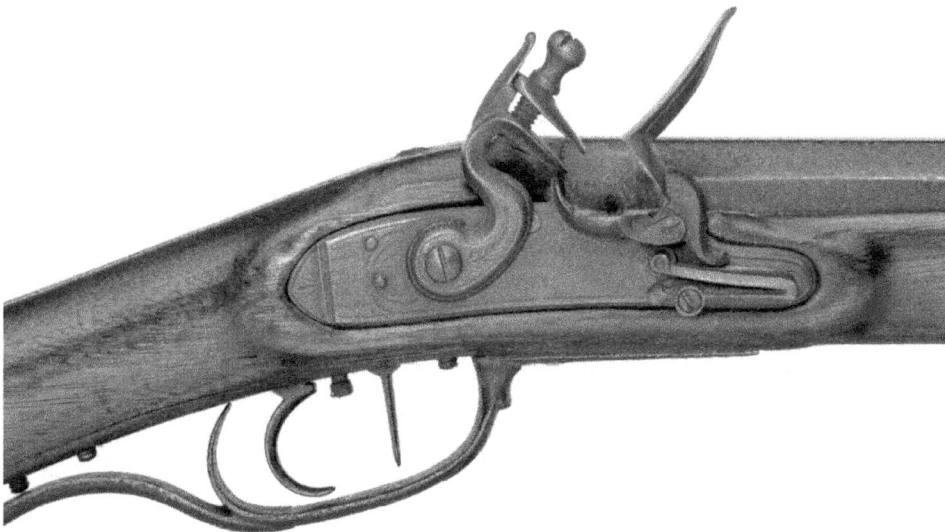

John Valentine Bull, Marion County, AL

James Conning DB, Mobile County, AL

James Conning DB, Mobile County, AL

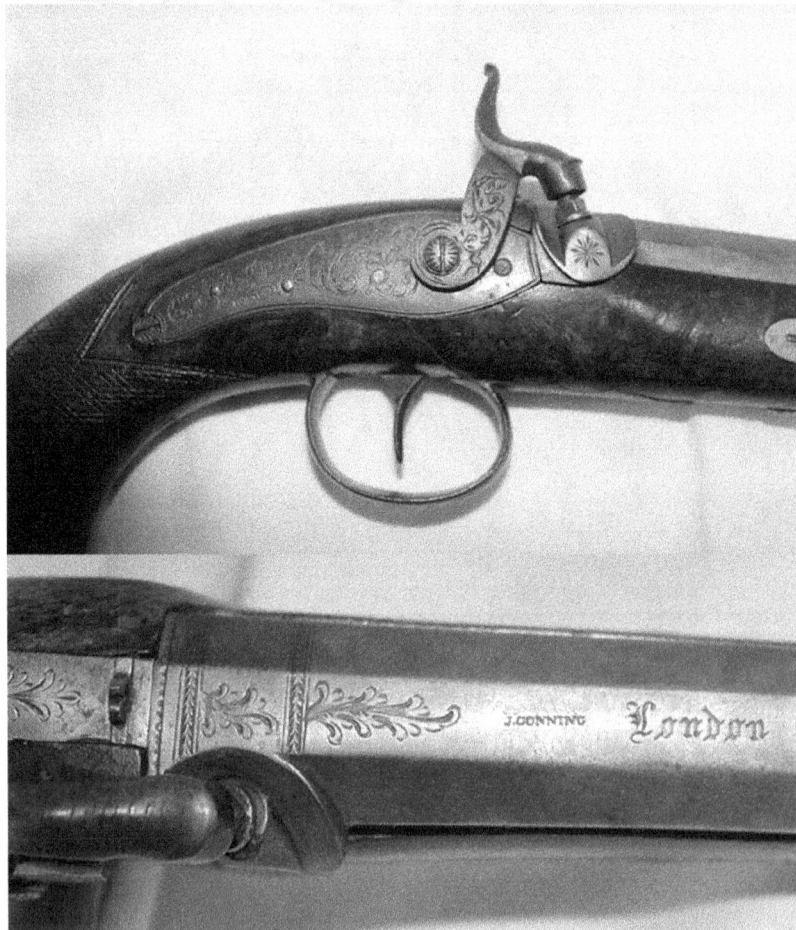

James Conning Pistols, English Imports, Mobile County, AL

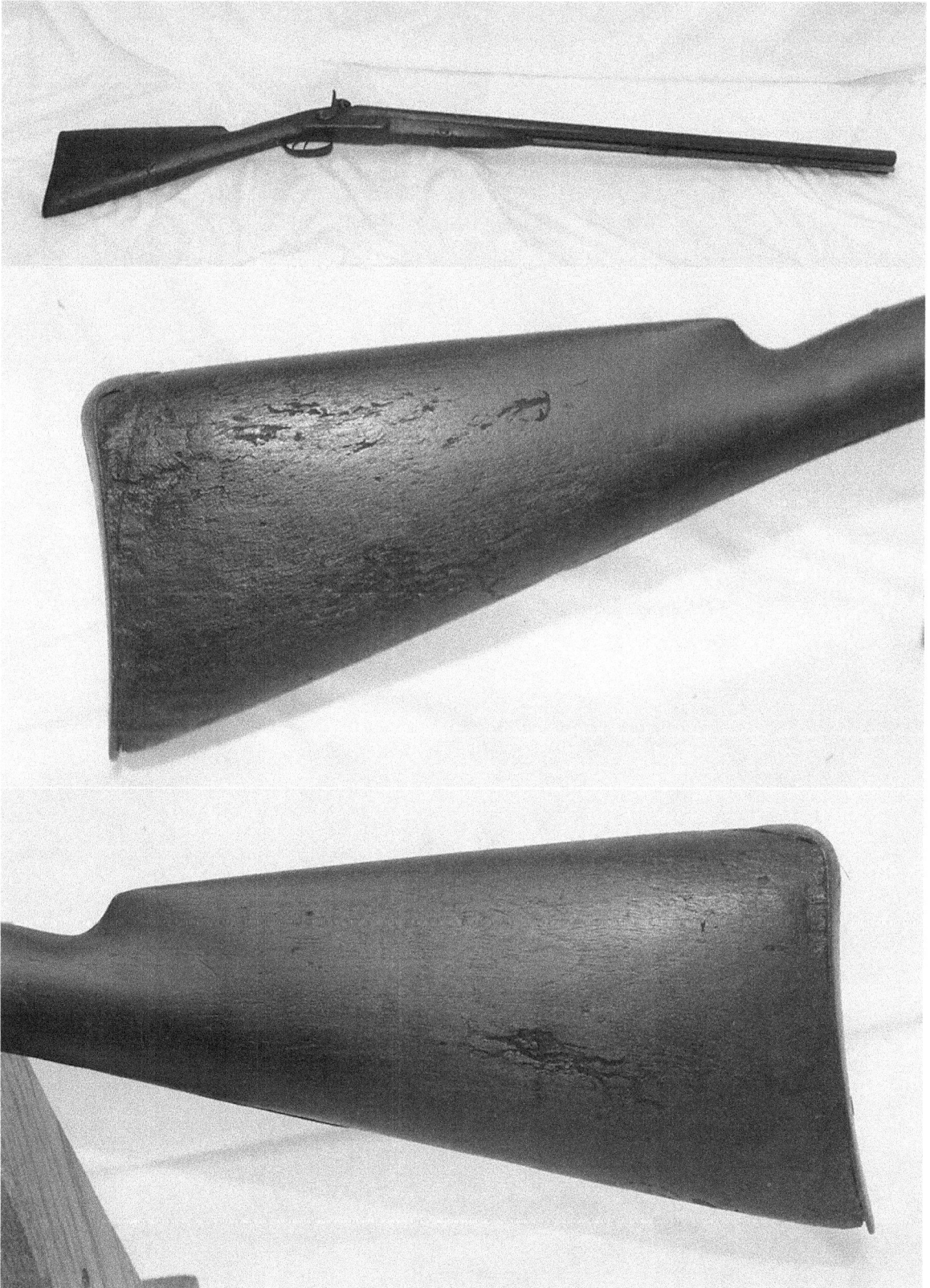

J. W. Danne, Mobile, Mobile County, AL

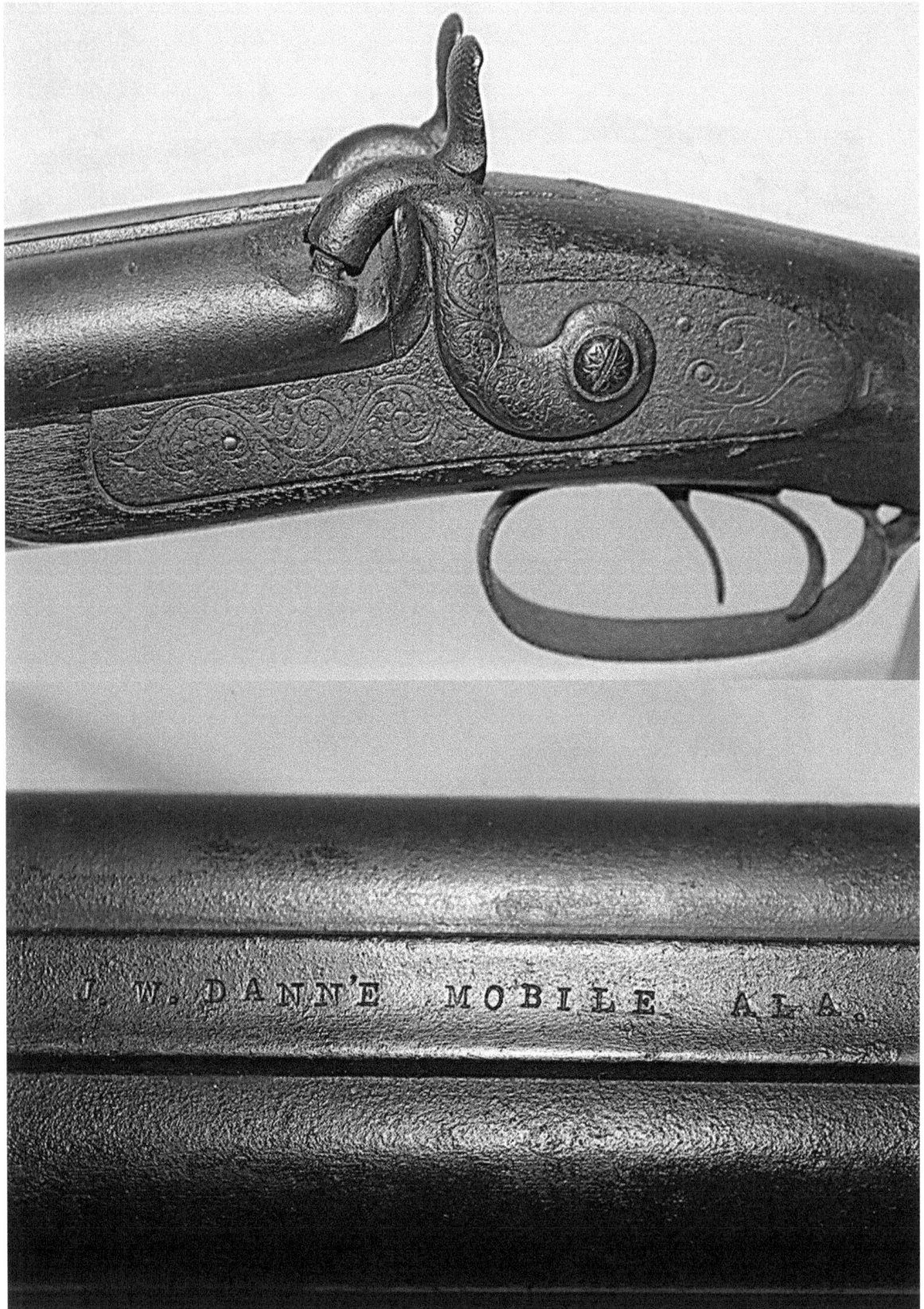

J. W. Danne, Mobile, Mobile County, AL

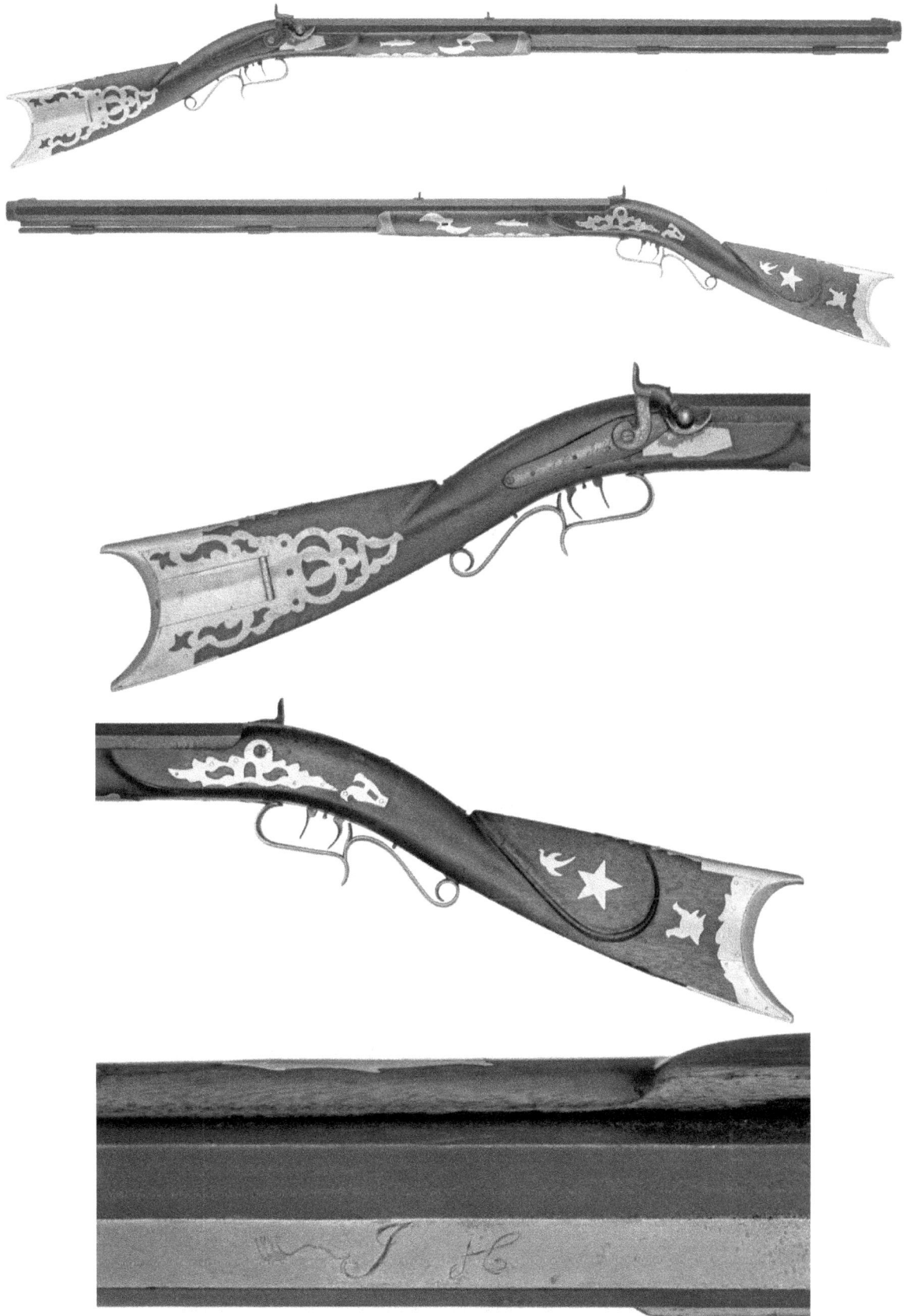

Joseph Higgins, Chambers County, AL

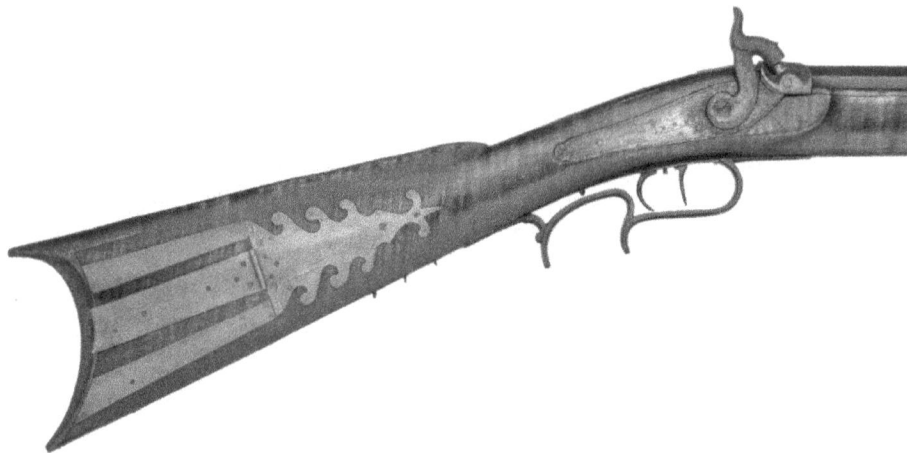

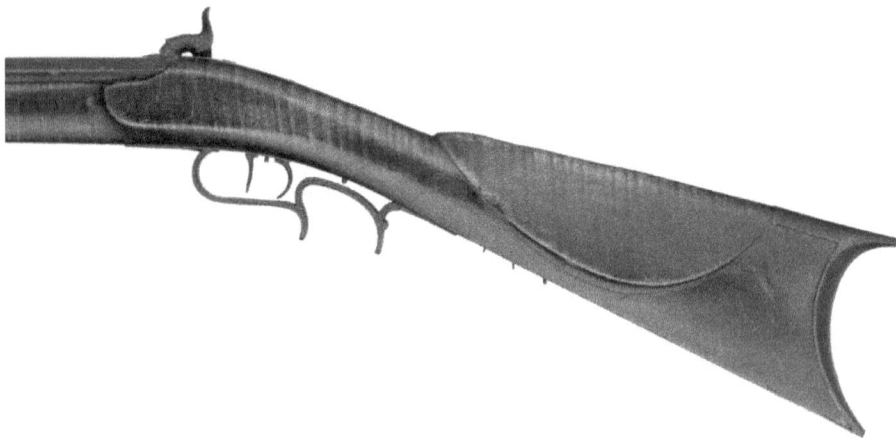

William Horton Hobbs, Talladega County, AL

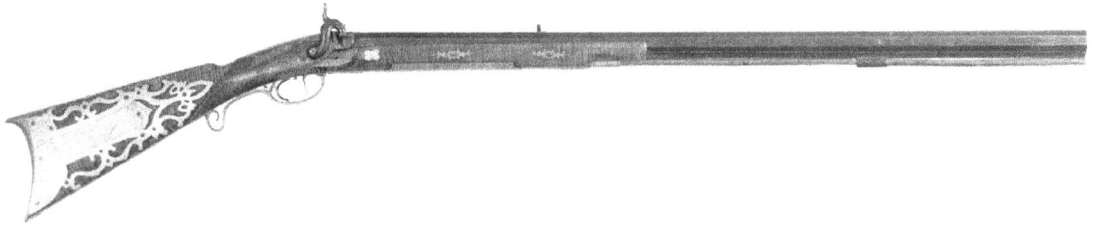

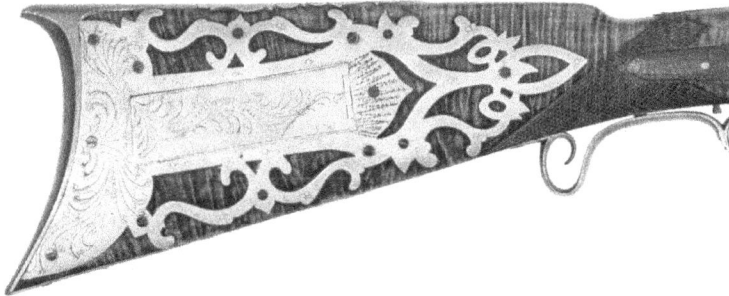

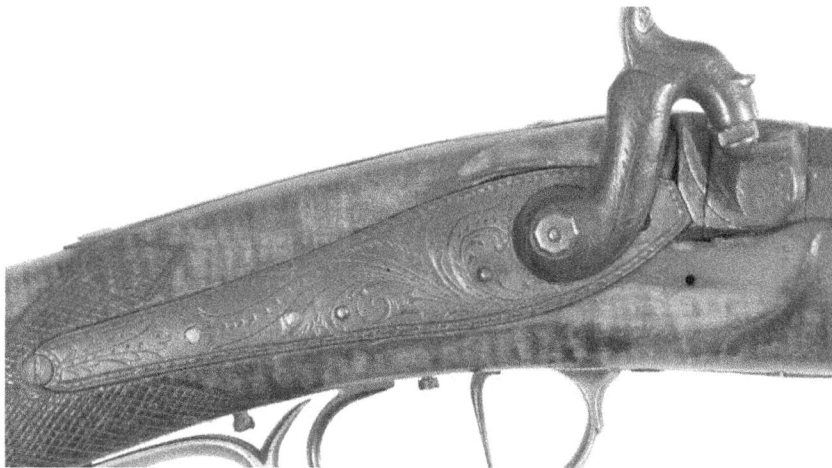

John H, Howard, New Market, Madison County, AL

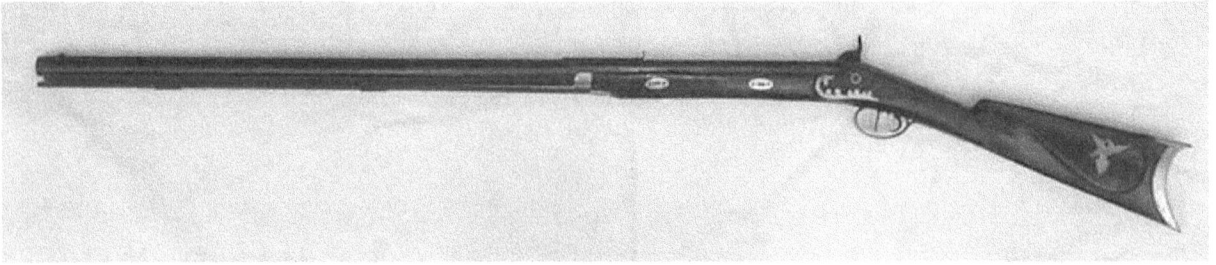

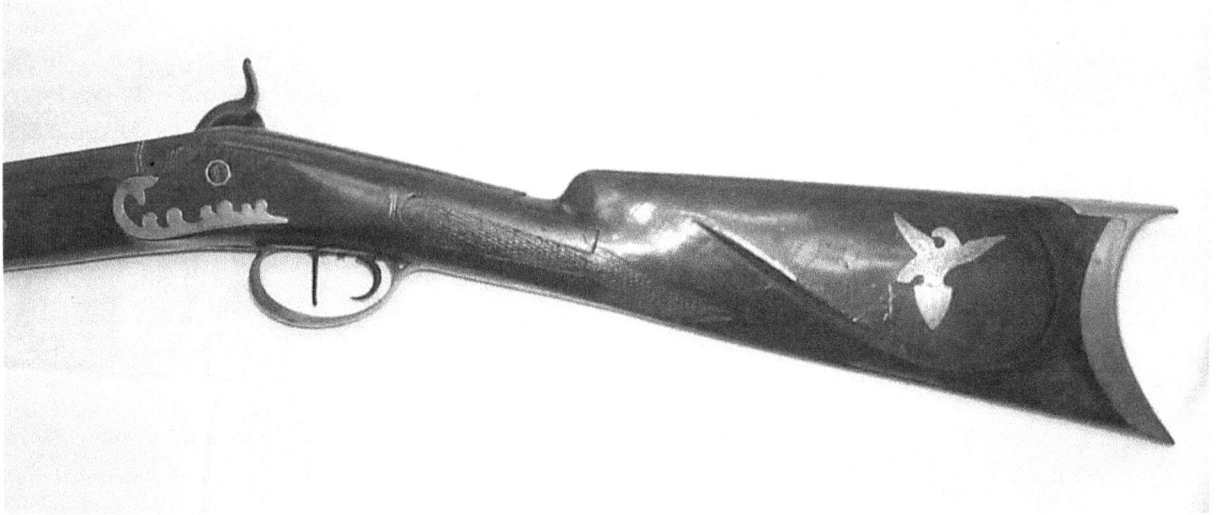

A. S. Jones, Montgomery County, AL

102

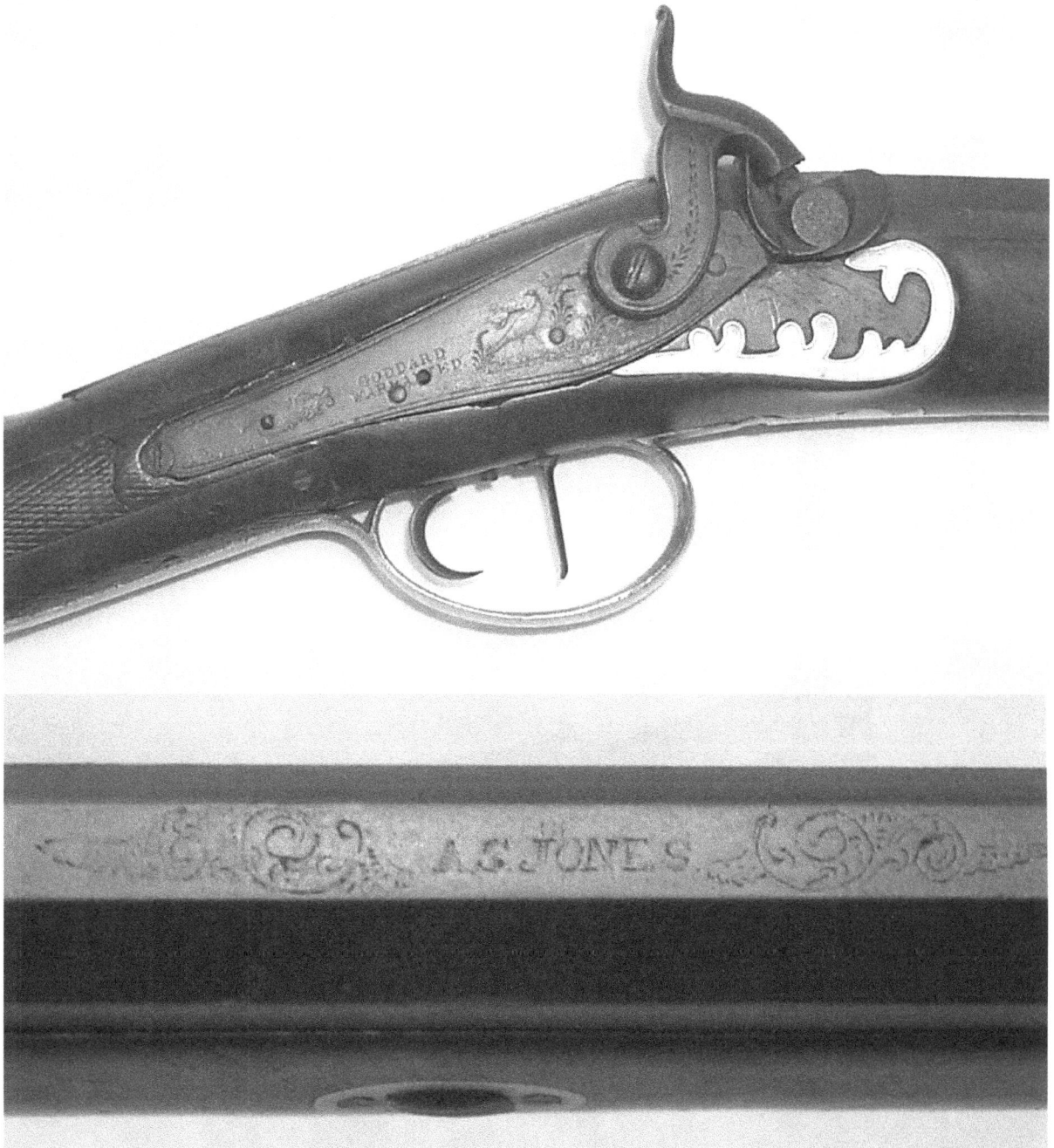

A. S. Jones, Montgomery County, AL

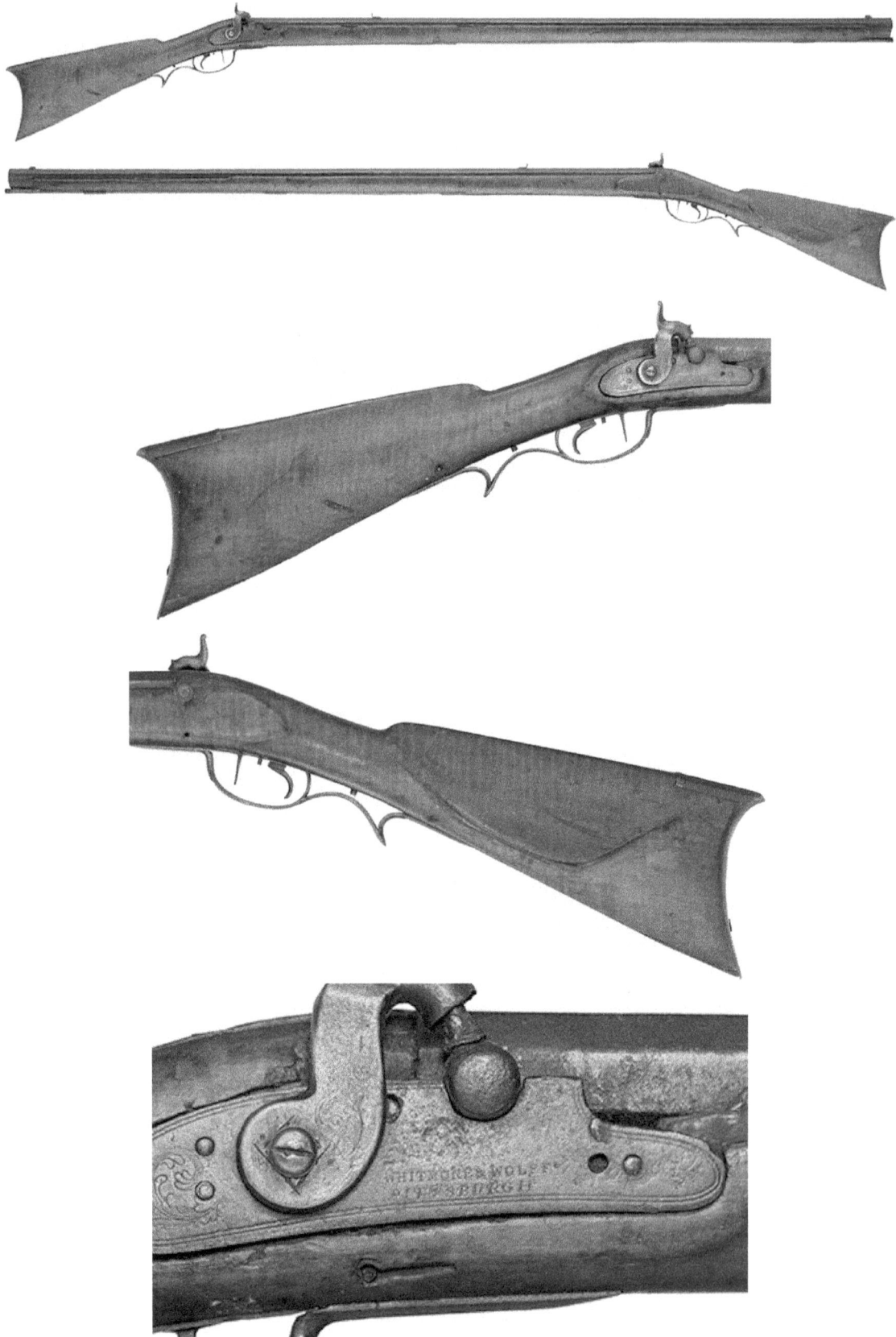

Kennedy Gun Factory, Green Hill, Lauderdale County, AL

Rufus King Plantation, Imported Parts, Dallas County, AL

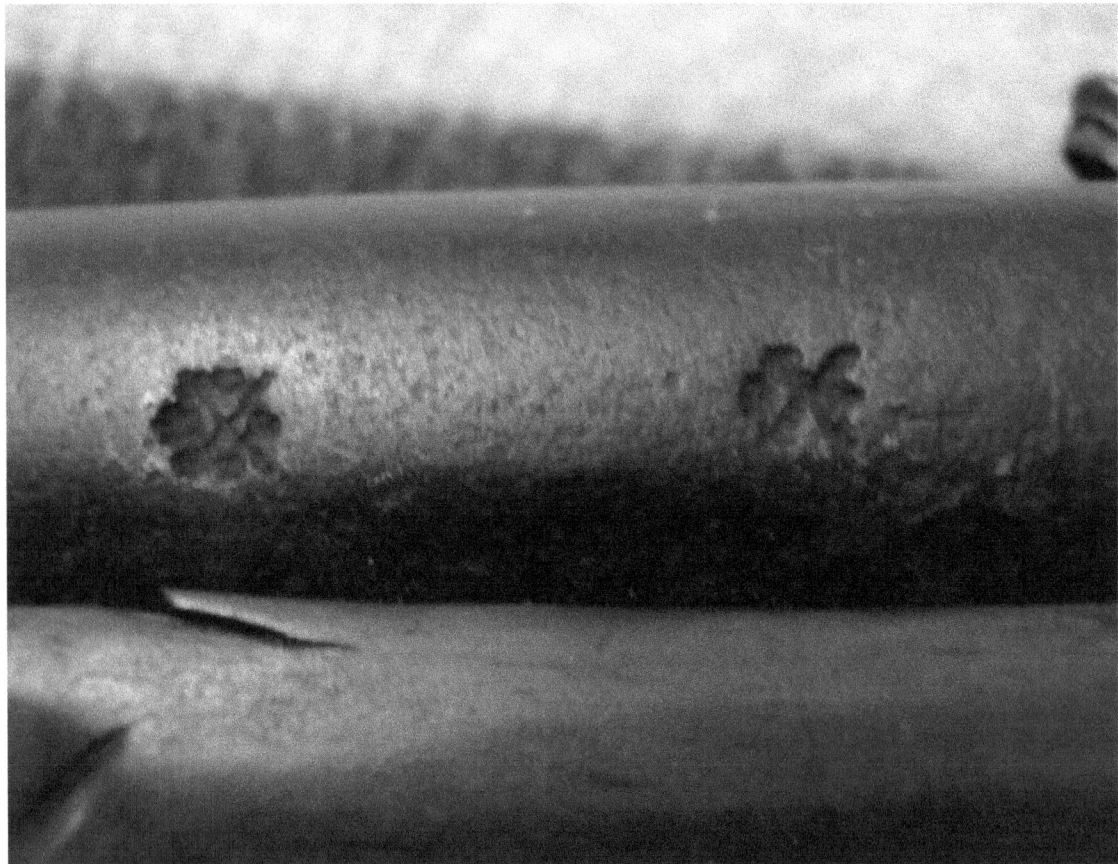

Rufus King Plantation, Imported Parts, Dallas County, AL

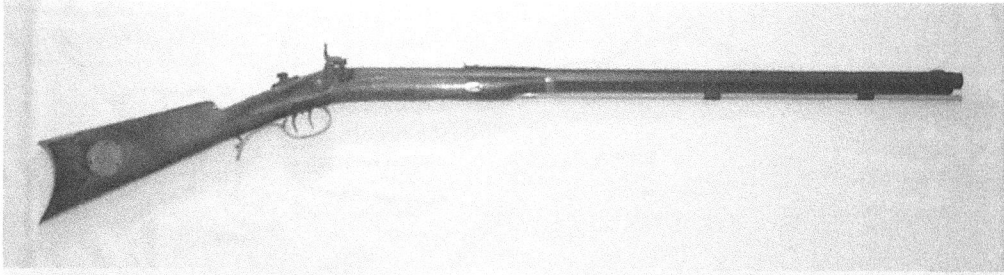

C. Kreutner Target, Montgomery, Montgomery County. AL

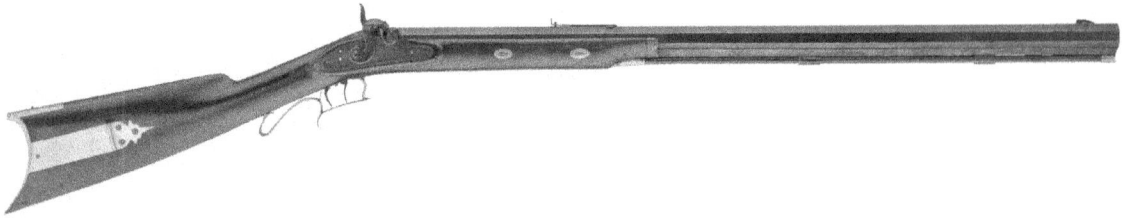

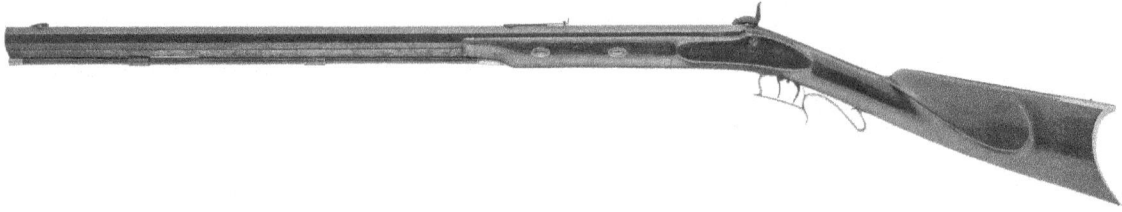

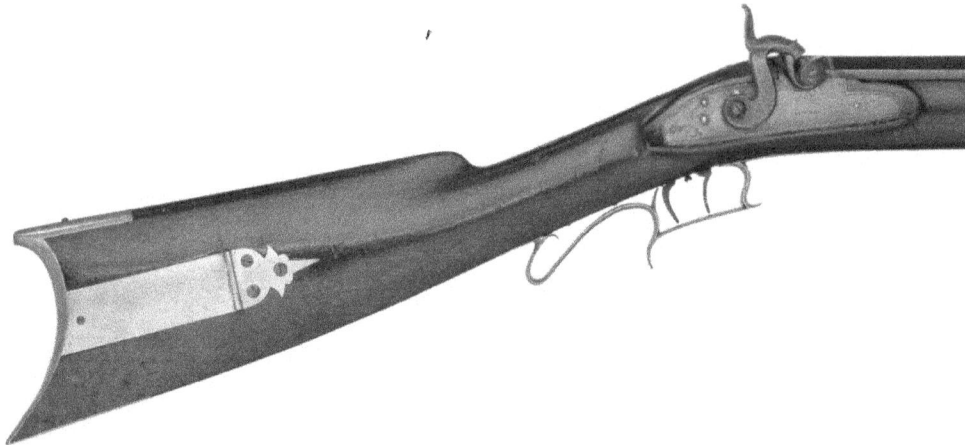

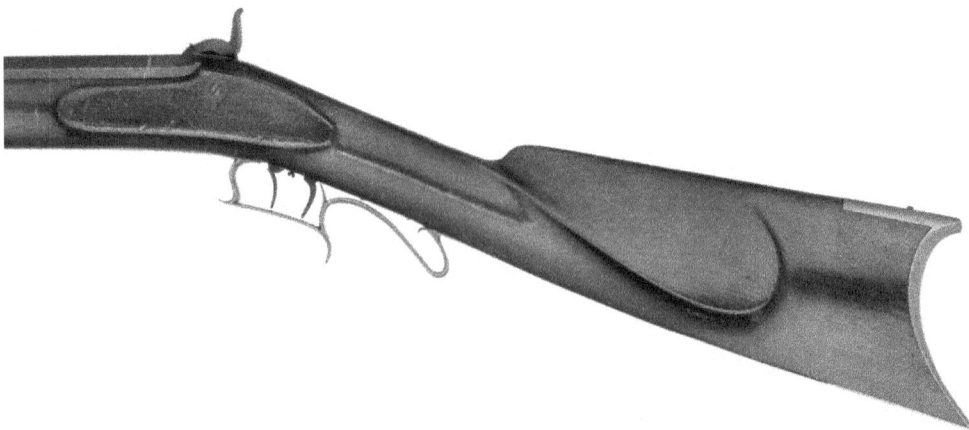

C. Kreutner Silver Mount, Montgomery, Montgomery County, AL

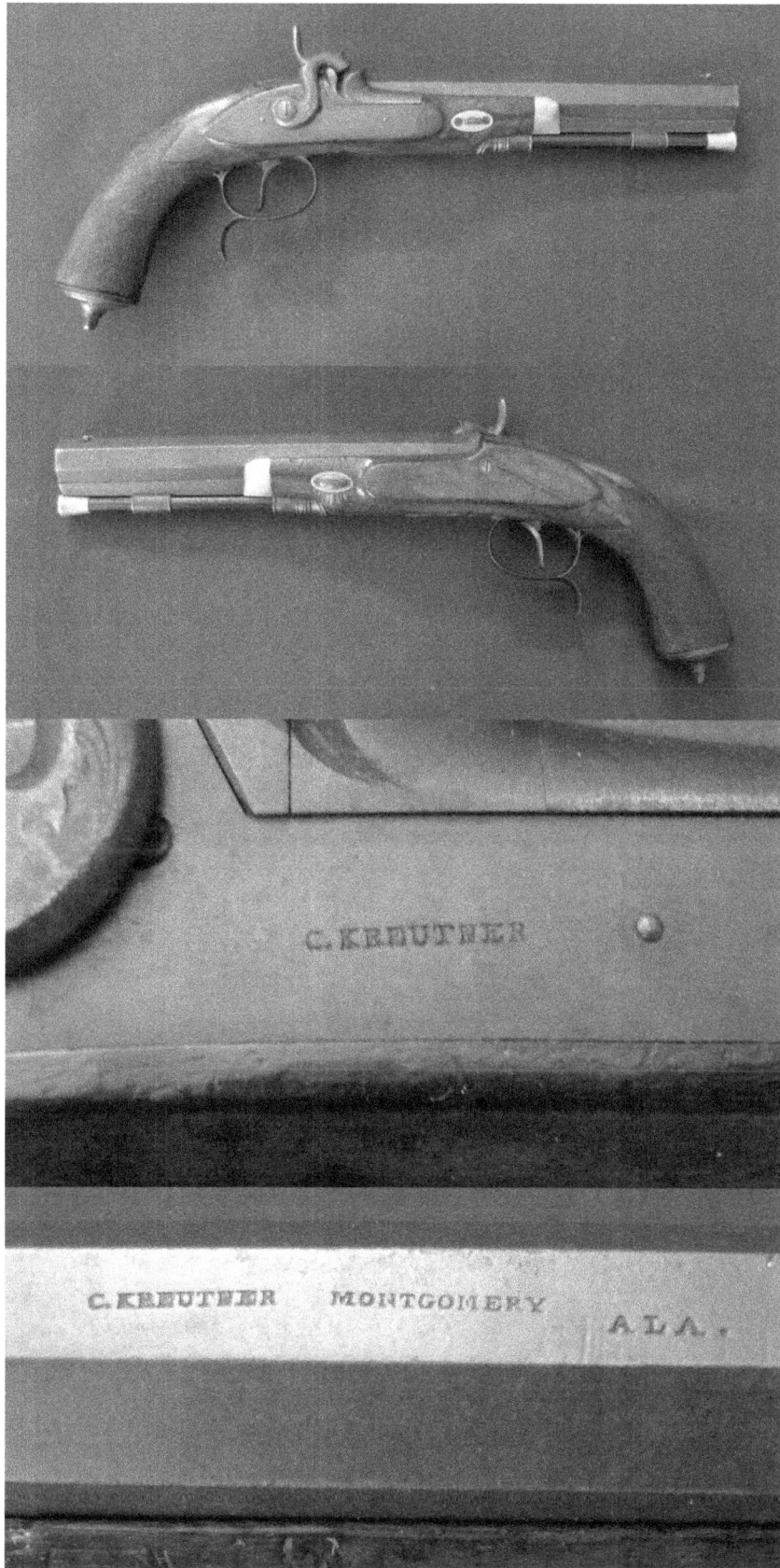

C. Kreutner Pistol, Montgomery, Montgomery County, AL

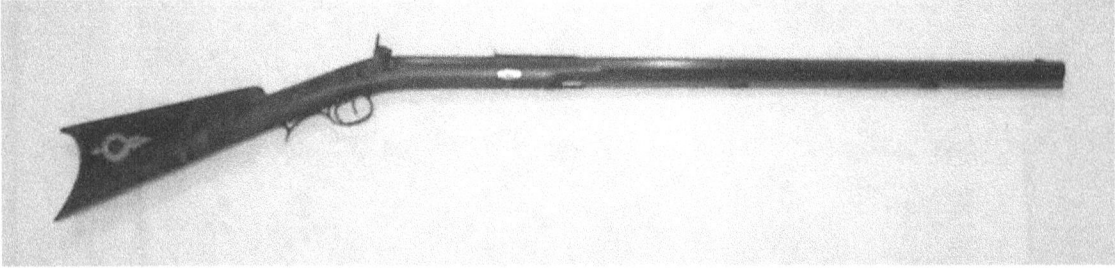

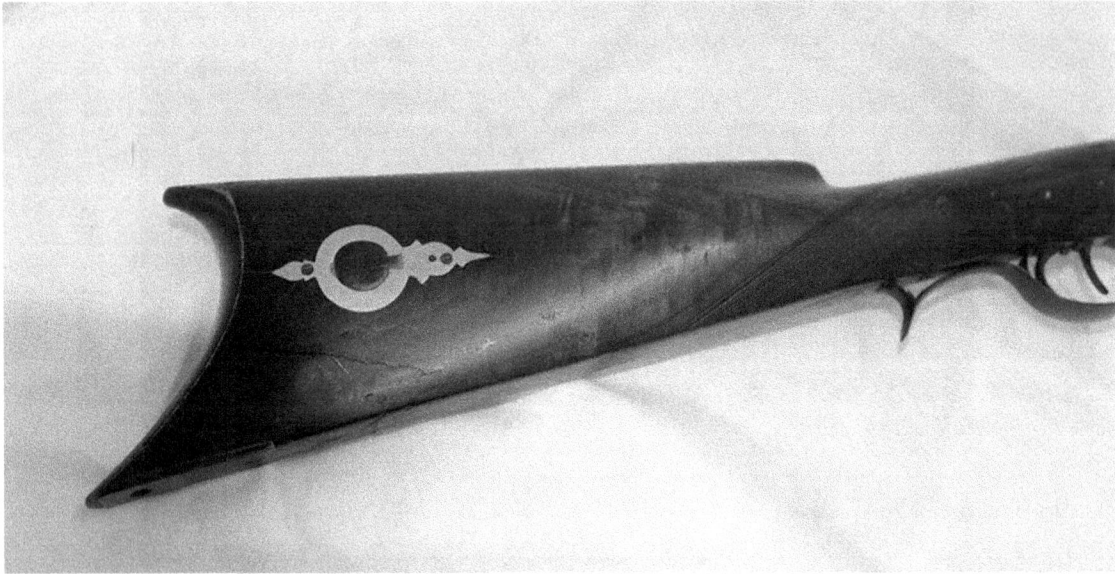

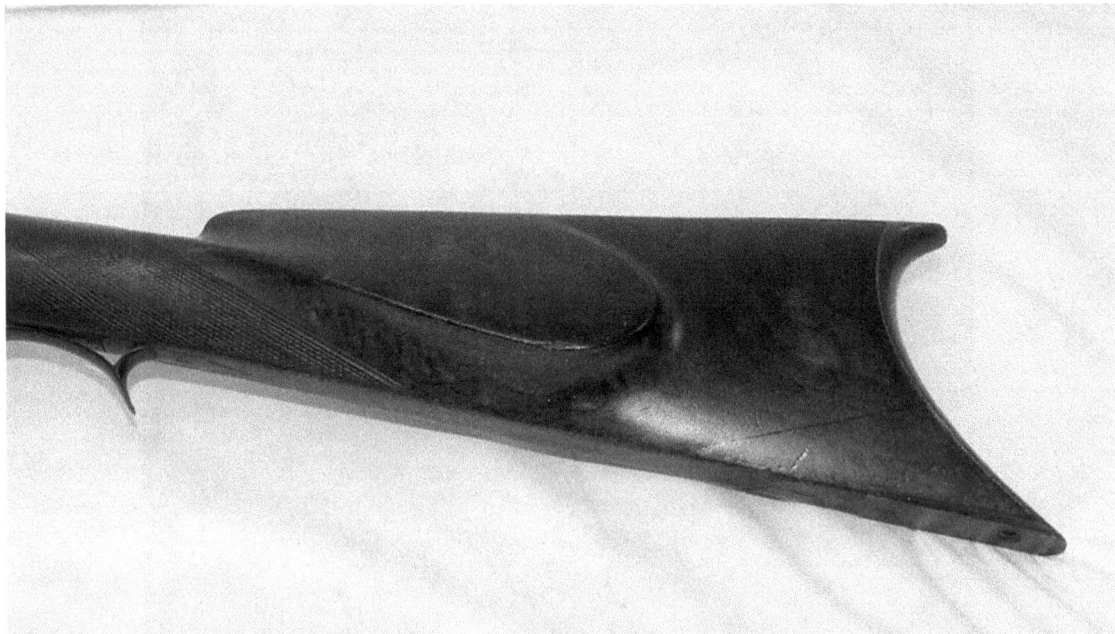

C. Kreutner Iron Mount 1, Montgomery, Montgomery County, AL

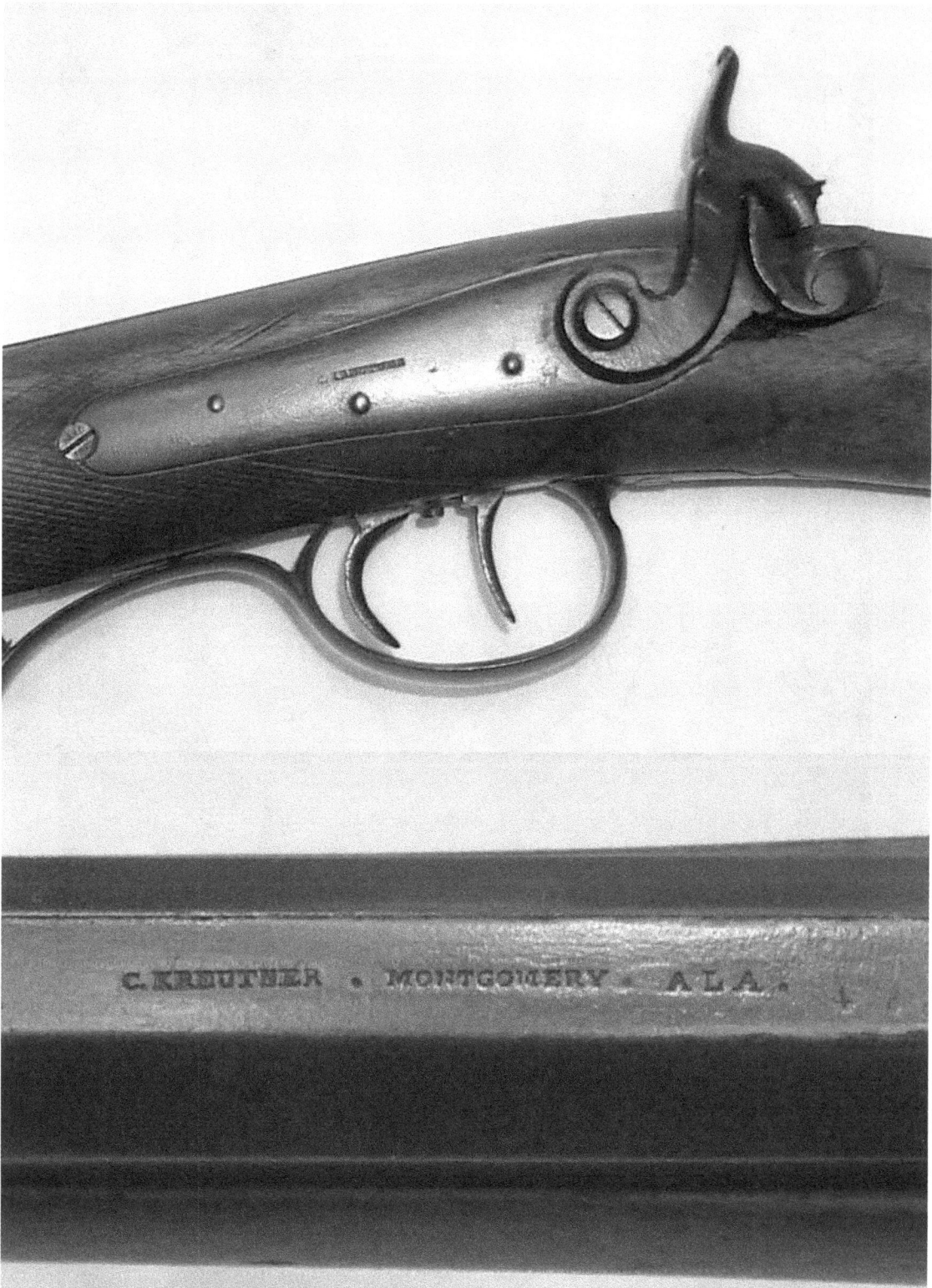

C. Kreutner Iron Mount 1, Montgomery, Montgomery County, AL

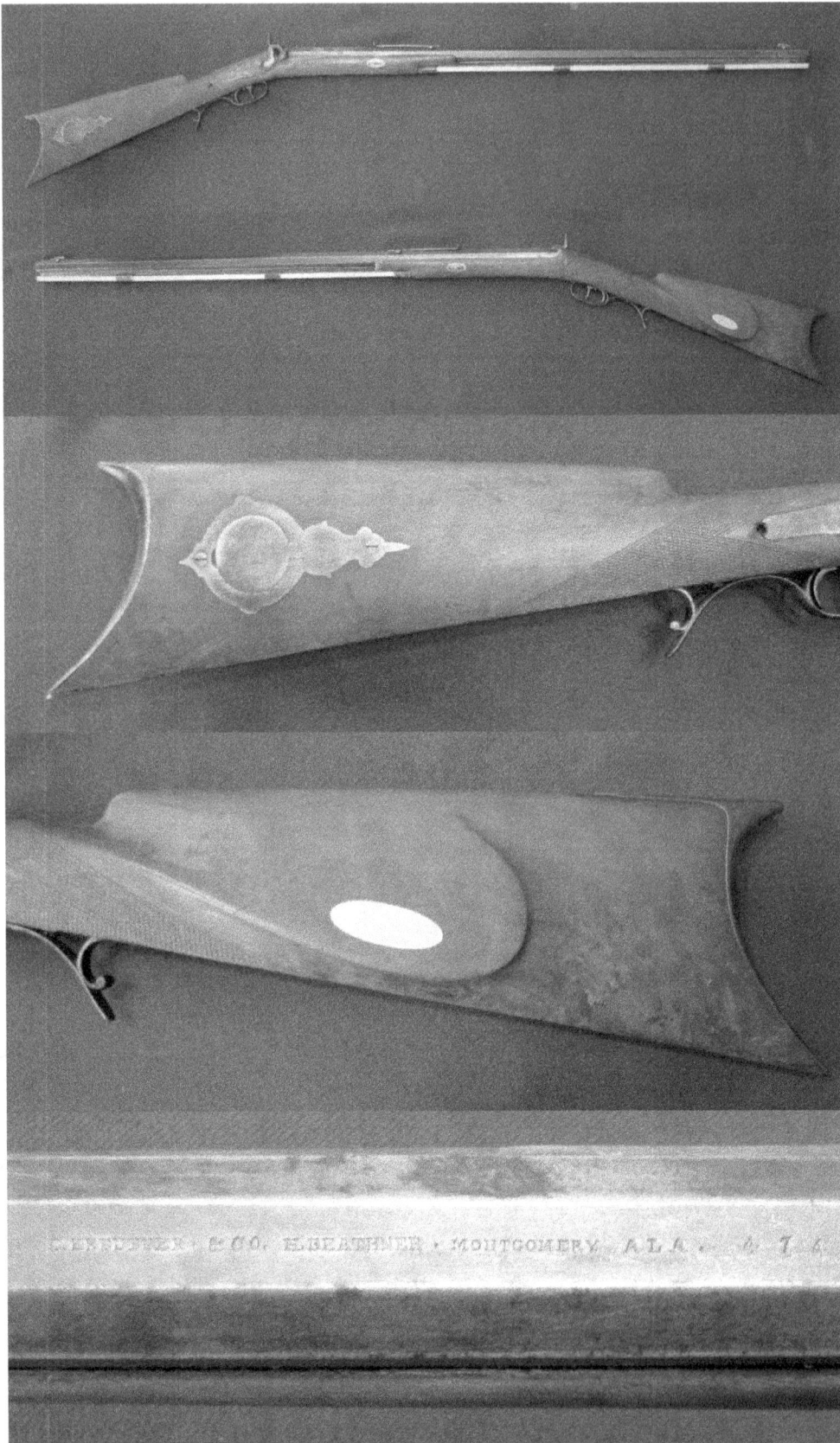

C. Kreutner & H. Beathner, Montgomery County, AL

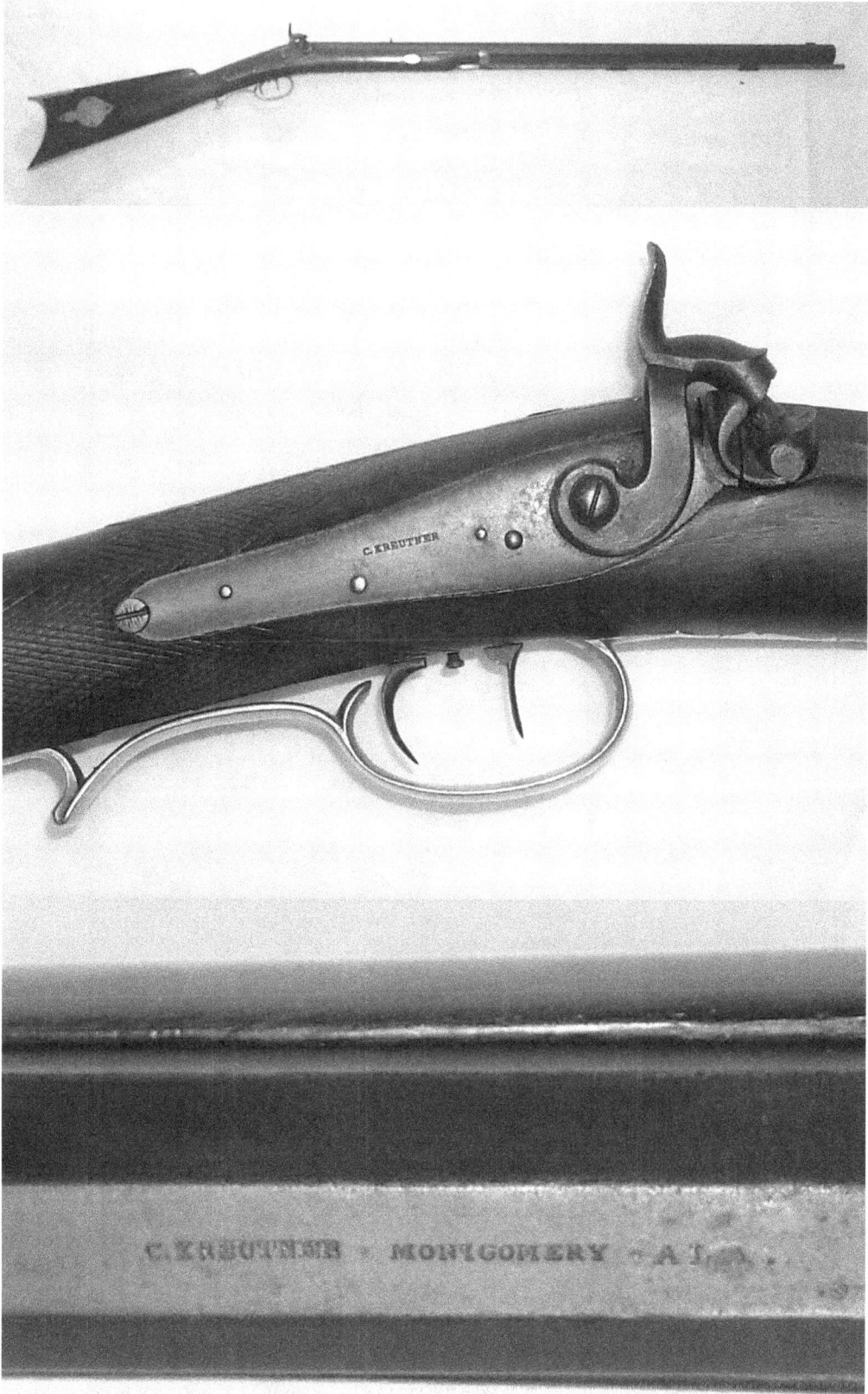

C. Kreutner German Silver Mount, Montgomery, Montgomery County, AL

C. Kreutner Buggy Rifle, Montgomery, Montgomery County, AL

C. Kreutner & H. Beathner Deringer, Montgomery County, AL

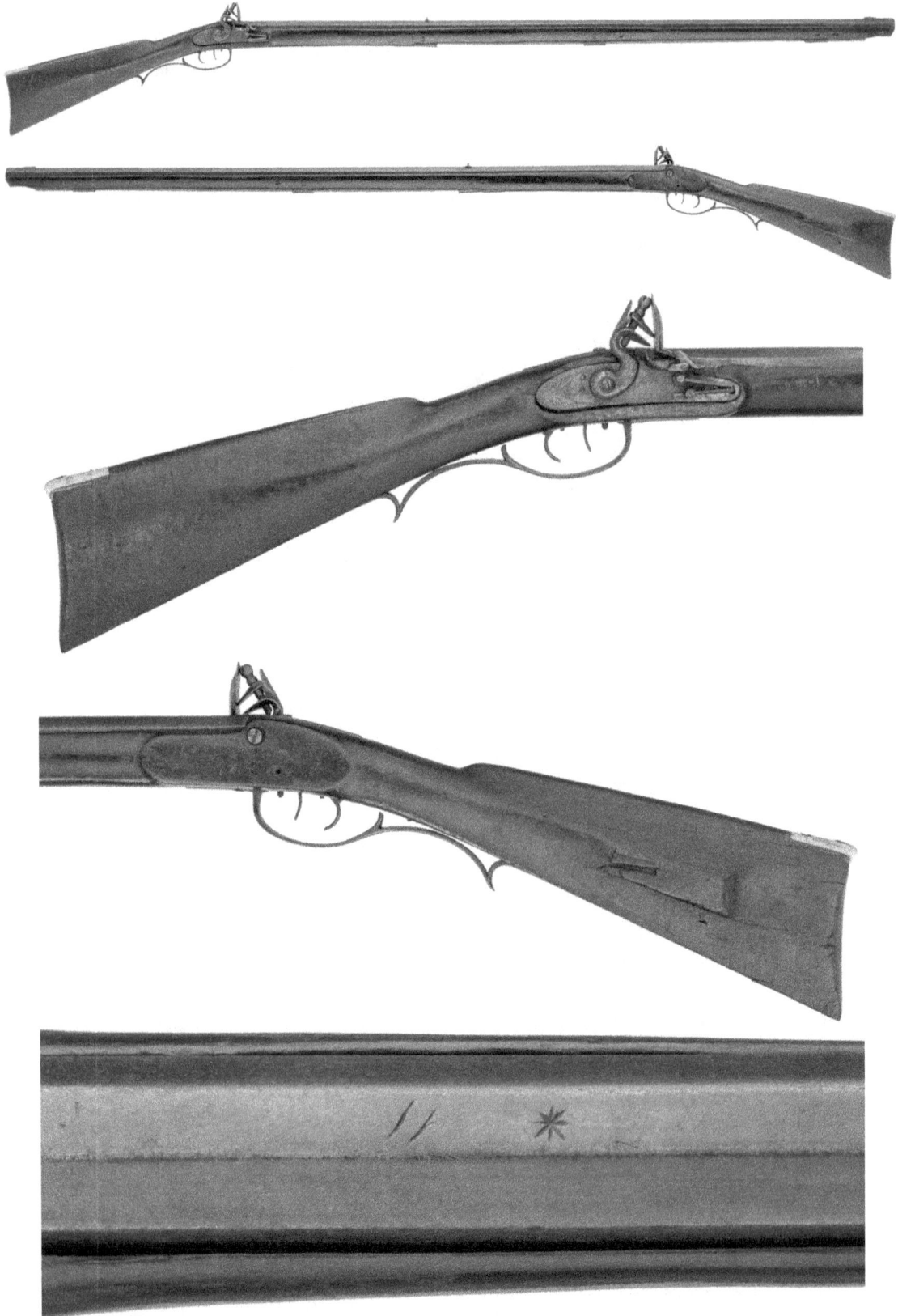

William Landrum, Washington County, Mississippi Territory

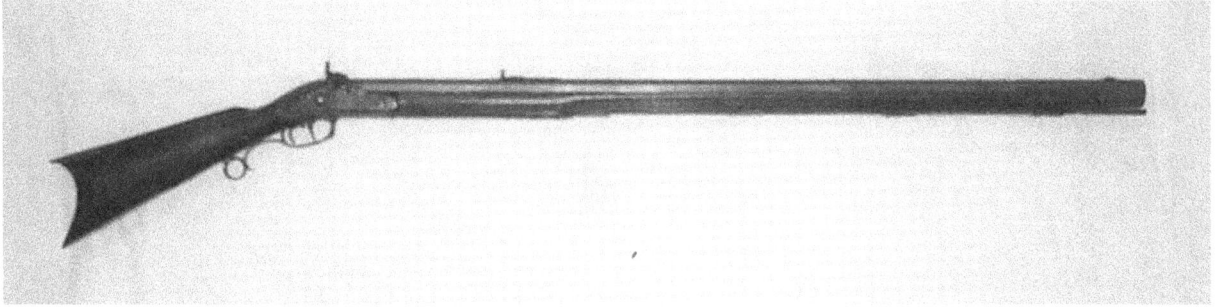

James G. Perry, Limestone County, AL

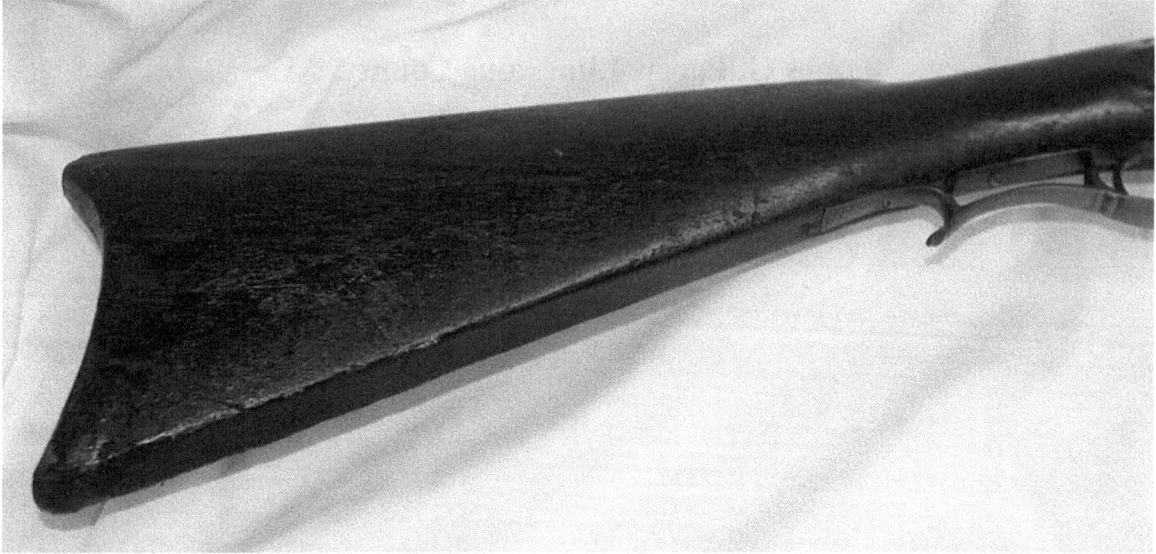

H. W. Ryburn, Madison County, AL

H. W. Ryburn, Madison County, AL

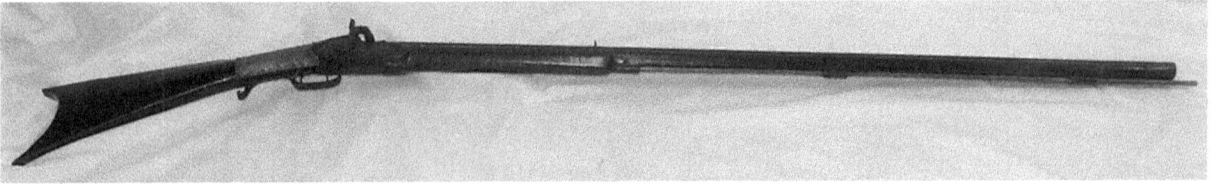

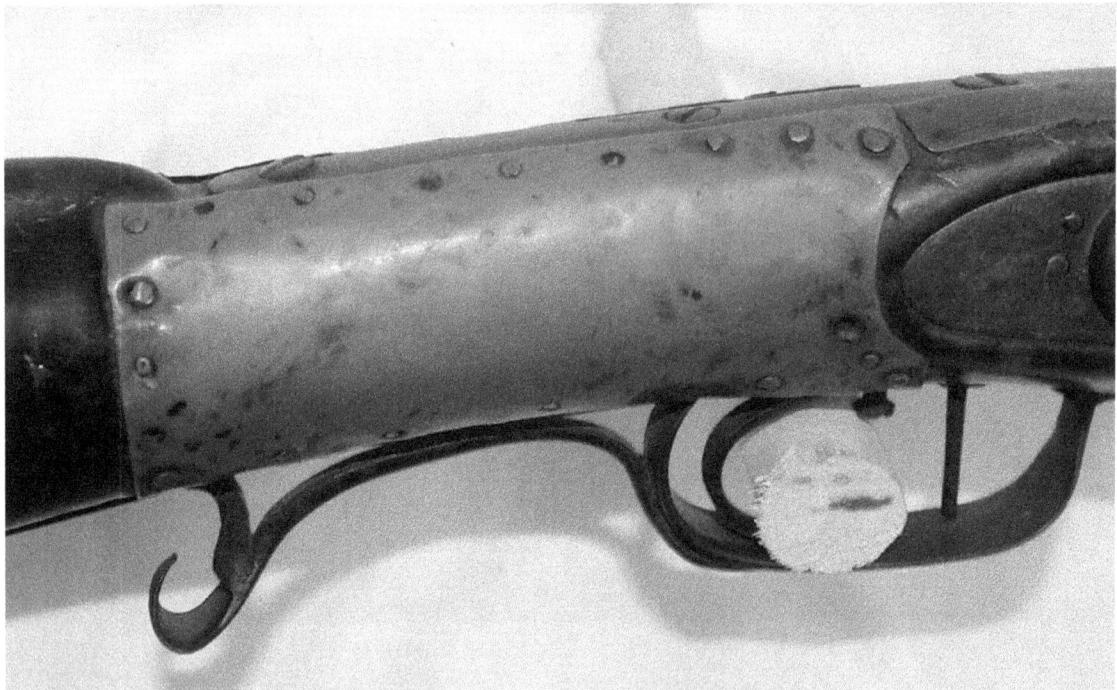

E. H. Smith, Jefferson County, AL

E. H. Smith, Jefferson County, AL

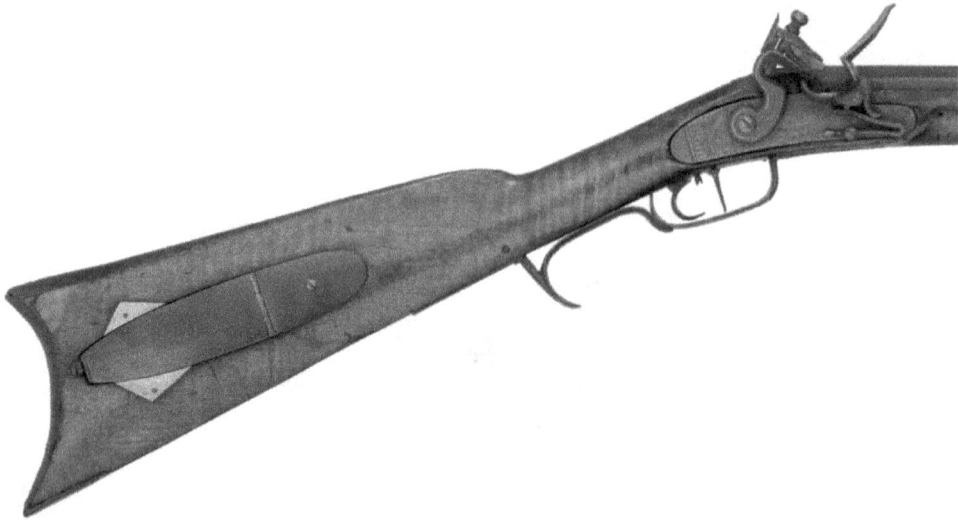

Jacob Stutts, Lauderdale County, AL

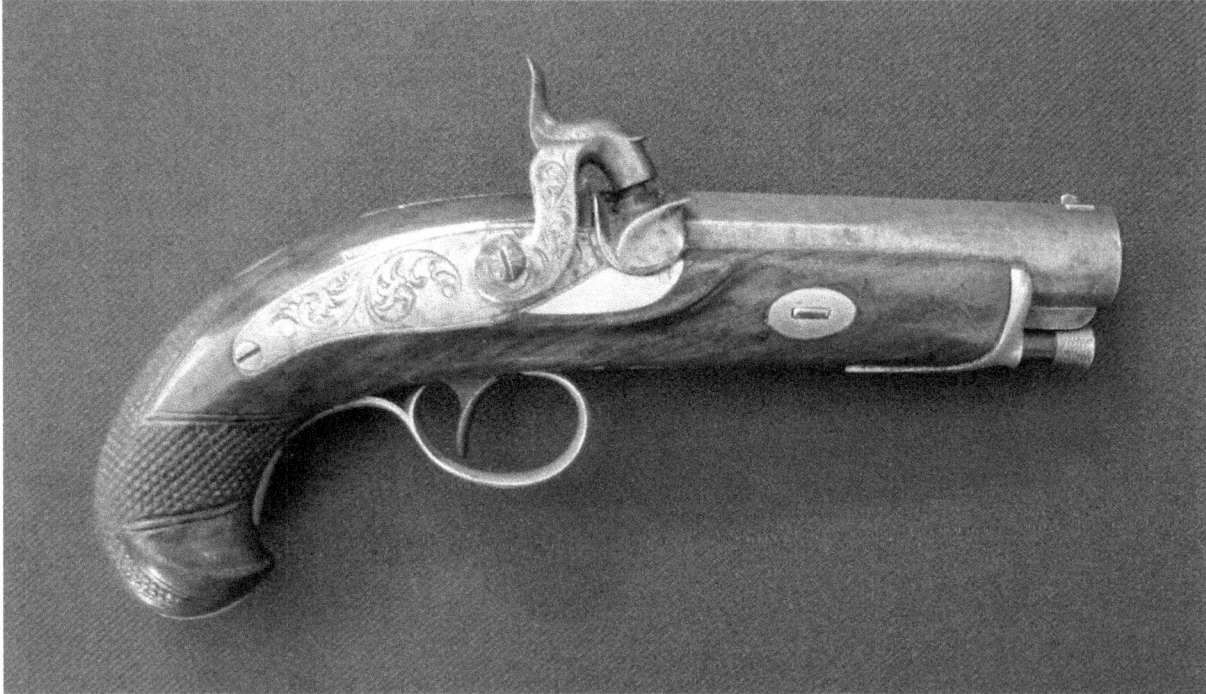

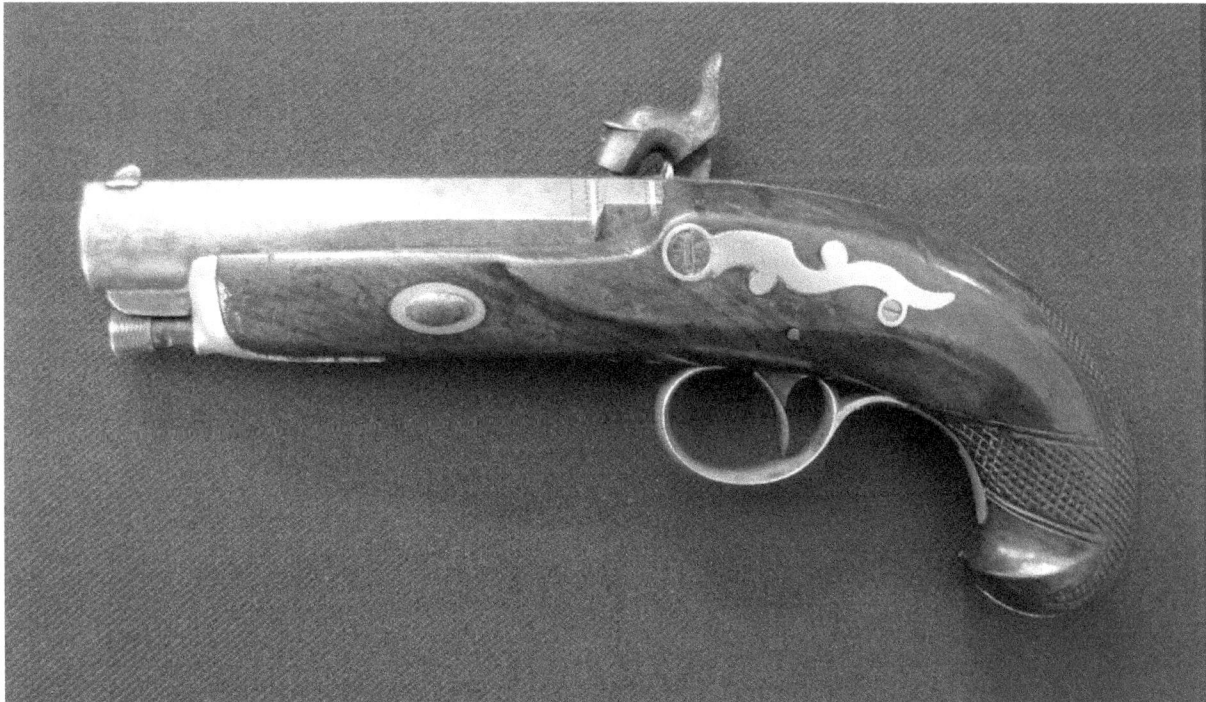

C. Suter, Selma, Dallas County, AL

C. Suter, Selma, Dallas County, AL

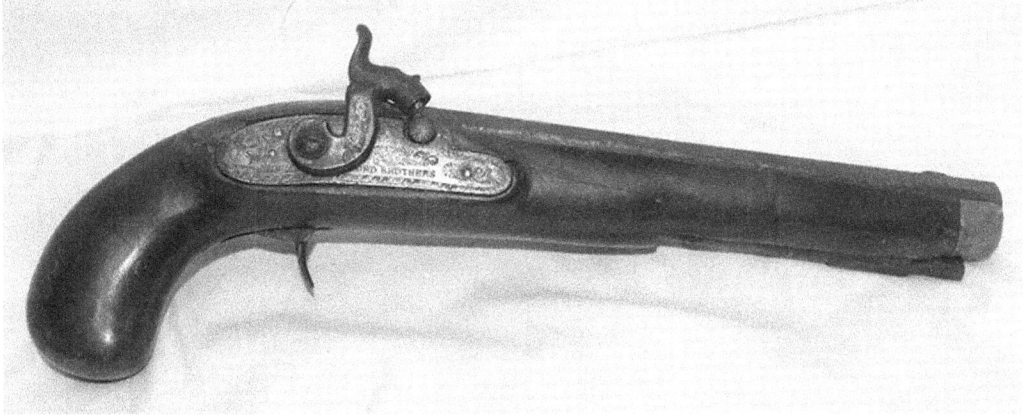

Unknown, Pistol With Ford Bros. Lock, From AL

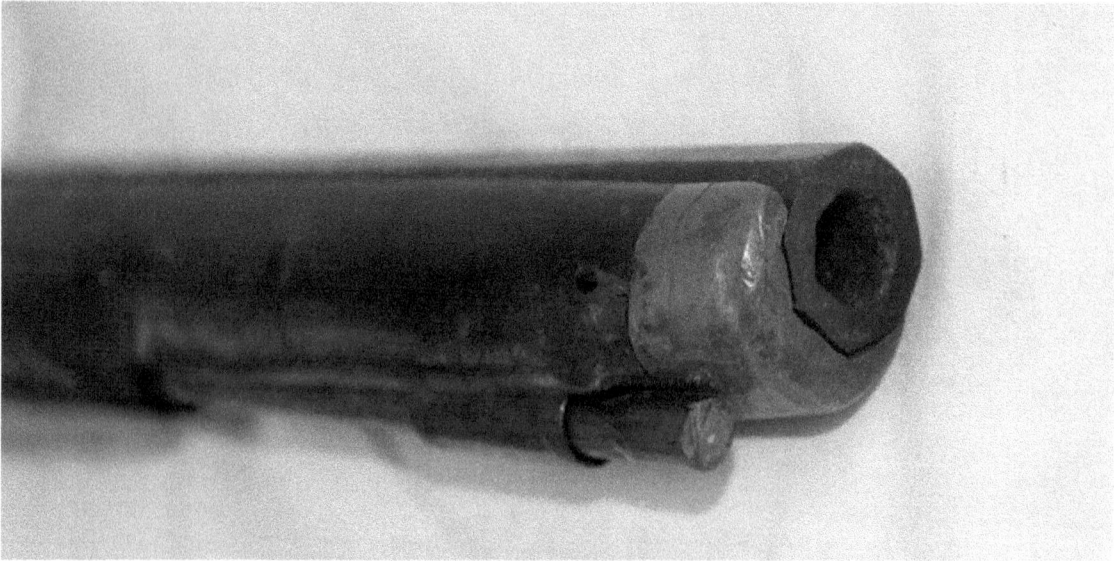

Unknown, Pistol With Ford Bros. Lock, From AL

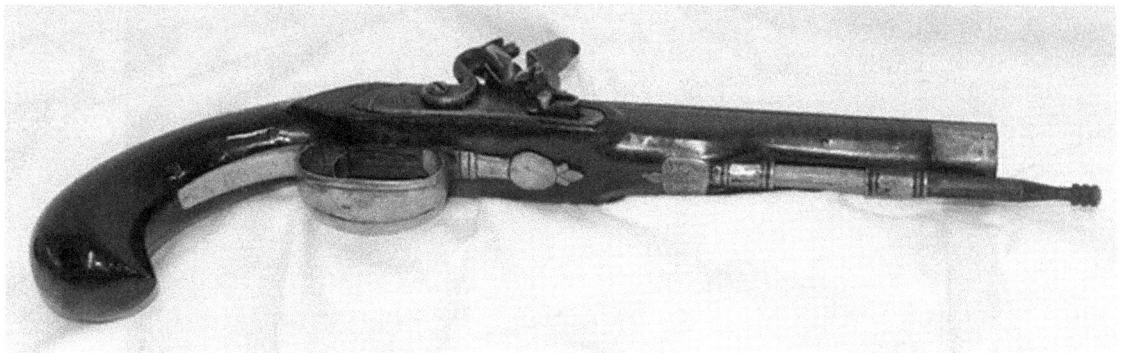

Unknown, Pistol With Spearman Lock, From AL

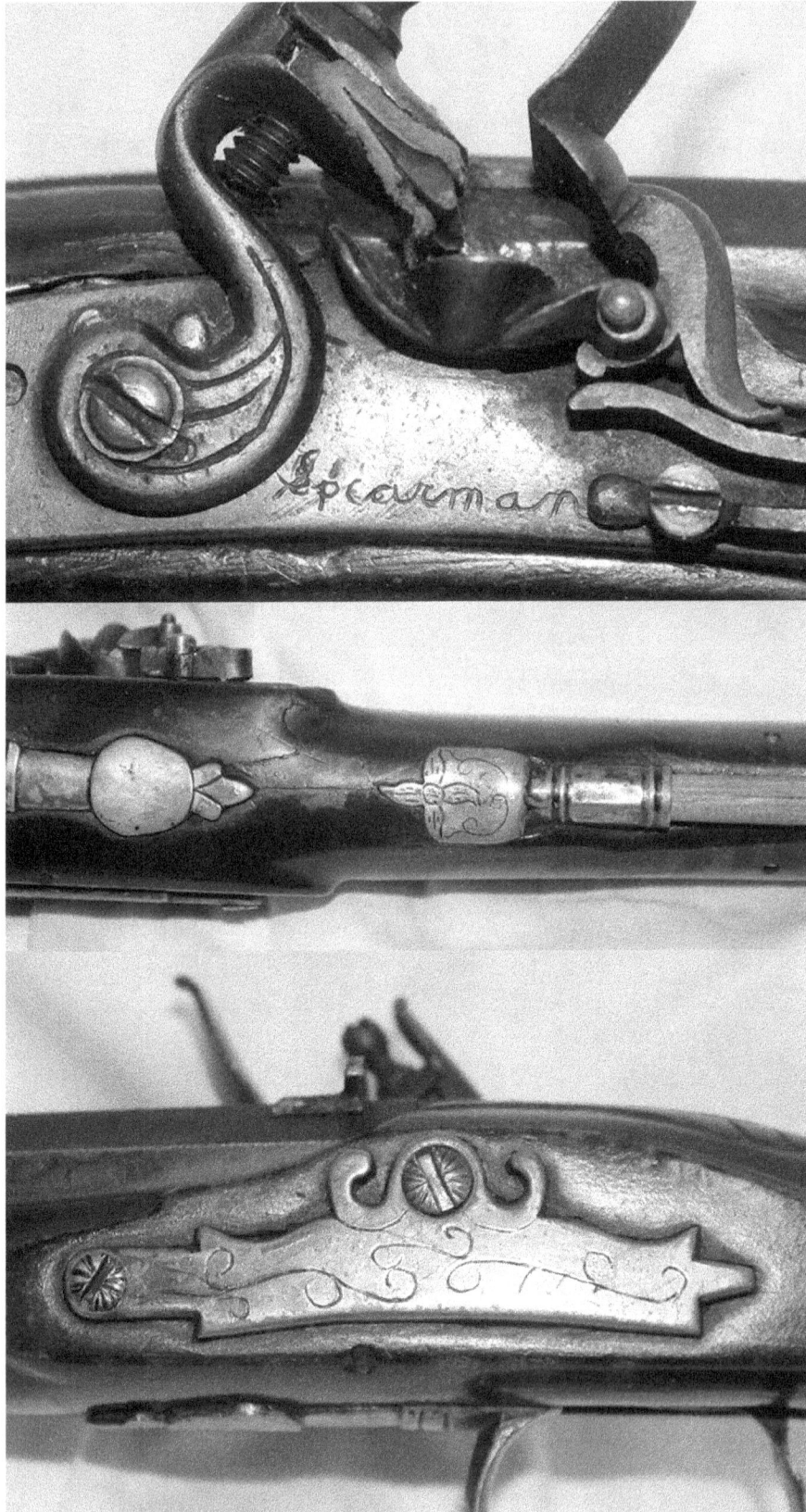

Unknown, Pistol With Spearman Lock, From AL

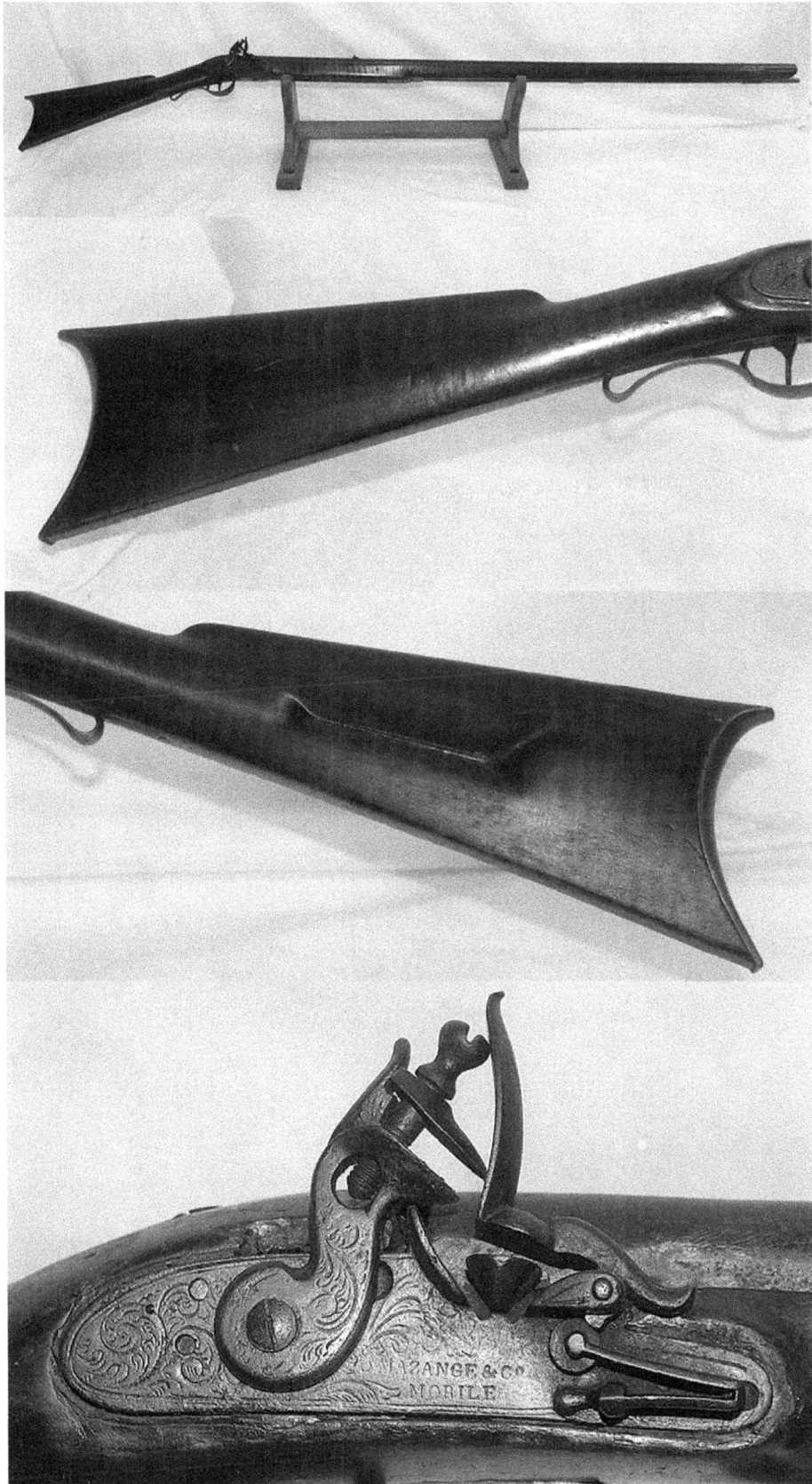

Unknown, Rifle With O. Mazange & Co Lock., Mobile County, AL

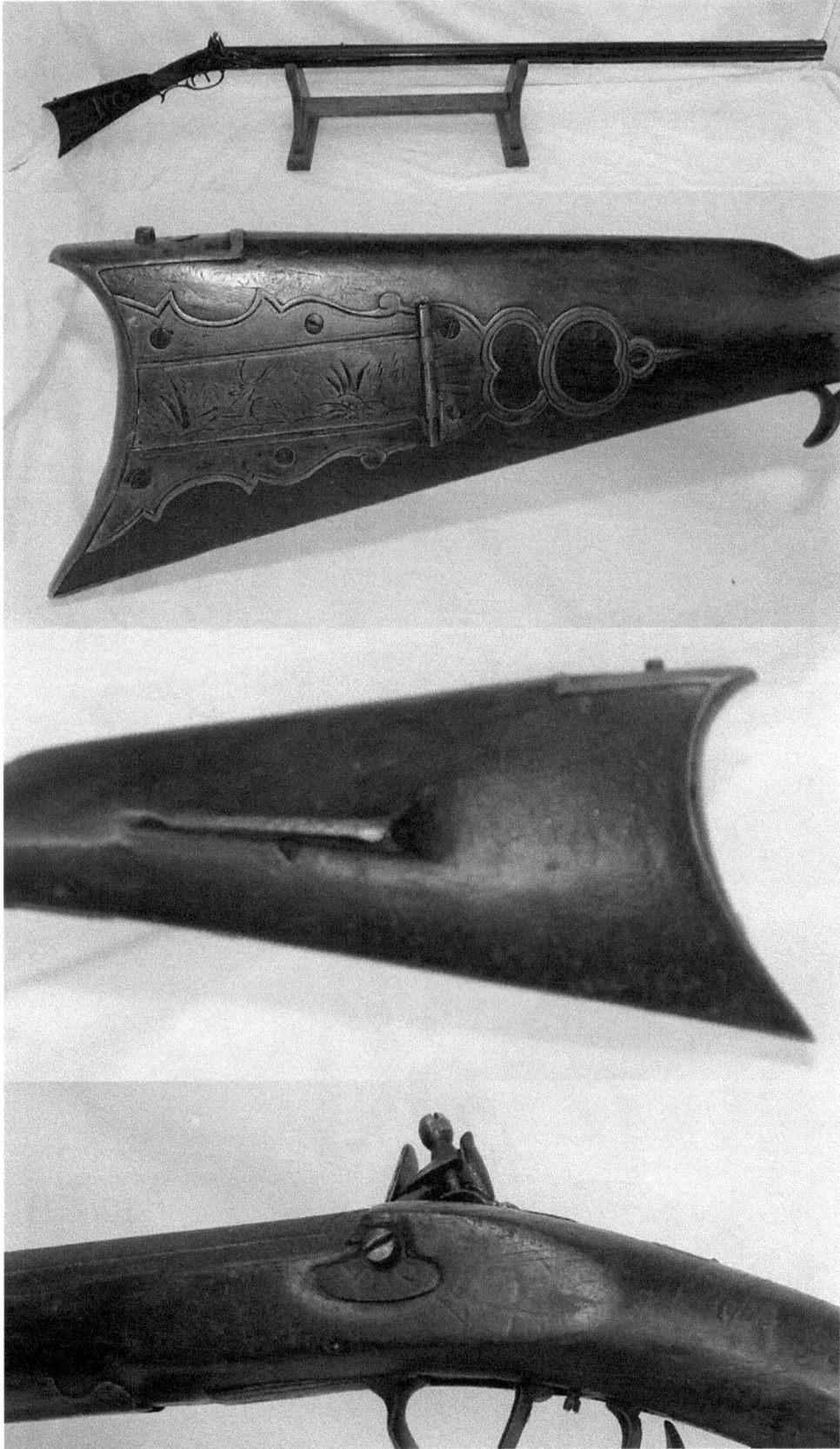

Unknown, With W. Jacot Lock, Marengo County, AL

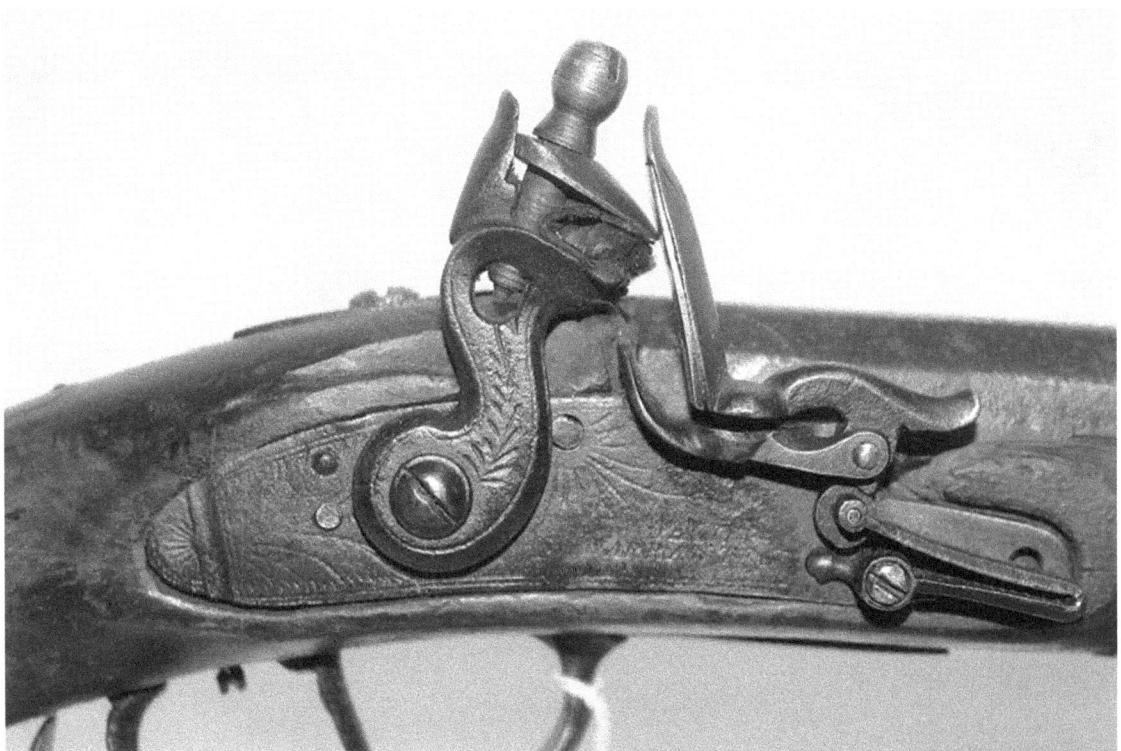

Unknown, With W. Jacot Lock, Marengo County, AL

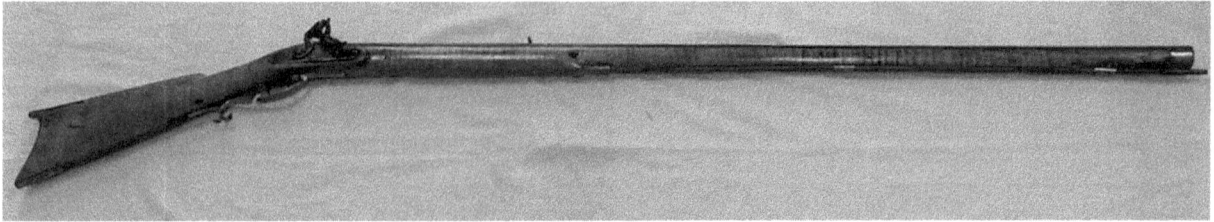

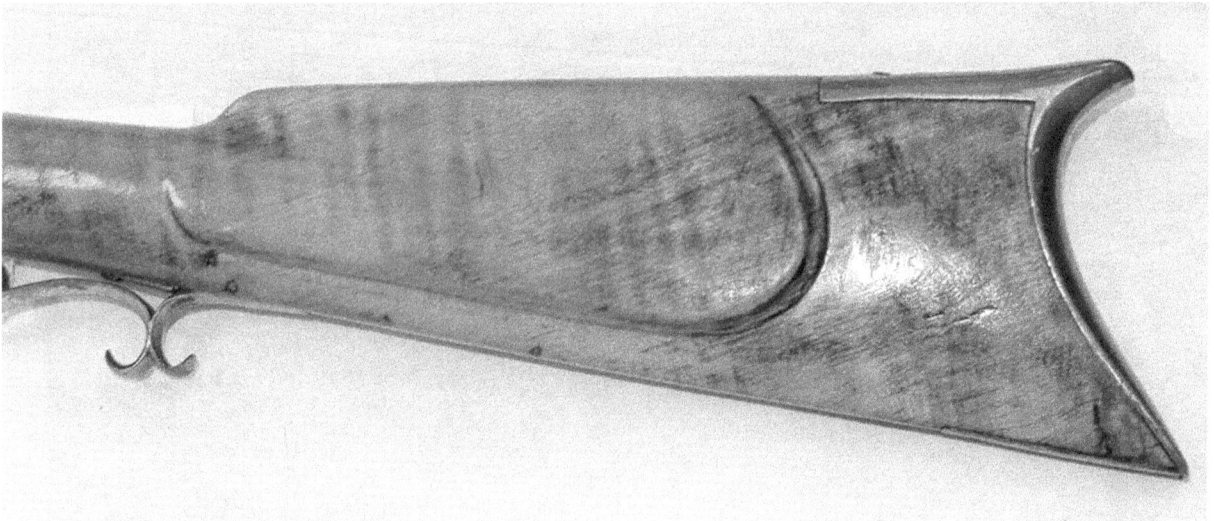

Unknown, Ashmore Lock Rifle, From Mobile County, AL

Unknown, Ashmore Lock Rifle, From Mobile County, AL

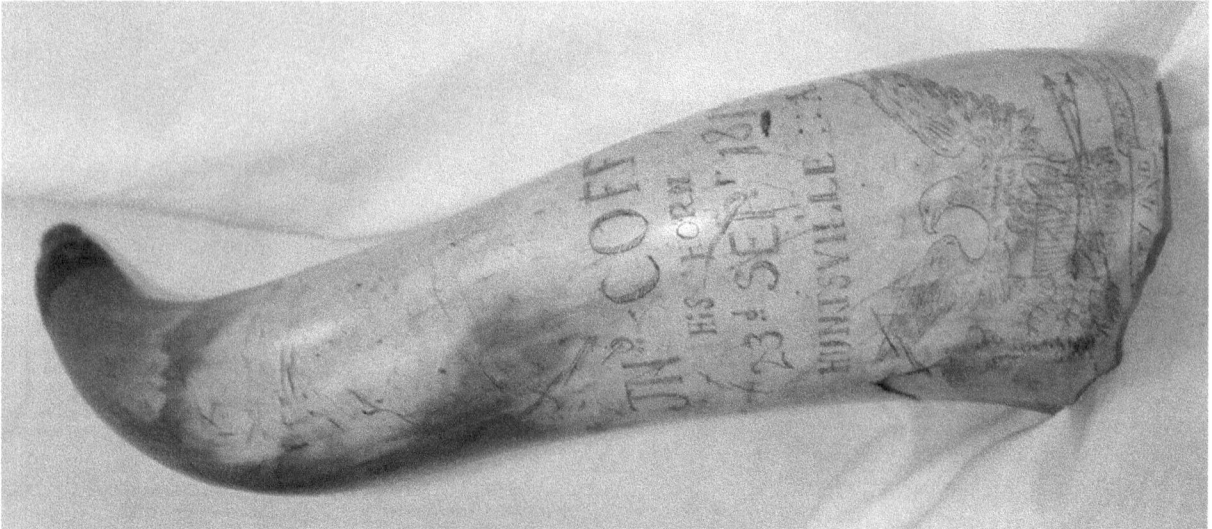

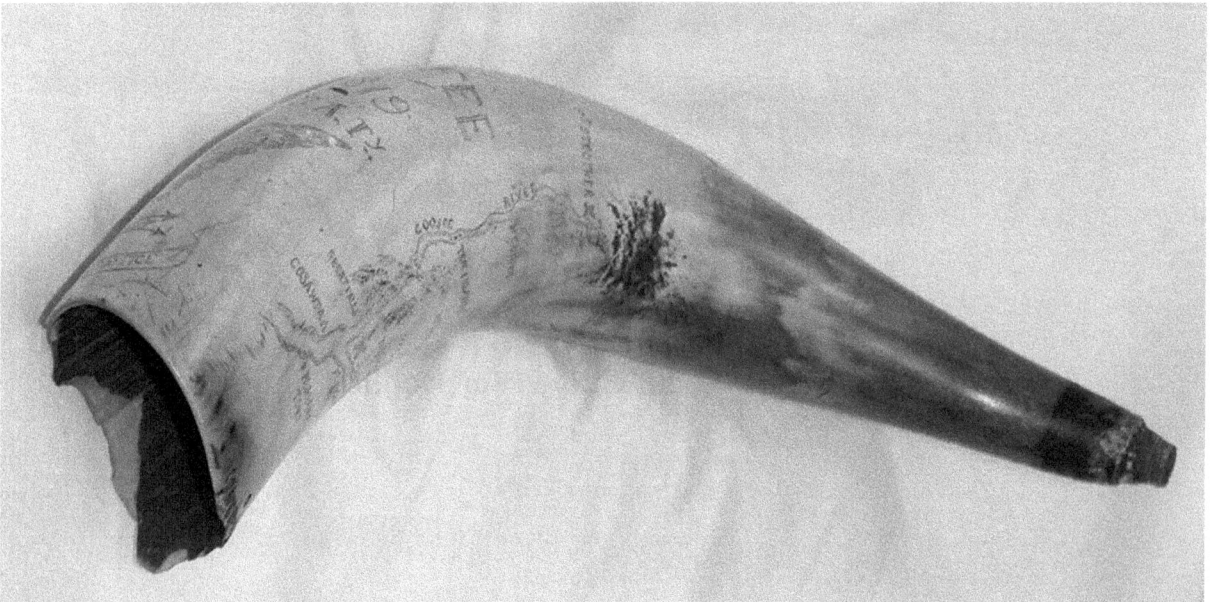

General John Coffee's Powder Horn, Huntsville, Madison County, AL

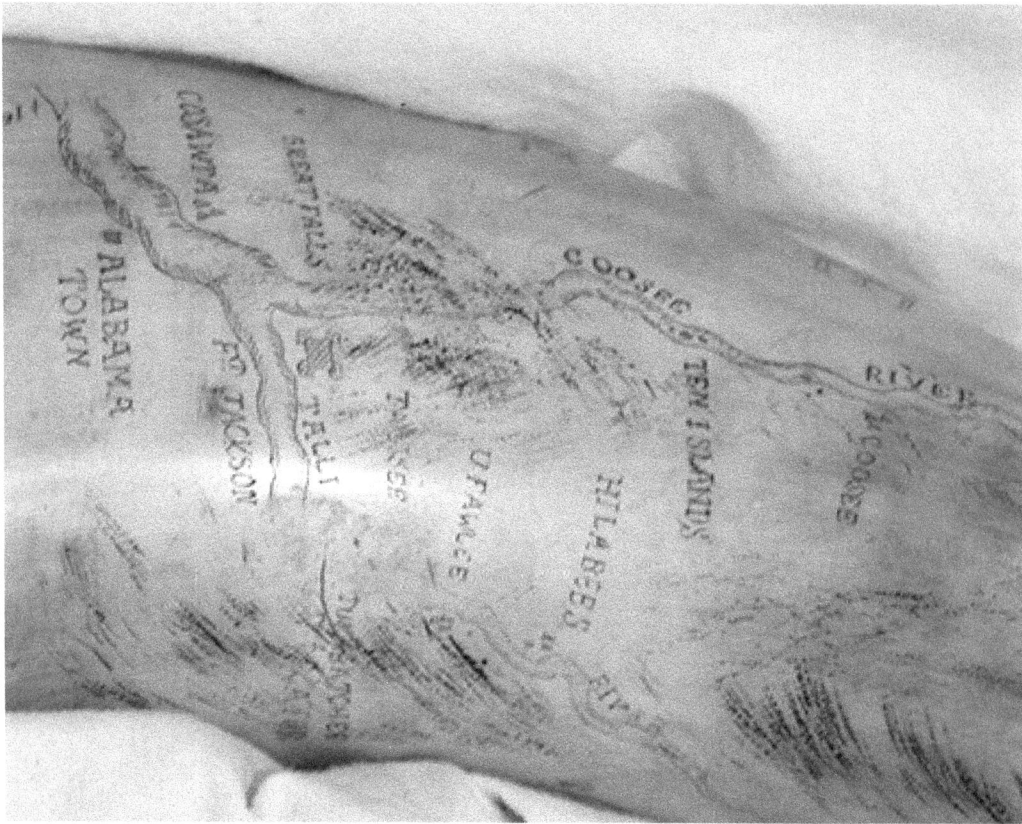

General John Coffee's Powder Horn, Huntsville, Madison County, AL

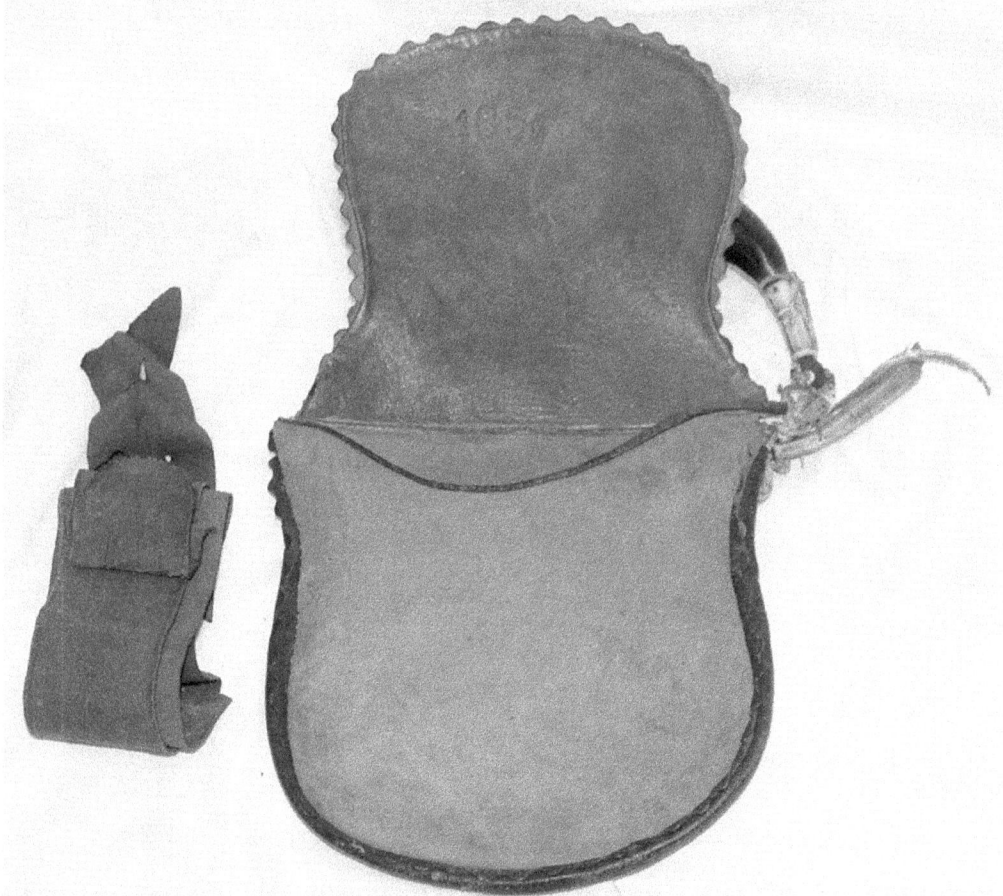

I. W. Possibles Bag Dated 1851, Double Horn, Powder Measure

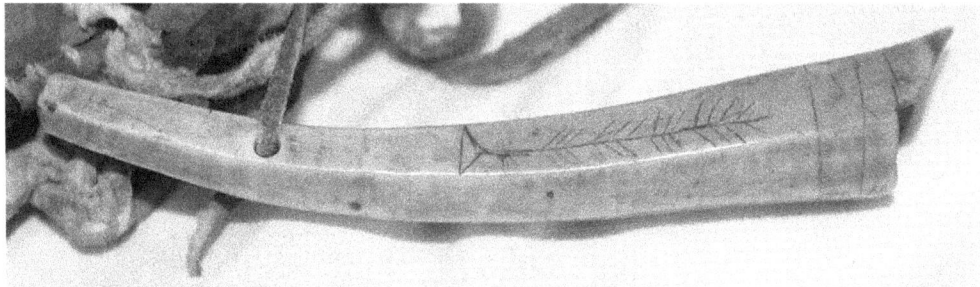

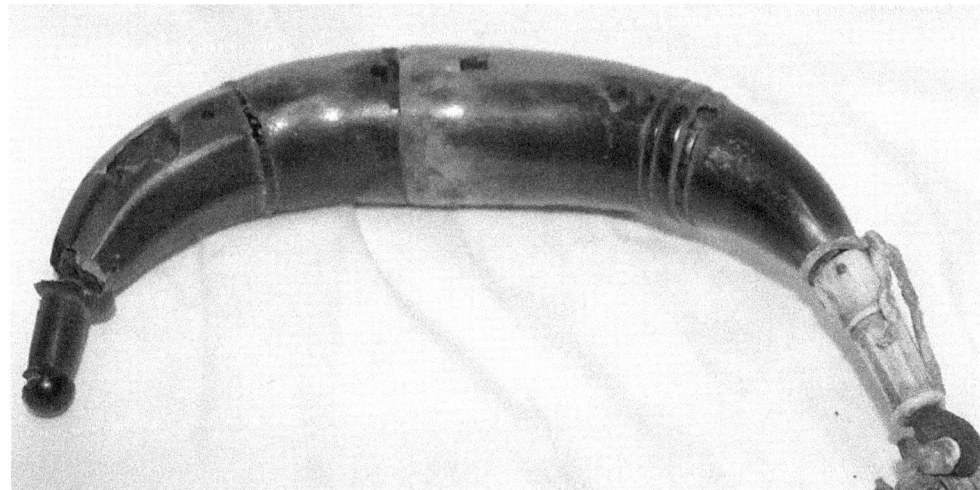

I. W. Possibles Bag Dated 1851, Double Horn, Powder Measure

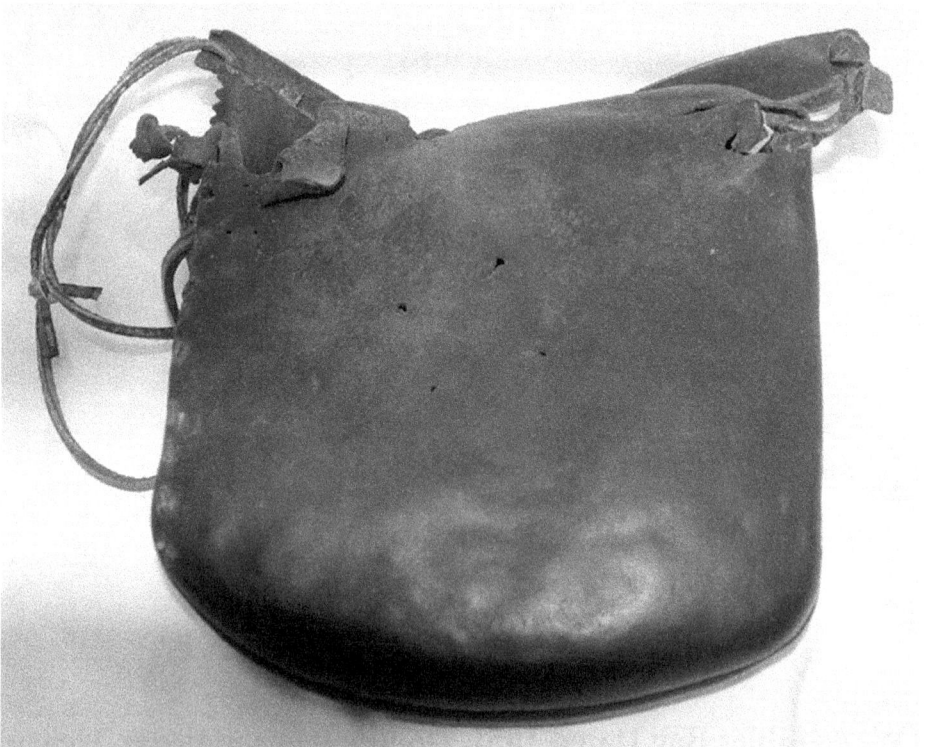

Early Southern Possibles Bag

Early Southern Possibles Bag

Early Shot Pouch

Powder Flasks

Powder Flasks

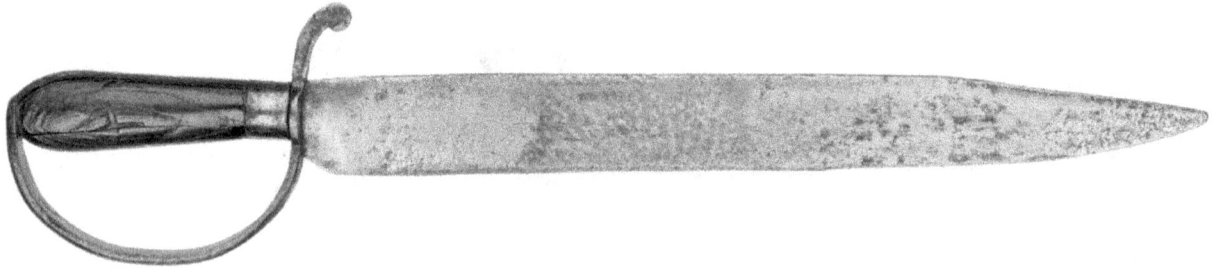

Alabama CSA Contract Bowie Knife

Index

Adams, Stephen Thomas, 4
Adamson, William Colt, 4
Adare, William Branch, 4
Allen, Robert, 4
Allen, William, 4
Alley, William, 4
Anderson, James, 4
Anderson, Samuel, 4
Angel, Elizabeth, 5
Angel, Joseph W, 5
Armstrong, Levi, 5
Austill, Evan, 5
Bailey, James W, 6
Bailey, W. J., 6
Balzer, George, 2, 6
Barber, W. A., 6
Barbour, Richard, 6
Barnard, William, 6
Barnerd, Elisha Smith, 6
Barnerd, Jesse, 6
Barnerd, Oliver, 6
Barnes, Z. A., 7
Barnett, Thomas M., 80
Barnett, Warren Hocksley, 7
Barton, James A., 7
Bassett, Henry, 80
Bates, Riley, 7
Beasley, Abraham, 7
Becker, Nicholas, 7
Belew, John J, 7
Bell, David, 7
Bellamy, John, 7
Beltz, D. C., 8
Bender, Antonio J., 8
Bender, Ignatious, 2
Bender, Ignatius, 8
Bender, James, 8
Bender, John, 8
Bender, John L., 8
Bender, Joseph A., 8
Bcyseigal, Charles F., 8
Biford, William, 8

Bill, W. R., 78
Binder, Charles, 8
Birmingham Arms & Cycle, 8, 23
Blackburn, Joel, 9
Blackwood, William, 9
Bluis, James, 9
Boatwright, Daniel Thomas, 9
Boatwright, James William, 9
Bohna, Joseph, 9
Bolles, C. P., 81
Bon, Jean, 9
Bourdin, A., 78
Boyer, 10
Boyles, James, 10
Bozeman, David Wood, 10
Brackner, Joey, 2
Broadnax, H. P., 10
Brog, Adolph, 10
Brooks, Dan C., 10
Brooks, John Thomas, 10
Brouse, William, 10
Broyles, James C., 10
Bruce, Wilson Pulaski, 11
Buchanan, James, 11
Buckner, Walker, Sr., 11
Bull, John Valentine, 11
Bull, Russell Samuel Sellers, 12
Burke, Solomon, 12
Burriss, Isham B., 13
Burroughs, Berny, 13
Burson, Walter C., 13
Burton, James H., 81
Buys, Jeremiah, 13
Campbell, Colin, 14
Campbell, Hiram W., 14
Cannon, Berry, 14
Cardener, C., 14
Carleton, Charles H., 14
Carmichael, Hugh, 14
Carmouche, Jean Baptiste, 14
Carpenter, Barto Davis, 14
Carroll, W. B., 15

Caruthers, Joseph, 15
Cedar Creek Furnace, 15
Chamberlain, John W. R., 82
Clark, Isaac, 15
Cole, William F., 15
Coleman & Duke, 15
Cone, L. T., 15
Conner, John M., 15
Conning, James, 15
Connor, Hugh, 15
Cook, Ferdinand W., 77
Cook, Francis, 77
Corun, Hugh, 16
Coruse, Hugh, 16
Cowen, H., 16
Craddock, David, 16
Cradner, C., 16
Craig, John A., 16
Crain, John, 16
Culpepper, David, 17
Cuyler, R. M., 82
Dalton, John Washington, 18
Danley, James, Jr., 18
Danne & Zepernick, 18, 71
Danne, Arthur O., 18
Danne, John W., 18
Davidson, A. S., 18
Davidson, William Riley, 18
Davis and Bozeman's Gunshop, 18
Deene, William, 19
Dewitt, A. H., 77
Dittrich, John F., 19
Dobson, W., 19
Dod, Jonathan, 19
Dolphus, Adam, 19
Doty, James J, 19
DuBois, Barent, 80
Dudley, Oliver, 19
Duncan, Jonathan, 19
Eckard, George, 20
Eckard, William, 20
Edgar, James, 20
Edwards, Henry B., 20
Edwards, Thomas, 20
Eiland, Judge Stephen, 20
Eldridge, Charles, 20

Elston, Allen, 20
Estes, Henderson, 20
Farragut, David, 80
Farrin, John, 21
Faulkner, William L., 21
Ferguson, Bartholomew, 21
Ferrie, James, 21
Fettback, I., 78
Fisher, W. B., 21
Fisher, William, 21
Flautt, Jerome, 21
Fleming, William, 21
Flynn, James, 21
Foley, Watson, 21
Forem, G., 22
Foster, James Daniel, 22
Foster, Walter V., 22
Franks, Benjamin R., 22
Freeman, Fineas, 22
Gamble, Harry, 23
Gammell, Harry M., 23
Ganmiel, George, 23
Garner, Lewis, 23
Gast, E. H., 23
Gay, Alexis, 23
Gelbke Brewery, 23
Gelbke, Charles, 23
Gelbke, Frederick L., 24
Gesslin, Robert, 24
Giesel, Jacob, 24
Gorgas, Josiah, 24, 81
Goubil, Benjamin, 24
Graham, John C., 78
Graves, Charles Henry, 24
Graves, James, 24, 25
Graves, James C., 24
Gray, Adolphus, 25
Gray, William C., 77
Greenberry, Franklin, 25
Greenwood, Eldridge S., 77
Griffin, Green, 25
Haag, G., 26
Haiman, L., 77
Hanley, Michael, 26
Hanna, John, 26
Haralson, Jonathan, 78

144

Hardin, Morris, 26
Harris, Andrew Green, 26
Harris, John H., 26
Harris, Virginius C., 26
Hasting, John P., 27
Hatcher, Jordan, 27
Hatcher, S. G., 27
Haughton, W. A., 27
Haughton, William W., 27
Hennington, 28
Henry, Edward, 28
Hidle, John B., 28
Higgins, Alexander, 28
Higgins, Benjamin F., 28
Higgins, James, 29
Higgins, John, 29
Higgins, Joseph, 29
Higgins, Josiah, 29
Higgins, Michael, 30
Higgins, Palmer, 30
Higgins, Robert, 30
Higgins, Sterling T., 30
Higgins, Uriah D., 30
Higgins, William Fleming, 28
Higgins, William H., 30
Hill, Joseph, 31
Hill, Wiley Williamson, 31
Hobbs, Charles H., 31
Hobbs, Erasmus Marion, 31
Hobbs, James W., 32
Hobbs, William George Thomas, 32
Hobbs, William Horton, 32
Hodges, James, 32
Hodgkins, Walter E., 82
Holder, John L., 32
Honiker, W. H., 32
Horton, Henry, 33
Horton, James R., 33
Houston, Alex G., 33
Houston, Hartwell, 33
Howard, Jno, 33
Howard, John H., 33
Howard, William, 33
Hudgins, Ambrose, 33
Humphreys, F. C., 77
Humphries, Benjamin, 33

Hunt, William H., 33
Huroy, George, 33
Hurt & Schevenel, 33
Irons, H. R., 34
Ivy, John, 34
Jackson, Andrew, 1
Jacobs, B., 35
Jessel, Peter, 35
Johnson, Arcy, 35
Johnson, Felix, 83
Johnson, James, 83
Johnson, Mary, 83
Johnson, William P., 83
Jones, A. S., 35
Jones, J. W., 35
Joplin, A., 35
Joulin, Jacques, 35
Juallain, François C., 35
Keable, W. B., 36
Keeling, William, 36
Keesee, William, 36
Keipp, S. P.., 36
Kelly, Samuel S., 36
Kelper, John, 38
Kennedy, Alexander, 36
Kennedy, Enoch Spinks, 37
Kennedy, Hiram, 37
Kennedy, John Spinks, 38
Kennedy, Josiah S, 38
Key, Calvin Domas, 38
Key, Thomas, 39
King, Joseph, 39
King, Samuel D., 39
King, William Rufus DeVane, 39
Knight, James Allen, 40
Knowles, William J., 40
Knox, W. S., 78
Kreutner, Christian, 2, 40
Kreutner, Henry, 40
Laborne, J. T., 41
Lamberth, A. F., 41
Landrum Family, 41
Landrum, Benjamin, 41
Landrum, George, 41
Landrum, John, 41
Landrum, Meridith, 42

Landrum, William Ellis, 42
Landrum, Zachariah, 42
Lee, Robert E., 80, 81
Leonard & Day, 42
Leslie, J. D., 42
Lewis, Thomas D., 42
Ligon, E. T., 42
Liles, John Madison, 42
Liles, William, 43
Lindfors, John F., 43
Lindsey, W. H., 43
Ling, O. C., 43
Linkham David W., 43
Marin, Edmund C., 46
Marin, Oscar E., 46
Marks, William M., 80
Mattei, Peter, 46
May, William Green, 46
Mayhall, William, 46
Mazagne, Oliver, 47
McClanahan, William, 44
McClung, John Richard, 44
McCravy, Jonathan, 44
McCravy, William, 44
McDaniel, Archie, 44
McDennat, Matthew, 44
McDonald, Archibald, 44
McDonald, E. B., 45
McDonald, Elias, 45
McDonald, John, 45
McGee, David G., 45
McGee, Jacob, 45
McKinney, John, 45
McLauren, Dan, 46
McRae, Colin, 79
McRae, Colin J., 79
Merrell, Benjamin, 47
Meyer, M., 78
Michant, Peter, 47
Micou, B. H., 81
Micou, Benjamin, 81
Milican, John, 47
Miller, Henry, 47
Millican, Benjamin F., 47
Millican, Francis Marion, 47
Montgomery Arms, 47

Mooney, John, 48
Morales,, 48
Morris, James B., 48
Morrison, John C., 48
Mullins, Albert Clay, 48
Murray, John P., 77
Mycick, James C., 48
Nalors, B. N., 49
Norwood, Thomas Edward, 49
Nunis, Samuel Unis, 50
Nunn, Elijah, 50
Ogleby, Jesse L., 51
Opelika, John Thomas Brooks, 51
Orr, William C., 51
Palmer, Amansa Marlin "Mace", 52
Palmer, Joseph Washington, 52
Peck, William, 52
Perkins, William P., 52
Perry, James G., 52
Person, William Davis, 53
Pessou, L., 53
Peterson, George W, 53
Peterson, Karsten, 53
Pettis, William R., 53
Phillips, Elisha L., 54
Pierce, S. C., 78
Pierce, Thomas B., 78
Pinkston, Rid, 54
Pisson L., Sr, 54
Pisson, L., Jr., 54
Poyas, Francis Delisseline, 54
Poyas, James Osgood, 54
Price, Isaac, 55
Price, William, 55
Prickett, William Parks, 55
Pruett, T. L., 55
Pugh, Isaac, 55
Pugh, Stephen, 55
Raynolds, D. H., 57
Read, John B., 57
Reedy, Logan B., 57
Respess, A., 57
Rews, B. B., 57
Reynolds, H. L., 57
Richardson, Asa, 57
Richardson, David, Jr., 58

Richardson, Isham, 58
Richardson, John David, 58
Richardson, Wiley, 58
Ricketts, William A., 58
Rider David, 58
Riley, John Frederick, 58
Rison, Archibald, 59
Roberts, Colbert, 59
Robinson, William, 59
Rogers, George W., 59
Rogers, J. B., 59
Rose, Tom, 59
Rousseau, Lovell H., 82
Ryan, William T., 59
Ryburn, Hyrum W., 59
Salisbury, William L., 60
Salle, Nicolas de la, 1
Salter, William Joseph, 60
Saltsman, Daniel, 60
Sanders, Benjamin, 60
Sanders, Levi Lindsey, 61
Saunders, C. W., 61
Schley, William, 61
Sellers, Young, 61
Senn, James, 61
Sewall, A. F., 61
Shipp, William, 61
Short, Samuel Andrew, 61
Shotts, David Hilliard, 62
Singer, Edgar C., 62
Sloat, L. W., 63
Smith, Edmund Cape, 63
Smith, Henry, 63
Smith, Robert W., 63
Solomon, Olivia, 83
Starkey, Calvin, 63
Stover, Nathan, 63
Stuart, J. E. B., 81
Stuart, J.E. B., 80
Sturdivant, Lewis G., 64
Stutts, George, 64
Stutts, Jacob, 64
Summersett, James Monroe, 64
Suter, Casper, 64
Suttle, William, Jr., 65
Swain, Charles, 65

Taylor, W. V., 83
Thames, C. E., 78
Thomas, N., 66
Thomas, William, 66
Thomas, William B., 66
Thompson, J., 66
Thompson, James O., 66
Thompson, Seth, 66
Thompson, W. P., 66
Thoss, Eugene, 66
Tissier, Charles George, 67
Tissier, P., 78
Tissier, Peter, 67
Todd, David, 67
Todd, George H., Sr., 67
Todd, John Norton, 67
Todd, Joseph, 68
Tolbert, Edward, 68
Tolbert, Samuel, 68
Toomer, F. C., 68
Traylor, William P., 68
Turner, Frank, 68
Tyrey, Jesse, 68
Vaughan, George, 70
Vincent, David, Sr., 70
Wagner, C. G., 77
Wallace, Dan, 3
Walls, Ellis, Jr., 71
Ware, Jeptha M., 71
Washburn, B. M., 71
Weeks, Oscar, 71
Weidman, Felix, 71
West, George Jr., 72
West, George W., 71
Wettman, 72
White, J. L., 78
White, John, Jr., 72
Wilcox, T. D., 72
Williams, David, 72
Williams, Job, 72
Williams, William F., 72
Williamson, Robert, 72
Willis, John, 73
Wing, M., 73
Winslow, Edward P., 78
Wise, I. A., 73

Wooten, Isaiah, 73
Wooten, Jonathan, 73
Wright, James A., 73
Wright, William, 73

Young, J. R., 84
Youngblood, R. C., 75
Zeperick, Charles, 76

Bluewater Publications is a multi-faceted publishing company capable of meeting all of your reading and publishing needs. Our two-fold aim is to:

1) Provide the market with educationally enlightening and inspiring research and reading materials.
2) Make the opportunity of being published available to any author and or researcher who desire to be published.

We are passionate about preserving history; whether through the re-publishing of an out-of-print classic, or by publishing the research of historians and genealogists. Bluewater Publications is the *Peoples' Choice Publisher*.

For company information or information about how you can be published through Bluewater Publications, please visit:

www.BluewaterPublications.com

Also check Amazon.com to purchase any of the books that we publish.

Confidently Preserving Our Past,
Bluewater Publications.com